ENGLISH DRAMATISTS OF TO DAY

ENGLISH DRAMATISTS OF TO DAY

WILLIAM ARCHER

GYAN

Published by

Gyan Publishing House
5, Ansari Road
Daryaganj, New Delhi-110002
Phone: 011-47034999, 9811692060
E-mail: books@gyanbooks.com

Distribution Network
gyanbooks.com
India, USA, Canada, UK, Australia

ISBN: 978-93-7225-279-8 (PB)

First Published, 1882

2nd Impression 2026

Printed at: Gyan Press, Delhi.

ENGLISH DRAMATISTS OF TO DAY
Author: WILLIAM ARCHER

ENGLISH DRAMATISTS

OF TO-DAY

BY

WILLIAM ARCHER.

1882.

CONTENTS.

INTRODUCTION.

BEFORE asking the reader to follow me through the detailed examination of the works of our present-day dramatists contained in these pages, I wish to define my point of view and lay down clearly the latitude and longitude of my position.

A very short glance at any of the following essays will show that I take a somewhat gloomy view of the present state of the drama. In this I am not singular. Pessimism is the prevailing attitude of the critical mind with regard to the theatre. The higher criticism despises and ignores it. One might examine the volumes of our great quarterlies ever since their foundation and find scarcely a word in which the existence of an English theatre is recognized. In one or two of the more modern reviews the weight of a name like Mr. Matthew Arnold's procures at long intervals the admission of a thoughtful but unpractical paper upon the theatre of the day. The lower criticism, again, in its more serious moods, inclines to despondency and lamentation. It sighs for a past golden age, commonly designated the "palmy days" of the drama; or it mourns in sackcloth and ashes the prevalence of French adaptations.

My own dissatisfaction arises from quite other grounds. I am no profound believer in the palmy days, and in any case I do not care to cry over spilt milk. As for our indebtedness to the French, I do not deny it, but I do not regard it as an unmixed evil. The comic servant in the farce, who, being discovered poring over a French grammar, gives as his reason that he is anxious to study the English drama in the original, might just as well have said that he was anxious to go to the fountain-head of the world's drama. I am not aware that Augier and Sardou have penetrated to the Chinese stage, their pieces being rather too short to please celestial taste; but it is certain that their career of conquest has only been stopped by the great wall of China. The Jeremiahs of our dramatic criticism seem to hold that we are the only people who go to France for our dramatic supplies. The case is not so. In Germany, Holland, Scandinavia, Russia, Italy, America, the novelties of the French stage are seized upon more eagerly than they are here. More eagerly, I repeat, because in these countries the French drama is accepted with scarcely any selection as an illustration of French life and an important factor in European culture. We, on the other hand, fastidiously select only such plays as can be tortured into a certain fitness to English life—a very wrinkly and baggy fitness at best—and which, moreover, do not tread on the toes of our insular prejudices. Sardou's "Divorçons!" has been played with success in Germany, in Denmark, in Italy: for us it is much too lively. Pailleron's "Le Monde où l'on s'ennuie" has gone the round of Europe and America: for us it is much too dull. True, we appreciated "Les Dominos Roses" much more than any other nation; and indeed we are snappers-up of many of the unconsidered trifles of the French stage, neglected by others because they have not meaning and stamina enough to attract attention beyond the Rhine and the Alps. But the fact remains that the French drama is much more intimately known and thoroughly appreciated in every other European country than it is here. France is the only nation, with one exception, where for the last half-century the highest imaginative and wittiest comic literature has taken dramatic form. It would be mere senseless chauvinism, worthy of the French themselves, to ignore the existence of such pieces as "Les Fourchambault" and "Dora" merely because they were not written by a German or an Englishman as the case may be. Even if we ourselves had an English Augier and Sardou, I, for one, should be sorry if their works excluded those of the great Frenchmen from our stage. Our weakness does not lie in the fact that we borrow from France; it lies in the fact that we have no contemporary drama of our own such as almost all our neighbours possess and appreciate along with the French masterpieces.

I shall be asked how I have managed to write half a score of essays upon a dramatic literature, which, by my own showing, does not exist. My answer is, that though the English drama does not exist as literature, it exists and flourishes as a non-literary product. *Hinc illæ lacrymæ*—hence my complaint, and hence my effort. I wish to show, by applying a moderately high standard of criticism to the body of our contemporary drama, how far it falls short of any literary merit, and in so doing, to indicate possibilities of improvement and elevation.

It is no very exalted standard that I apply. The ideal I adopt is a modest one. When it has been attained there will be plenty of room left for further aspiration; but I do not, in my most sanguine moments, venture to hope that this nineteenth century will witness its attainment. It may be shortly stated somewhat as follows:—I should like to see in England a body of playwrights, however small, whose works are not only acted, but printed and *read.* They might, of course, belong to every species of dramatic composition enumerated by Polonius or Geneste, but the large proportion of them, following the natural bent of the age, would probably deal with phases of modern life. In this sphere there would be room for comedy as light as Marivaux and drama as intense as Augier, but always, except in the merest farce, there should be at least an undercurrent of seriousness. Even the merest farce, be it noted, should be free from puerility and vulgarity, but with this reservation it might be as wild and fantastic as Labiche himself, if it were only half as witty. In comedy and drama again the element of seriousness might be purely poetic or sentimental, but it would generally arise from the relation of the work to some moral, social, political—may I add religious?—topic of the day, or better still of all time. Violent polemics of sect or party would of course be excluded, but there is an immense intermediate space between a drama of violent polemics, and a drama which is utterly irrelevant to any serious question of our daily life. The comedy of no manners, the farce of puns and quiproquos, the drama of furniture and fire-arms, would then cease to be the staple of our dramatic production, and would take rank as inferior branches of art. For my aspiration, or my provisional ideal so to speak, does not include the suppression of the non-literary drama, but only the creation of a literary drama. That is quite ambitious enough for the present, considering how small are the germs from which this literary drama must grow, and how unfavourable the surrounding conditions.

I should be quite content to see our drama in the condition, not of the French, but of the German, Italian, or Scandinavian drama of the day. In Germany, there are several writers of light comedy far more literary than ours, and such men as Freytag, Lindau, and Laube write plays which grasp moral problems or touch social topics,—plays which influence the national life and are literary as well as theatrical "events." In Italy, though the "teatro di prosa" is in a very low condition materially, it is intellectually far in advance of ours. The modern plays of Paolo Ferrari sometimes carry to an inartistic extreme the seriousness upon which I insist, and become positively didactic. Cossa and Giacosa are among the leading poets of the country besides being its leading dramatists, and Del Testa, Bersezio, Castelvecchio and others have written serious plays in which dramatic force and skill are combined with style and literary finish. In Scandinavia the highest literature of the past twenty years has taken dramatic form. Ibsen and Björnson are almost as popular in Germany as in their own country, and Molbech has written at least one exquisite idyll which has had the greatest success both as a book and on the stage. The names I have mentioned by no means exhaust the list of dramatists who write both for the stage and the study in Germany, Italy, and Scandinavia, but they are sufficient for my argument. I have named at least three in each country—what three English dramatists have been successful both before the footlights and in Paternoster Row? What three dramatists have even systematically published their plays, except in the quite unreadable form in which Mr. French presents them to the "profession" and amateurs? "Queen Mary" is the only play of Mr. Tennyson's which has been both published and represented. One play of Mr. Wills' has been published, none of Mr. Albery's. Some of Mr. Burnand's minor works have appeared in Lacy's series, and a good many of Mr. Byron's; but the very form of this edition is a negation of all attempt at literary effect, and proves that it is only a "trade" publication. Mr. Tom Taylor published a volume of "Historical Dramas," but it is a significant fact that the volume of comedies which he promised in his preface has never appeared. To Mr. Gilbert belongs the credit of always attempting to give literary form to his work, and the consequence is that his plays have attained a considerable sale among the general public; but even they scarcely take rank in the book-market with the last three-volume novel.

In any case, printed or not printed, the modern English drama is not *read*, and is not written to be read. The public has entirely lost the habit of reading fiction in dramatic form. The loss to itself, to the authors, and to art in the abstract is enormous. Until it regains the habit which exists throughout Europe and once existed in England, our drama will remain unliterary, frivolous, non-moral, unworthy of its past and of our present stage of advancement in other branches of literature and art.

The word "non-moral" may perhaps strike the reader as strange, seeing we have an irresponsible official specially engaged to devote his whole omnipotence, if I may be allowed the phrase, to keeping our stage moral. He may prevent it from being immoral—on that point the less said the better—but at the same time he most successfully hinders it from being in any true sense moral. M. Got, of the Comédie Française, in an article written shortly after the last visit of that company to London, remarked:—"If, after rendering justice to the actors, I now ventured to go further and hazard some judgments on the moral side and the tendencies of your stage, I should then, without doubt, be more exclusively in our own favour." This may seem a case not of the pot calling the kettle black, but of the frying-pan insinuating that the porcelain vase is grimy. And yet, properly understood, M. Got is right. Our stage, if it is not immoral, is certainly not moral, whereas the French stage is moral in its very immorality. Our dramas have no relevance to the moral facts and problems of English life, as the dramas of Augier, Dumas, Feuillet, and Sardou have to those of French life. Our "original" comedies never venture beyond the economic problems of love in a cottage, or the social difficulties presented by a marriage between the Lord of Burleigh and his village maiden. These matters are very nice and interesting, but there are harder problems to be solved in life, and the stage which merely shirks moral questions altogether cannot in any sense be called moral. That is the reason, I think, why many of our French adaptations are comparatively harmless. An audience never thinks of getting moral instruction either for good or evil in a theatre. When a French moral problem is placed before it in English guise, as in "The Crisis," it scarcely recognizes the utter lack of truth and nature in the whole situation. Our drama, with all its moral safeguards, is what Mr. Matthew Arnold calls "fantastic"—the French drama, in its higher phases, is always moral, though it may now and then be gross and impure.

This fact is not to be attributed solely to the censorship of the stage. No one can be more convinced than I am of the injustice, illogicality, and futility of that office; but even a nominally irresponsible censor is after all responsible to public opinion. It is with the public, I believe, that the fault lies, though in this, as in everything else, cause and effect act and re-act, so that it is difficult to discover where an evil actually begins. Modern Englishmen cannot be got to take the drama seriously. The theatre is supported by the most Philistine section of the middle class, and by the worse than Philistine, the utterly frivolous section of the upper class. People of intellect and culture go at long intervals to one or two theatres, and are perfectly in the dark as to what is really good and bad. A theatre supported mainly by people who have no taste or thought whatever, and partly by people who have taste and thought for everything except the drama, cannot be expected to take a serious hold of life. Pleasure, and that of the least elevating sort, is all that the public expects or will accept at even our best theatres. People talk of the theatre as an instrument of culture, but they take very good care that it shall be nothing of the sort. A drama which opens the slightest intellectual, moral, or political question is certain to fail. The public will accept open vice, but it will have nothing to do with a moral problem. It likes to go to the theatre to-night, and to forget the name, plot, and characters of the piece to-morrow. It will laugh always, cry sometimes, shudder now and then, but think—never. Especially it will have nothing to do with a piece to whose theme the word "unpleasant" can be applied. This epithet is of undefined and elastic signification, but once attach it to a play and all chance for it is past. Nothing can be more deplorable. Theatrical audiences are seldom entirely composed of young ladies' boarding-schools, and in a world constituted as ours is, the serious facts of life cannot be seriously treated without touching on subjects which may be classed as "unpleasant." The fault lies not with the dramatist, but ultimately with Eve and the serpent, but for whom the Licenser of Plays would have had a sinecure. There can surely be no logical defence for the ostrich-like tendency of the public to escape from the inevitable problems of life by burying its head and refusing to look at them.

Of late years I remember to have seen five actually or potentially moral plays upon the London stage. "The Old Love and the New" is the best instance, and it succeeded mainly on account of an episodic duel scene. In "Forget-me-not," on the other hand, the moral interest was episodic, but strong and ably handled. Strange to say it too succeeded. "Coralie" failed because the adapter had managed to make a feeble play of it. "Duty" and "Honour" failed solely on account of the "unpleasantness" of their subjects. And here I should like to draw a distinction which the two last-named plays serve to illustrate. "Honour," I grant, deserved to be branded as unpleasant; "Duty," I submit, did not. In the former the problem presented was artificial, a problem of mere French society, starting from premises almost repulsive and working through emotions largely conventional to a conventional solution. In the latter the problem was one of very general relevance, and of interest not merely local but universal. The difference between the two plays is curiously typified in their titles—"Duty" and "Honour." The one is elemental, the other conventional. Honour is Duty in stays and a stock—warped and distorted to suit local and temporary fashions. Duty reigns absolutely in all times and places—Honour bears limited sway in a limited realm. Therefore, I hold that the public was right in refusing to accept the "unpleasant" materials of a far-fetched problem of French Honour, but was wrong in rejecting the much less unpleasant foundation of a problem of universal-human Duty. I believe the true reason of the failure of "Duty" was that it was too interesting. It stimulated the mind instead of soothing it. People left the theatre asking themselves, "Was it his duty?" and the enigma interfered with the digestion of the solid supper, without which no evening at the theatre is complete. The British public wants sedatives and not stimulants in a theatre, and it is the essence of great and serious modern drama to be stimulant and not sedative. There lies the whole question in a nut-shell.

And now, with fear and trembling, I approach a difficult question—that of the influence of criticism. In no country in the world is the drama so much criticized as in England. Even in France the theatrical *chroniqueur* is often content to record in a paragraph performances which an English critic would treat in an essay of a column and a half. Instead of a single Monday *feuilleton*, our great newspapers devote three, four, five columns a week to the drama. The reason for this does not lie solely in the greater fecundity or prolixity of the British critic, nor in the greater appetite of the British public for theatrical comments. It is largely explained by our advertising system, since the manager who gives a good advertisement has a right to a detailed "notice," good or bad. I do not mean that in any respectable paper criticism is warped by a desire to retain any particular manager's advertisements. This I do not for a moment believe. What I wish to point out is that the length and fulness of English criticisms is part of the commercial rather than of the artistic policy of the different newspapers, and that quality does not always stand in a direct proportion to quantity.

So far as my own observation enables me to judge, I should say that nowhere is criticism more honest than in England—less influenced, I mean, by direct or indirect pecuniary considerations. On the other hand, it is nowhere more empirical, more superficial, more warped by considerations of personal friendship or enmity towards authors, managers, and actors. The critic is very often a man of great ability, still oftener a man of immense experience; but as a rule he has no fundamental principles, no fixed, not to say lofty standards—in short, no ideal. He may have started with one, as I do here, but the wear and tear of English theatrical life soon rubs the gilt off the brightest ideal. Criticism, like the dyer's hand, quickly assimilates itself to the medium in which it works. The critic assumes an easy-going cynicism, gives up the hopeless task of reform, is grateful for small mercies, and shrugs his shoulders over what falls below even the modest standard which experience has shown to be practicable. He may have started with instruments to take the height of the pyramids; but when he finds that mole-hills and not pyramids are what he has to measure, he leaves his quadrant at home and gauges them with his walking-stick. Involuntarily too, but quite inevitably, he is trammelled by feelings of personal kindness and good fellowship, feelings which are very amiable, but destructive to criticism. The theatrical clubs which bring together authors, managers, actors, and critics are the bane of critical frankness and impartiality. I speak feelingly, for I know the thousand little galling trammels to which a critic is subjected. I too have been a newspaper critic, and though none of the fraternity, probably, had fewer personal relations with authors and "the profession," yet it was often impossible for me to speak my innermost thoughts of a play or player. Not that I ever wrote deliberate falsehoods, and asserted that black was white and white black; rather I toned down everything to an inoffensive grey. Let us suppose that a new comedy by a popular writer is produced at a theatre owned by a popular manager. I know perfectly well that the piece is absolutely worthless, both from a literary and dramatic point of view. It is a mere collection of puns, old and new, placed without rhyme or reason in the mouths of some half-dozen grotesquely-dressed puppets known as characters. To me, personally, it is a weariness of the flesh, and I have no acquaintance with author or manager to warp my judgment. But do I say, even in the politest phrases, that the piece is puerile, and beneath the notice of intelligent men? No. I remark that, "Judged by his own standard, Mr. X. has surpassed himself." I then devote half a column to describing how the audience dutifully laughed at every quibble, all of which is literally and exactly true; and I wind up with some complimentary remarks, generally sincere enough, upon the actors, and a description of the "gorgeous and tasteful" *mise-en-scène.* In fact, every sentence, taken by itself, is literally true, but the whole article conveys a false and distorted impression. If I dared to apply even a moderately high standard and speak "from the liver out," the public would exclaim against my stupidity and spite, managers would place me under a taboo, while my editor would tell me that he could not afford to have his dramatic critic playing the part of Alceste, and would replace me with one of the hundred Philintes who are always ready to hand. Yet I appeal to all who know the *métier* to say whether the above description of the way "notices" are compounded is not literally correct in a large percentage of cases, even where absolute personal friendship does not complicate the problem. I say nothing of the cases, though they are not very rare, in which personal enmity, or even the mere exclusiveness of a clique, blinds the critic's eyes to the merit of comparatively good work.

All this applies mainly to newspaper criticism. Let us now look at the magazines. The great reviews, as I have said, ignore the drama, and nothing proves more clearly than this how entirely outside the literature of the country our theatre is held. In France the *Revue des Deux Mondes* follows carefully the leading productions of the literary theatres, and in the most influential German reviews great prominence is given to theatrical criticism. Our minor magazines in dealing with theatrical matters usually confine themselves to gossip and anecdotes of the "palmy days." Now and again a piece of serious criticism appears, but it is too often by a writer who imagines that a knowledge of the Greek dramatists qualifies him to criticize modern dramatists and actors without more study than is involved in going to the Lyceum or the Haymarket once or twice a year. Nothing can be more fallacious. General culture, apart from special study, no more fits a man to criticize a stage-drama than it fits him to criticize a steam-engine. Even the one or two writers of some authority who occasionally treat of the stage in the magazines, almost always confine their attention to Shakespeare and the poetic drama. This general feebleness of magazine criticism has long been a matter of regret to me. I believe that the magazines, or more probably some particular magazine, might become a power in the dramatic world. The critics of the daily and even of the weekly press labour under certain obvious disadvantages. Generally, and very properly and necessarily, their articles are news as much as criticism. Sometimes they are cramped for space, sometimes they are forced to give a subject much larger space than its intrinsic merits demand. The result is in one case perfunctory generalities, in the other misleading verbiage. They indicate rather than guide public opinion. Of the influence of personal relations with actors and authors I have already spoken. The duty of seeing everything, good, bad, or indifferent, dulls their sensibilities and renders them blasé. From all these disadvantages the magazine critic is, or might be, free. He can write with all advisable deliberation and at what length he pleases. He can avoid personal relations with the profession, which a critic who is also a purveyor of news cannot. He can run boldly counter to public opinion and declare that a great success is a bad play, and—rarer but not inconceivable case—that a dismal failure is a masterpiece. He can confine his attention to leading and representative productions, and does not need to breathe the gas of the footlights until he sinks into a sort of intellectual asphyxia. Last, but not least, *he can criticize the critics*, or at any rate can comment upon the attitude of the public mind towards a play or actor as affected by the professed organs of criticism. In short, I am convinced that "the coming critic" who must certainly precede "the coming dramatist" is to be looked for rather in the magazines than in the daily press. I, for one, am eagerly on the look-out for this protagonist. When he appears, I shall begin to have some hope that the day of regeneration is at hand.

For the present we can only labour to improve the conditions, material and intellectual, under which "the coming dramatist" will have to work. Were he to make his appearance to-morrow, he would find no public to applaud him, no critics to appreciate him, and consequently no manager to put his pieces on the stage. Suppose a dramatist like Augier to arise in our present-day England, he would probably carry a play from stage-door to stage-door for ten years. If at last by some happy chance he got it accepted, the Lord Chamberlain would insist on the suppression or falsification of its moral or political meaning, and it would make at best a success of esteem with the critics and a dead failure with the public. He would then take to writing ephemeral three-act farces, or to adapting the works of MM. Gondinet and Meilhac; or he would try novel writing, and as the dramatic faculty is quite different from the narrative, he would very likely fail at that. We have got into a vicious circle, and seem likely to go on turning in it indefinitely. A frivolous public calls for frivolous plays, and frivolous plays breed a frivolous public. The public degrades the managers, the managers the authors, the authors the actors, the actors the critics, and the critics the public again. It is impossible to tell in which the impetus towards degradation originates, or where first to attempt to check it. Time, however, works miracles, and we must trust to its beneficent power. In sanguine moments I sometimes dream of a "great Perhaps" in the shape of an Endowed Theatre—not necessarily endowed by the State, but in some manner or other raised above the necessity of being always and immediately a remunerative speculation. But the words "Endowed Theatre" open a large and terribly vexed question, on whose merits my own mind is as yet quite undecided, and upon which, in the present work at any rate, I cannot enter.

Some portions of the following articles have already appeared in periodical form. In one or two essays I may seem to devote too much attention to comparatively unimportant works, and to ignore or slur over more characteristic or successful plays. This is generally due to the fact that much of the English drama remains in manuscript, so that I have sometimes been obliged to fall back upon vague recollections, or even to omit all notice of a play, not having seen it and being unable to procure a copy. At the same time I have not failed to make use of every opportunity I could find to refresh my memory or to gain a knowledge of works hitherto unknown to me. In this effort I have been much aided by several gentlemen who have kindly thrown open to me their dramatic libraries, and to whom I desire to convey my warmest thanks. To show how small is the proportion of important plays published, even in Lacy's modest series, I may mention that an expenditure of about a pound at Mr. French's in the Strand procured for me every play included in his list which could possibly be of the slightest use to me.

PLAYWRIGHTS OF YESTERDAY.

TIME runs faster in the theatrical world than anywhere else. The stage clock, it is well known, often moves an hour while the watches of the audience record barely a quarter; and when the curtain is down a score or two of years pass as quickly as so many bars of the entr'acte music. The same rapidity characterizes theatrical life as a whole. The playwright whose name is to-day figuring in big capitals on every hoarding finds himself to-morrow forgotten even by the myrmidons of the Messrs. Willing. It is very hard indeed to distinguish a playwright of to-day from a playwright of yesterday. As for the playwrights of to-morrow one may guess or hope that this or that promising writer may be among the coming men, but anything like scientific prediction is impossible.

There are one or two writers who may perhaps be best described as playwrights of the day before yesterday. To this category belongs Dr. Westland Marston, whose works have disappeared from the stage with unaccountable completeness. To this category, too, one would like to consign Lord Lytton, but three of his plays die very hard indeed.

When Bulwer, on the well-merited damning of his "Sea-Captain," appealed from his contemporaries to posterity, Thackeray, in the character of C. J. Yellowplush, asked him pathetically if he really imagined that posterity would occupy itself with his "tradgadies." "This is sheer misantrofy, barnet," he added, "reglar Byronism, and you ot to have a better apinion of human natur." Yet it seems as if Bulwer were right and Thackeray wrong. Posterity does busy itself with his "tragedies," and, what is still more marvellous, with his comedy as well.

Within the last two or three years we have seen the two leading actresses of the day struggling with the pinchbeck sorrows of Pauline, and have heard two of our leading actors inform their audiences that "no divorce can separate a man from his mother," and that every penny of the spoils gathered by a successful officer in one of Napoleon's armies is "hallowed in the cause of nations." Neither of these revivals was particularly successful, it is true, and even the genius of Mr. Edwin Booth failed to secure more than a slight measure of acceptance for "Richelieu," though it is the least objectionable of the Lyttonian plays. Moreover, "Money," which is perhaps the most offensive of all, was far from proving a great attraction on the opening of the new Haymarket Theatre. But in spite of this undoubted decline in popularity we have probably by no means heard the last of Lord Lytton as a dramatist. His reputation still "walks" like a persevering ghost, more among actors, perhaps, than among the public. So long as staginess of the old type survives, the stagiest of plays will probably survive with it. Their very "flatchulency," again to quote Mr. Yellowplush, makes it difficult for them to give up the ghost. There is no saying how long they may gasp and pant on, in the provinces if not in London.

And here I may mention the name of Mr. Browning, not as a playwright of yesterday or the day before, but rather, perhaps, as a dramatist of the day after to-morrow. If his dramas with all their poetry and power are ever to become living works on the stage, it must be before audiences such as are not to be dreamt of under existing circumstances. The mere difficulties of his diction would preclude their general acceptance by even the most cultured audiences of to-day. For that reason it is no part of my purpose to examine them in detail. "The Blot on the 'Scutcheon" was produced at Drury Lane many years ago, but neither it nor its fellows have had any influence on the life of the stage. The "Antigone" of Sophocles, which has once or twice been played of late years, is as much a portion of the living stage-drama, with which alone I deal. For the same reason I say nothing of Mr. Swinburne's tragedies and several other remarkable works which form an additional proof of the total divorce of literature from the stage.

Of the playwrights of yesterday the first in point of merit and influence is undoubtedly Mr. T. W. Robertson. For the past twenty years he has been the ruling spirit of English comedy. He has had many direct imitators, and even those writers who have not precisely imitated him, such as Mr. Albery and Mr. Byron, have been indirectly influenced by the taste he fostered among audiences and the style he created among actors. The story of his short career of success is soon told. After years of chequered fortune he produced "Society" at the Prince of Wales's in November, 1865, and the success of that famous work changed the fortunes of the theatre, converting it from a burlesque house into the home of drawing-room comedy. "Society" was succeeded by "Ours" in September, 1866, by "Caste" in April, 1867, by "Play" in February, 1868, and by "School" in January, 1869, while "M.P.," the last of the series, produced in April, 1870, could not, despite the charming Cecilia Dunscombe of Mrs. Bancroft, be included among the Robertsonian successes. All these pieces, except perhaps "Play" and "M.P.," may be said to belong to the living drama, and yet it is distinctly the drama of yesterday. Not long ago "Society" was revived at the Haymarket, and the performance was altogether melancholy. It confirmed the observation that it is not always pleasant to meet an old friend after a lapse of years. Time has probably changed both him and you, and pleasant recollections are apt to be rudely effaced. There was still much to be amused at in "Society," but there was more to be wondered at, if not mourned over. There were touches of dialogue and character still fresh and true, but it was quite evident that the play as a whole was to be regarded mainly as a curiosity. It is at least half-way on its journey towards that haven of rest for theatrical *invalides*, Mr. Hollingshead's "educational" repertory. Anything more threadbare in the matter of construction it is hard to conceive. As no one ever did or ever will remember the plot of a Robertsonian comedy for more than a week after having seen it, a sketch of the plot of "Society" may have the charm of novelty.

Sydney Daryl, younger brother of a baronet, is in love with Maud Hetherington, niece and ward of Lord and Lady Ptarmigant. The latter wishes her to marry Mr. John Chodd, Junior, whose character may be guessed from his name, and a paragraph to the effect that a marriage has been arranged between them finds its way into the newspapers. Daryl, on reading this, goes to a party at the Ptarmigants', insults Maud, and wins 1000*l.* of Chodd at cards, by the most extraordinary run of luck on record. Just then a dissolution of Parliament takes place, and Chodd stands for the seat which has long been an heirloom in the Daryl family. Daryl opposes him on the strength of his own 1000*l.*, wins the election, which, so far as I can make out, takes place on the day after the dissolution, succeeds to the baronetcy, and is accepted by Maud, who, a few minutes before, has formally accepted Chodd. Such is the plot, and Mr. Byron himself could scarcely have invented a balder one.

I have said nothing of the child episode, which has the advantage of being unpleasant as well as absurd. Sydney Daryl secretly pays for the board and lodging of a little girl, innocently unconscious of the injurious suspicions to which this very secrecy must give rise. One fine morning his Bohemian friend Tom Stylus conceives the bright idea of calling at Lady Ptarmigant's along with the child. When asked who she is, he naively, not to say fatuously, replies, "Daryl's little girl." Lady Ptarmigant and Maud at once jump at the only possible conclusion, and by this ingenious device the author explains Maud's consent to receive the addresses of Chodd. Could anything be more deliciously simple in the way of dramatic construction? Of course we learn in the end that the child is really Lady Ptarmigant's own grand-daughter, her only son, now dead, having contracted a private marriage and left his child to Daryl's care.

The scenes in the Owl's Roost remain genuinely amusing, though the sort of life represented, or rather caricatured, in them is more or less a thing of the past. In the scenes between Lord and Lady Ptarmigant and Tom Stylus, on the other hand, the action degenerates into mere farce. Lady Ptarmigant's perseverance in calling Stylus "Mr. Silenus" becomes in the end amusing; but is there any so-called comedy in any other European language, in which such tricks as this are tolerated for the sake of a laugh? Or is there any comedy, farce, or burlesque, from Cadiz to Archangel, in which one of the leading characters has nothing whatever to do but to drag a chair after him wherever he goes and to fall asleep on every possible occasion, leaving his legs sticking out for the other characters to tumble over?

I dwell on "Society" partly because it was the play which made Robertson's reputation, partly because it is the last of his I happen to have seen. The last revival of "Caste," however, was an almost equally melancholy performance. The crudity of its construction, especially in the scenes where the Marchioness is brought into contact with the Eccles-Gerridge family, is almost incredible; and only the character of Eccles, which is really finely observed and strongly drawn, raises the play above the level of the merest commonplace. "School," on the other hand, is to my mind the very pleasantest of all Robertson's works. It has not the strong character-drawing of "Caste," but neither has it the glaring faults of that unequal play. It lacks the picturesque military element of "Ours," but its story is much more evenly developed. Its morality, as I shall afterwards have occasion to remark, is questionable, but fortunately no one thinks of drawing a moral from it. In fine, it is a charming woodland and garden comedy, full of grace, and with an atmosphere of freshness and health about it.

Yet withal what a trifling and flimsy work it is! It takes no hold of real life, it illustrates no point in dramatic art, except the possibility of keeping an audience of Britons amused for two hours with cleverly flippant and feebly sentimental small-talk. As Mr. Ruskin has aptly said:—"Its 'hero' is a tall youth with handsome calves to his legs, who shoots a bull with a fowling-piece, eats a large lunch, thinks it witty to call Othello a 'nigger,' and having nothing to live on, and being capable of doing nothing for his living, establishes himself in lunches and cigars for ever, by marrying a girl with a fortune. The heroine is an amiable governess, who, for the general encouragement of virtue in governesses, is rewarded by marrying a lord." And this is the best work, or one of the best, of the founder of modern English comedy! The fact is wonderful but undeniable; and another undeniable and sad fact is that this dramatist of yesterday lives again in a degenerate and time-hardened form in more than one prominent dramatist of to-day—"for what we have been makes us what we are."

If Mr. Robertson had had some of Mr. Tom Taylor's culture, taste, and constructive instinct, or Mr. Taylor some of Mr. Robertson's fresh humour, and mastery of the minutiæ of stage business, we should have had one admirable instead of two imperfect playwrights. Mr. Taylor's mind was exclusively prosaic. There was nothing of the *genial* about him—I use the word in its German sense—while T. W. Robertson was undeniably *genial* with all his shortcomings. Mr. Taylor, on the other hand, possessed this merit, that his work was almost always of some literary value. He was a very fertile, but at the same time a very painstaking writer. His best work had a solidity and a lack of obtrusive mannerism, which we look for in vain among other writers of the present day. Many of his best plays, it is true, were suggested by foreign works, but in most cases he so thoroughly remodelled his original as to make the result to all intents and purposes entirely his own. Those of his works which are likely to be longest remembered are "Still Waters Run Deep" and the "Ticket-of-Leave Man," which thoroughly deserve to hold the stage. "The Fool's Revenge," "Plot and Passion," "'Twixt Axe and Crown," "Clancarty," and "Arkwright's Wife," are stirring and able dramas, which will probably be occasionally revived for many years to come. "To Parents and Guardians" affords in M. Tourbillon a part which will always be a favourite with character actors. "Our American Cousin" has probably died with Mr. Sothern. Among his less important works are "Victims," "An Unequal Match," "To Oblige Benson," "A Sheep in Wolf's Clothing," "The Contested Election," "The Overland Route," "The Serf," "Joan of Arc," and "Anne Boleyn;" but some of even these are not likely to be entirely forgotten for a long time to come. Mr. Taylor was very fortunate, too, in works written in collaboration. "New Men and Old Acres" and "Masks and Faces," of which Mr. Dubourg and Mr. Charles Reade respectively were part authors, are among his most successful plays.

The mention of Mr. Charles Reade brings me to another dramatist of yesterday, and one who has at least that first requisite of greatness, faith in himself. In speaking of him I should perhaps confess that my estimate may be warped by the personal repulsion which Mr. Reade's style tends to create in me. He is always in a bad temper. Anger is not with him a "short madness." His controversial style is violent to a degree, and he carries the same mannerism out of the sphere of controversy into that of art. It is a question of temperament, and to me such a temperament is antipathetic. Hence I may possibly be unjust in my estimate of his absolute merits.

That he is a great dramatist if not *the* great dramatist of the age, he himself has perseveringly informed us, in the manifestoes and controversial effusions which every now and then ornament either the advertising or the correspondence columns of the newspapers. His theory is that he is a born dramatist driven into prose fiction by unjust and unwise copyright laws. In this theory there is a certain amount of truth. Let any one compare "Peg Woffington" with "Masks and Faces" and he will find in the spasmodic style of the novel a defect which disappears in the play. On the other hand let any one sit out "The Scuttled Ship" or "It's Never Too Late to Mend" and he will find it difficult to believe that such crude, ill-digested, and often conventional matter is the work of one of "nature's dramatists." *Poeta nascitur, non fit,* does not hold in regard to the drama. A dramatist must be "made," as well as born. Mr. Reade may have been born a dramatist, but he has certainly not been shaped into one.

"Masks and Faces" is probably his best work. It is a genuine comedy of interesting intrigue and well-marked character. The dialogue, too, is above the usual level. It is true that in many cases, the wit belongs to the "comedy of no-manners" school, which seems strangely inappropriate in a piece whose dresses and surroundings are eminently those of a comedy of manners. Half the fun of the piece, moreover, is got from two or three themes mechanically worked out to the very last echo. The number of jokes, for instance, extracted from the subject of painting of the face, is something wonderful—at a rough guess I should say about a score. The authors seem to have taken a rouge-pot, powder-box, and hare's foot, and worked out mathematically all their "combinations and permutations." The weight of poor Triplet's tragedies, too, is a subject for witticisms of which the authors appear to have held that "age cannot wither nor custom stale its infinite variety." But with all this the dialogue remains more than usually interesting from its occasional touches of true wit and genuine feeling.

Its construction is in several respects interesting. The first point to be observed, as a peculiarity rather than a fault, is that, like "Vanity Fair," it is a play without a hero. More correctly, it has in Triplet a hero who is almost entirely unconnected with the plot. He is concerned in the *dénouement*, it is true, but quite passively, and upon the course of the first two acts he produces absolutely no effect beyond that of accidentally opening Mabel Vane's eyes to the true state of matters in her husband's house. He is evidently one of the original elements in the play, which probably grew out of the idea of the picture scene, to which everything leads up; yet, up to the end of the second act, one is apt to believe that the authors have worked him in without rhyme or reason, merely to give a touch of character and sympathy to their otherwise rather unsympathetic matter.

A much more serious defect is the conduct of the *dénouement.* From the moment when Triplet leaves the room to allow Peg Woffington and Mabel Vane to have it out alone, the authors seem to have lost all grasp of their subject. They needlessly protract the action through several tedious and illogical scenes, which have to be led up to by means of very strained devices. The paper bearing Mabel's name, Peg Woffington's personation of Mabel, the incident of the diamond ring, and several other touches, are equally improbable and ineffective. The authors have not even taken the trouble to provide an adequate motive for Mabel's leaving the stage after her scene with her rival. The latter merely remarks, "I have need of being alone," and Mabel, instead of taking her coach and driving home, as she would naturally do, retires into the inner sanctum of the Triplet family, where one would imagine that she must be rather *de trop.* All this leads one to suspect the previous existence of a fourth act, in Mr. Reade's imagination if not actually on paper. The play is like the human body as represented by the Darwinian theory—it has caudal vertebræ which seem to indicate that, at some earlier stage of its development, it rejoiced in a tail. I should not be at all surprised to find that the curtain was originally intended to fall upon Mabel's discovery of the tear on Peg Woffington's face, which would reduce the third act to a reasonable length, and leave matter for a short fourth act. There would have been obvious difficulties in this arrangement, which perhaps tempted the authors to compress their fourth act into the end of the third, making it inordinately long, and resorting to strained expedients necessitated by the inconvenience of the scene. The fault lies in their desire to give Peg Woffington a scene of self-sacrifice, after the fashion of "David Garrick," by which she shall effectually restore Vane's affections to Mabel. They do not succeed in the attempt, and would not have succeeded had they written a fourth or even a fifth act. The audience does not feel at all satisfied of the sincerity of Vane's repentance. The difficulty lies in the original design of his character, which precludes a really satisfactory *dénouement* by any possible scenic means. It would have been much better frankly to accept the impossibility, make Vane enter immediately after Mabel's appeal to her rival, and close the play with a short scene, in which Peg Woffington restores Vane to Mabel as well as she can, by naturally and simply refusing to have anything more to do with him. Her self-sacrifice would then lie in her renunciation of the schemes for revenge, which she confesses to Triplet that she is meditating.

I have dwelt thus at length upon "Masks and Faces," because I believe it is the only one of Mr. Reade's works, so far as they are known to me, which is likely to hold the stage. He, on the other hand, believes in the immortality of "It's Never Too Late to Mend," which, he says, has outlived a hundred French dramas, and will outlive a hundred more. This is in a sense unquestionable—my only wonder is that it does not outlive its audiences. It has outlived me twice, so that after mature deliberation I have come to the conclusion that there is an M too much in its name, and that "It's Never Too Late to End" was the title to which it was "specially written up." On its last revival at the Adelphi, when I left the theatre at 11 p.m. the "humours of Jacky" were still in full swing, and there seemed every probability of their proving inexhaustible. And this was only the third act: when the fourth act ended, the gods only know. Yet had I gone to the theatre with a stern determination to sit it all out at all costs. I remembered how, on its revival at the Princess's, I had fled, weary and dispirited, at the end of the hut scene in the third act. This time I remained at my post half an hour longer. But though the spirit was willing the flesh was weak. When the irrepressible Jacky took the centre of the stage and set himself to solve the mysteries of a cotton umbrella, I reflected that art is long and life is fleeting, and went. The problems presented by that umbrella to the aboriginal intellect of Mr. Calhaem were no doubt of absorbing interest, but one cannot sacrifice everything to scientific curiosity. I went, "not that I loved Jacky less, but that I loved home more."

The play was mounted with the realism on which Mr. Reade always insists. The curtain rose upon "The Grove Farm with all the details of agricultural life—the farm-yard, wall and gate—the straw-yard—the duck-pond—the barn—the barley-mow—pigeons, ducks, poultry, animals, &c., &c." So the programme set forth the charms of the opening scene. Only a real pump was required to make the realism perfect, but that was reserved for the third act, where it produced a thrilling effect under the disguise of a mountain-lake and waterfall. As for the pigeons, ducks, poultry, and animals, they were all letter-perfect in their parts, and played, on the whole, with excellent spirit and discretion. One of the geese, it is true, seemed to labour under the very pardonable delusion that it was the star of the piece, and manifested a desire to take the centre of the stage—an ambition which was promptly checked by the string attached to its leg. The dog, too, showed a tendency to irrelevant "gagging" when it got its chain caught round its foot, and seemed, on the whole, to feel that, being a greyhound, it was derogatory to its dignity in the profession to be cast as a watch-dog. Otherwise the pigeons, ducks, poultry, and animals did not o'erstep the modesty of nature, and thoroughly carried out Hamlet's instructions so far as in them lay.

The &c. &c.—under which symbols I presume the men and women to be designated—were almost as good in their way. The matter of the play may be said, in Mr. Gilbert's words, to consist almost entirely of

> Blessings and curses
> And ever-filled purses,

judiciously tempered by the humours of Jacky. The ever-filled purses and Jacky do not come in until the third act, so the first two are entirely given over to the blessings and curses. Before the curtain has been up five minutes we have "the gentle Jew," Isaac Levi, cursing "the hard hristian" Mead ows. Then George Fielding alternately blesses and curses his friends and acquaintances, until his sweetheart very sensibly remonstrates with him, and asks him how he can use language like that "within a stone's throw of a Christian church." In the second act most of the comminatory eloquence falls to the share of Tom Robinson. I did not see the first production of the play in 1865, so cannot tell what were the horrors of the prison-scene which led to its rather stormy reception. If the scene was more horrible and more absurd than it is at present, it must have been a wonderful production. In the Australian scene we have only one curse, but that is the most original of all. When Abner deserts him in his distress, George Fielding remarks, "Wherever you go may sorrow and sickness—! No, I leave that to Heaven!"—a piece of self-abnegation and effacement which cannot be sufficiently admired. After this the humours of Jacky predominate and carry everything before them. It is marvellous with what precision Mr. Reade has managed to avoid every touch of character, habit, or dialect which could by any possibility suggest the actual Australian native, who is a lethargic individual with an extremely limited command of language, which, moreover, he is very chary of using. Jacky is a garrulous, volatile, monkey-like personage, with a very full English vocabulary, only marred by a few malapropisms. His favourite phrase is "a good deal," which no Australian aborigine ever used in his life. "Plenty," a word which Jacky never uses, is always in a blackfellow's mouth. Jacky makes fire by means of rubbing two sticks for something under a minute—a feat which would astonish a genuine

Australian native far more than the box of lucifers which exercises Jacky so greatly. He talks, too, about "the happy hunting-fields," an idea quite foreign to the blackfellow's order of things, and generally conducts himself like a cross between a Christy Minstrel and a Red Indian of the conventional type. In short, in all this portion of the play, Mr. Reade shows a perfectly Victor-Hugo-like power of moulding facts to fancy—a power to whose exercise one would not object so much, were it not that, like Victor Hugo, he insists upon his fancies being taken as fact. Of the fourth act I cannot speak, for I have never seen it.

One achievement of Mr. Reade's, perhaps his greatest, I should like to treat at more length than my space permits. He has informed us that "Drink," his adaptation of "L'Assommoir," is the greatest drama of the century, and it is certainly a very remarkable play. It is hard to over-estimate the difficulties with which he had to contend. He had to transplant a piece depending for its success on its realistic reproduction of the lights and shadow of low life in Paris, to a theatre whose audiences, for the most part, have no special knowledge of or interest in Parisian life. Another dramatist might probably have destroyed the reality and diminished the picturesqueness by removing the scene to England. Not so Mr. Reade. He saw that there was enough of universal-human interest in the piece to overcome the insular self-sufficiency which makes us unwilling to undergo the effort of putting ourselves in the place of a foreign people. He had the great central theme suggested by his title, coming home, alas! even more forcibly to the audiences of the Princess's than to those of the Ambigu, round which to group his characters and situations. He acted on the hackneyed truth that "one touch of nature makes the whole world kin." So long as his heroine speaks in the genuine tones of a suffering and struggling wife and mother, it matters not whether she be called Gervaise Coupeau or Susan Johnson. So long as his central character—one cannot say his hero—gives a faithful picture of the ravages caused by the great vice of modern times, it matters not whether absinthe or gin be the demon that destroys him. I am no great believer in the direct and immediate moral effect of stage representations, but if there ever was a drama which could cause instant conversions from evil ways, "Drink" was that drama. Mr. Reade and Mr. Charles Warner between them made a terrible "call to the unconverted." So completely was this the case, that the total-abstinence sermons put into the mouth of Goujet produced the effect of mere anti-climax and bathos. They put into words, and these not very just or logical, what the whole piece put in the terrible logic of action and fact. Every one has heard Goujet's homilies over and over again; almost every one has seen through their fallacies; but it is not every one who has seen the gradual decline of a working man from sober domestic happiness to a degraded and ghastly death, set forth with such striking and concentrated reality. Mr. Warner's rendering of the part of Coupeau was beyond doubt in its way the most extraordinary piece of acting the English stage has seen for many a day. There is a story of Dickens, after a trial-reading of the death of Nancy, going up to a distinguished actress in the audience and asking her what she thought of it. She rolled her eyes and slowly replied, "The public has long been on the look-out for a sensation, and, by heaven, they have got it now!" The same might be said of Coupeau's death-scene. In face, in voice, in figure, in everything, he was transformed. The management of his voice was perhaps the most wonderful part of the whole. M. Gil Naza's voice lent itself readily to the horrible huskiness required, but Mr. Warner must have laboured hard to produce the effect with his naturally fine organ. I do not know whether the realism was exact to nature. It produced the effect of reality, and that is the main point. When some actors writhe and wriggle on the stage in so-called realistic deaths, one is inclined to laugh rather than shudder. No one, I venture to say, ever laughed at Mr. Warner. I can imagine people screaming, fainting, leaving the theatre, even hissing, but not laughing. And just on this account I venture to defend the scene and the play. No one has less taste than I for horrors of this sort. They affect my nerves most painfully. During the death-scene I sat grasping the arms of my seat so as to repress my impulse to get up and leave the theatre. Having once seen it, no reasonable consideration would have tempted me to see it again. But after it was over I was glad to have seen it once. It had placed before me one of the realities of life, not otherwise likely to come so livingly under my ken. It had given me a vivid glimpse into one of the abysses which underlie the thin crust of society. It had not increased my knowledge, but vivified my perception of life. Its merits as a matter of art I shall not discuss. "Art" is a question-begging word in such a connexion, unless one has space to enter into the precise definitions which are necessary before it can be used with any hope of profit. My contention is that, art or no art, "Drink" was an instructive play of distinctly moral tendency, though I am not prepared to guess the probable extent of its direct moral effects. It rose in several respects above the level of conventional melodrama, and was a more or less truthful illustration of life. I know I shall be accused of rank Zola-ism in putting forward this plea. So be it. If it be Zola-ism to demand that the stage shall "hold as 'twere the mirror up to nature," then Hamlet and I are Zola-ists.

The last of my dramatists of yesterday is Mr. Dion Boucicault, certainly one of the most gifted "dramaturges" that ever lived. Were it worth while, one might write a book on Mr. Boucicault, in which would be resumed the history of English—and French—drama, properly so called, for the last half-century or so. He is the Scribe, the Dumas père and the D'Ennery of the English stage. With a little culture, a little thought, in short a little earnestness of character, he might have become a great and original dramatist. As it is, he has been the supreme showman of the Victorian stage. Mr. Percy Fitzgerald has summed him up in the phrase "the adaptive Mr. Boucicault." With the whole range of

English and French drama and fiction at his fingers' ends, he can piece together an original play out of half a score of scenes and situations gathered from every possible source. He is the great picker-up, or rather user-up, of unconsidered trifles. He knows every papier-maché property, every paste-board character, every threadbare phrase, every tough old ficelle of the theatrical lumber-room. He is the author or adapter of half the fossil dramas which some theatrical convulsion is every now and then throwing to the surface. How often have playgoers of the younger generation been surprised by the information that such and such a play, which to them seemed a relic of bygone ages, was the work of Mr. Boucicault. It is to be hoped that he has written or will write his memoirs; they would rival those of Dumas in interest and variety.

To him, for instance, we owe the two great supernatural plays of the stage, "Rip Van Winkle" and "The Corsican Brothers." There are some misguided parents who carefully prevent their children from imbibing in youth a taste for the supernatural through the medium of ghost-stories. They taboo as injurious alike to the intellect and the nerves those "old-wives' tales" which are at once the terror and delight of less scientifically educated children. This superstitious dread of superstition is fortunately rare, and most of us have learned in our childhood to appreciate the weird picturesqueness of a good ghost-story. Its attraction is scarcely increased by the fact that some people, even of intellect and education, are beginning to believe the "night side of nature" scarcely so apocryphal as it was once supposed to be. Mesmerism, spiritualism, clairvoyance, and their kindred "discoveries," if the word may be used in this sense, are undeniably placing the minds of many in an attitude of suspended judgment rather than of the absolute disbelief which formerly reigned. But a belief in its possibility rather detracts from the artistic charm of a good ghost-story. The supernatural is being vulgarized and is becoming a matter of science rather than of imagination. Our philosophy is determined no longer to admit Hamlet's reproach, and not merely to dream of but investigate everything in heaven and earth. But this is not the spirit in which ghost-stories are to be approached. We do not care whether they are true or possible—we believe in them because they are picturesque, because they satisfy a want in our nature. In this "painful kingdom of time and space" we feel ourselves cabined, cribbed, confined. Gravitation and evolution, the parallelogram of forces and the law of supply and demand, hem us in on every side. Euclid and Newton tyrannize over us. We long for a realm where apples shall fall upwards, and any two sides of a triangle shall be less than the third side—where nature shall no longer abhor a vacuum, and where "the inverse ratio of the square of the distance" is an unknown quantity. All this we find in ghost-land. It is the great privilege of a ghost-story that it is above, or rather beyond, criticism. It must be judged, not by the intellect, but by the nerves and the spinal marrow. If it sends a shiver down one's back, and a thrill to the roots of one's hair, it is a good ghost-story—if not, it is a bad one. Judged by this standard, "The Corsican Brothers" and "Rip Van Winkle" are excellent ghost-plays, and will probably remain the last great representatives of their class, since the tendency of the day is to "lay" imaginary ghosts, while it attempts to conjure up real ones, unavailable for stage purposes.

And if the ghost-play is an institution of yesterday, what of the Irish drama? "The Colleen Bawn" was played the other day at an East End theatre with Mr. Boucicault himself as Miles-na-Copaleen, and as I saw it I could not but wonder if this were actually the play which the whole West End was rushing to see not twenty years ago. I believe the result of a revival of "The Shaughraun," though its success dates from less than half that distance of time, would be very much the same. So, too, with Mr. Boucicault's last effort in the same field, produced only a year or two ago at the Adelphi. We felt that we were assisting at a drama of yesterday. As "The O'Dowd" illustrates very fairly not only Mr. Boucicault's dramatic manner, but a peculiarity of his character which deserves to be noted, I shall give a pretty detailed analysis of it.

In the first act we are introduced to a party of young gentlemen who have been gambling all night in the Temple chambers occupied by Mr. Percy Walsingham and Mr. Michael O'Dowd. At nine in the morning they are "as fresh as paint," their evening dress faultless, their hair evidently fresh from the embraces of the curling-tongs. Mr. Percy Walsingham loses an immense sum of money, and all his friends take their departure except one, Bertie Talboys. Bertie remarks, with that poetic fervour so characteristic of the gilded youth of this metropolis, "My heart tells me that yours is in trouble;" whereupon the two young men paw each other for some time and talk of their mutual "love." Then Percy confesses that he and Mike O'Dowd are one and the same person. His father is the O'Dowd of Suilamore, descended of course from the Irish kings, but, until lately, a fish-salesman. He has made money and sent his son to Trinity College, Dublin, where Mike has acquired the purity of accent peculiar to that seminary of learning, and at the same time gained the friendship of a Mr. Percy Walsingham, heir to a great estate in County Something-or-other. Percy Walsingham dies, Mike writes poetry beside his death-bed, and signs it with Percy's name. He thus becomes famous in London under the name of Walsingham, and, coming over, has not the heart to admit that it is only a pseudonym, well knowing that O'Dowds descended from the Irish kings are too common to be made lions of society. On the strength of his supposed heirship to the Walsingham estate he has run into debt to the amount of 20,000*l.*, and now sees nothing before him but "suicide or a sheep-walk in Australia." Before taking his choice between these direful alternatives, he proposes to go and see his parents at Suilamore. In an access of chivalrous devotion, Bertie begs to be allowed to come with him, as pathetically as if he were claiming the right to accompany his friend, not to Ireland, but to

Australia or the tomb. Mike feels that he has no right to refuse this crowning proof of devotion, and the two go off, not to Ireland, but to a garden-party at Lady Rose Lawless's, leaving the chambers in possession of Leake and Chalker, a money-lender and a broker's man. To them enters the O'Dowd himself, who has come across from Ireland accompanied by Kitty McCoul, Mike's sweetheart. Kitty carries their joint luggage in a basket, and is dressed in the traditional dress of the Irish colleen. With feminine curiosity she pokes into every corner of the room, and is delighted to find her own photograph, under which Mike has written, with the unblushing mendacity characteristic of his conduct, "Drawn from memory with the help of my heart." Meanwhile, the O'Dowd confides to Leake and Chalker the origin of his fortunes. He and Mike had some years before gallantly rescued a Swedish ship in danger off the Skelligs, and brought her into port through a "sacred" (secret) channel only known to themselves. It seems rather selfish of them to keep this important knowledge "sacred" from the other pilots and Trinity House; but that is a detail. They receive 6000*l.* as salvage-money, and this has now rolled up to a fortune of 20,000*l.* This information is very satisfactory to Leake, as that is precisely the sum Mike owes him. He says nothing about it for the present, however, and sends off the O'Dowd and Kitty to find Mike at the garden-party.

The garden-party is given by Lady Rose Lawless, the head of a bevy of fast young ladies, apparently unembarrassed by parents or guardians, or by any considerations of ordinary propriety. Lady Rose is engaged to Bertie, and the two discuss the probable future of their children with a charming frankness worthy of solicitors drawing up a marriage-settlement. Mike O'Dowd, or rather Percy Walsingham, is offered a chance of standing for the borough of Bally-na-Cuish, the funds to be provided by a rich widow, whom he is to marry. He is on the point of consenting, regardless of the breach of faith with Kitty, and of the fact that whenever he presents himself at Bally-na-Cuish his identity as Mike O'Dowd will be discovered, when, fortunately, his father and Kitty arrive, and the old man explains that he himself has been invited to stand for Bally-na-Cuish, in opposition to Colonel Muldoon, but has retired in favour of his son. Mike thus finds himself nominated for the borough by both parties, his opinions being apparently considered of no importance. He chooses to stand in his own name, and, when he cannot help it, nobly introduces his father and his sweetheart to the whole "garden party," who accept his change of name without comment, and lavishly place a carriage apiece at the disposal of the O'Dowd and Kitty, who wish to visit a relation in Spitalfields. Kitty bundles into her basket a pair of extremely coarse worsted stockings, which Mike's mother has knitted for him, and we are left to imagine her and the O'Dowd each driving off in solitary grandeur to Spitalfields, and returning in the evening to take up their abode with the hospitable Lady Rose.

In the third act we have the Bally-na-Cuish election.

Mike O'Dowd, who was at first perfectly willing to be the nominee of the Sassenach, has now turned an ardent patriot, and developes what Thackeray would call an "'arty contamp" for political economy. His anti-Malthusian principles excite the open enthusiasm of the virtuous peasantry who crowd the stage, and he is on the point of being elected by acclamation, when, in the next scene, at the O'Dowd's home, Leake and Chalker put in an appearance with a warrant for Mike's arrest on a charge of having forged the name of Percy Walsingham. This warrant they agree not to put in force if the O'Dowd will assign to them his whole property of Suilamore to cover his son's debts. The old man does so, and is of course struck with paralysis immediately after.

An interval of three years ensues. Mike has gone to Arizona and is supposed to be dead, the O'Dowd is mad, and Leake and Chalker have lived on air and apparently thriven. They offer untold sums for the loaves and fishes which seem to abound among the proud peasantry, but not a crumb or a fish-bone can they get. They have presumably supported existence during the three years on their own potatoes at Suilamore, so no wonder they are anxious for a change of diet. Even the tailors seem to have Boycotted them, for it is to be noted that they have on their old clothes, fortunately very little the worse for wear. Lady Rose Lawless looks in promiscuously, and remarks that Bertie, who was with Mike in Arizona, has made a fortune, half of which would be Mike's were he alive. Bertie is returning in the *Prairie Belle*, which at that moment is most inopportunely sighted in severe distress off the fatal Skelligs. Enter the O'Dowd, and to him Mike, in deep distress. He tries to convince his father of his identity by crawling about the stage, presumably to show that his consistently crawling character has not changed in the three years. The old man, however, does not see the implication, and it is not until Mike starts in the old pilot-boat, and brings in the *Prairie Belle* through the "sacred" passage, that he regains his reason and all ends happily.

And now comes the point of character to be illustrated. Mr. Boucicault is not only a dramatist, but a patriot to boot. His patriotism has a knack of cropping up in manifestoes and so forth just at the time when his plays want a little infusion of fresh blood into their veins. But that is no reason for doubting its sincerity, and I, for one, do not doubt it. What I doubt is its judiciousness. No one would welcome more heartily than I a play with some genuine political bearing, if by the Lord Chamberlain's gracious permission such a thing were possible. But I cannot accept "The Shaughraun" or "The O'Dowd" as pieces even of political special-pleading, worthy of any serious attention. Let us look at "The O'Dowd." If a tyrannical Saxon had set himself to satirize Irish patriotism, he could scarcely have done it more cruelly. Who is the patriotic orator whom the peasantry idolize? He is the man who was mean enough to be ashamed of his father's name, who was reckless enough to run into debt to the whole amount of his father's fortune, who was dishonest enough to forge his dead friend's signature, who was base enough to be on the point of deserting his old love to make an ambitious match, who was unprincipled enough in politics to consent to stand on the "wrong" side until he found he would have more chance on the "right." If this is a specimen of Irish patriotism, Heaven help Ireland! Mr. Boucicault seems to hold opinion with certain theologians who maintain that the elect may commit any crime under the sun, so long as their name is written in the right place on high. His heroes, he thinks, may do anything they please, and yet retain the sympathy of the audience, so long as it is clearly set forth in the play-bill and in the dialogue that they *are* heroes. It may be said that Mike's errors, with the exception of the forgery, which was perhaps scarcely intentional, were merely the errors which too often grow out of the national character —vanity, improvidence, recklessness, lack of strict principle. This is very true. But why choose as the exponent of the rights and wrongs of Ireland this type of the worst elements in the Irish character? It is a piece of grim satire, all the more biting from the fact that there is not a little truth in it. Mike's patriotism is a good deal after the fashion of Catiline's—*alieni appetens, sui profusus*—and one has a pretty strong suspicion that, in a sense different from that which Mr. Boucicault intended, it is remarkably true to nature.

All Mr. Boucicault's later efforts on the stage have been of a style to justify my classing him as a playwright of yesterday. "The Bridal Tour," "Forbidden

Fruit," and "Mimi," met with different amounts of success, but had all one characteristic—old-fashionedness. Their author, or adapter, or translator, or compounder—it is hard to tell which word to apply in each different case—is no longer in the current of the time. I do not mean that it is impossible that Mr. Boucicault should yet give us one or two successful dramas. Nothing would surprise me less. But he is no longer a living and effective influence in the dramatic life of the country. He is one of the giants that were—yesterday.

ENGLISH DRAMATISTS OF TO-DAY.

MR. JAMES ALBERY.

HOW well I remember my first introduction to the works of Mr. Albery! Living in the country, I had not seen any of his earlier plays on their production in London. One evening I wandered into a little provincial theatre, very smoky and dirty, and full of the smell of stale gas which never leaves a badly ventilated house. It was the opening night of a travelling company specially organized to play Mr. Albery's pieces. They had chosen "Two Thorns" for their first performance. The scenery was meagre and the company mediocre as a whole, though it contained one admirable actor in the person of Mr. Flockton. I can well recall to this moment my disappointment with the thin and trivial first act of "Two Thorns," followed by my growing interest and pleasure as the piece proceeded. Some of its scenes seemed to me to possess the ingenuity and force of the old Spanish comedies, though the looseness of its structure was only too evident. I particularly remember a scene in which a young gentleman, who is, or considers himself, on the best terms with a married lady, mistakes her husband for the butler, and confides the whole intrigue to him with much ridicule of "the mouldy old husband." I left the theatre with the conviction that here at last was the work of a dramatist, with some power of construction and a mastery of dialogue. For the week or fortnight during which the company remained, I was an almost constant attendant at the theatre. Besides "Two Thorns" the repertory contained "Two Roses," "Apple Blossoms," and "Forgiven." I remember being most of all struck with the last. The concluding scene of one act—I think the third—seemed to me the most brilliant and poetic piece of dialogue I had heard in modern comedy. I state my impression of the moment for what it is worth, as I have not since had an opportunity of testing its correctness. The play is still in manuscript, and I have never again seen it on the stage. My recollection, however, has been confirmed on several occasions when I have heard "Forgiven" spoken of as being, with all its faults, the best of Mr. Albery's original comedies. This phrase "with all its faults" is one which must unfortunately be applied to most of Mr. Albery's efforts. Few writers are more faulty, but none redeem their faults by such striking beauties. Mr. Albery has narrowly missed being *facile princeps* among modern English playwrights. He has escaped that distinction by lack of constructive power, lack of taste, lack of earnestness. As it is, he stands unrivalled in the sphere of dialogue. His fanciful wit and witty fancy might under better direction and more favourable circumstances have contributed works of genuine merit not only to the stage, but to dramatic literature.

The fact that scarcely any of his plays are printed

renders Mr. Albery's work peculiarly difficult to criticize as a whole. On this ground I must claim indulgence for the unavoidable incompleteness of the following study.

Mr. Albery's reputation as an original writer rests mainly on "Two Roses." And indeed this comedy is, if not his best, his most characteristic play. It is full of small beauties, which, as in an ill-arranged mosaic, do not blend into a clear or harmonious design. Mr. Albery does not, like Mr. Byron, trust to providence for his plot. He tries to form a plot and to invent original scenes, but unfortunately plot, situations, and characters are not welded into one piece. They adhere to each other more or less closely, but do not chemically combine.

The skeleton of the plot is in the highest degree conventional. In Act I. the broken-down adventurer Digby Grant succeeds unexpectedly to a fortune, and breaks off the engagement between his daughter Lotty and Jack Wyatt. In Act II. the action stands absolutely still. In Act III., by a peculiarly improbable variation of the old trick of the long-lost heir, Grant falls from his high estate, and Caleb Deecie, the blind lover of his elder daughter Ida, turns out to be the rightful owner of his property, with results which can of course be imagined. This is literally the whole plot. The second act, with its elaborate concluding situation, is an episode; the characters of Mr. and Mrs. Jenkins, the former only second to Grant himself in prominence, have nothing whatever to do with the action; in short about two-thirds of the play could be cut away, and the plot properly so called, would be left intact.

Now let us glance at the characters. Digby Grant himself is certainly an ably-drawn figure, not very original, for he has had several prototypes in fiction, but new to the stage. There is a touch of caricature in the design, but it is nevertheless vigorous and consistent. Both the strength and the exaggeration are apparent in the opening and closing scenes of the first act, which are not unfair specimens of Mr. Albery's dialogue. Grant is discovered alone, and opens the play with a short soliloquy, whereupon Mrs. Cupps, the landlady, enters.

Grant. Ah, Mrs. Cupps, how do you do?

Mrs. C (*stiffly*). I'm very well, I thank you. I have called for my little bill, Mr. Grant.

Grant (*taking bill-file*). I'm glad to hear it. I was afraid you'd called for the money. (*Takes bill off file and hands it politely.*)

Mrs. C. Mr. Grant, this is not right!

Grant. Very likely not. I haven't cast it up. I never do. The tradespeople mean to rob me—I mean to pay them—we both fail, and the good intention is with me, thank heaven!

Mrs. C. Well, I've not robbed you, and you'll find this is a debt you can't help paying.

Grant. Mrs. Cupps, that's new. I've always found them debts I can't help owing.

Mrs. C. And yet you pay away money without occasion. Last night you gave my potman sixpence to fetch you a cab—but I must go without!

Grant. Mrs. Cupps, you do not understand the feelings of a gentleman. I cannot be under obligations to a potman—absurd! Your case is different. There's your account—I acknowledge the debt—I do not dispute it, or attempt to deduct overcharges, or take off a discount for cash like a common cad. If you bring it to me next year I shall still acknowledge it; I can do no more—I am a gentleman, I can do no less.

Mrs. C. I don't care for all your fine talk. I'll have my money or I'll know the reason why.

Grant. What can be fairer? You *shall* know the reason why—I haven't got it.

* * * * * *

Mrs. C. I haven't common patience. Good morning. (*Rises indignantly.*)

Grant. Mrs. Cupps, stay (*rises*). You shall be paid. I'll do it—I'll do it!

Mrs. C. (*returning*). Dear me, what?

Grant (*leans on a chair*). This little room, lowly indeed, for I do not hold the position I did, is still the abode of honour and innocence, of me a broken gentleman and my two daughters—two roses, as my very worthy, though plebeian, friend John Wyatt calls them—two roses, white and red. This floor shall never be polluted by the tread of a broker. I'll do it—

Mrs. C. Dear me, do what?

Grant. I will sacrifice myself.

Mrs. C. Not kill yourself, Mr. Grant?

Grant. No, I will only stay my pride. A lady who has wealth has almost asked me to share it. I will marry her for the sake of my daughters, and you shall be paid.

Mrs. C. I—I could wait a little while, Mr. Grant.

Grant. No, you shall not wait. She is not a fair woman, she has not your comely figure or pleasant smile, Mrs. Cupps.

Mrs. C. Oh, Mr. Grant.

Grant. She has not your gentle voice.

Mrs. C. Do you think my voice gentle?

Grant. She will not be such a mother to my girls as—as you would make. But I have pressing need, she will, I know, lend me 20*l.* at once, and you shall be paid. (*Sits as if to write.*)

Mrs. C. Oh, it seems a great pity you should sacrifice yourself, Mr. Grant. It's very noble, but—

Grant. I will do my duty.

Mrs. C. I would lend you 20*l.*, Mr. Grant, if—

Grant (*takes her hand*). Mrs. Cupps, these lips have touched the royal hand (*kisses her hand*). I—I cannot express what I feel at this proof of your high esteem. I would not have you see my emotion ; leave me—and—and bring the money.

Mrs. C. I will, Mr. Grant ; good-bye.

Grant. Good-bye ; I shall never be able to repay you for your kindness. Allow me ! (*Opens the door and bows her out ; closes the door.*) That's a damned silly woman.

With all its exaggeration, and in spite of one or two clearly false touches, this scene is a piece of true comedy. So is the concluding scene, which takes place after Grant has been informed of his accession to fortune, and has been provided by his lawyer with a cheque-book.

Grant. My dear children (*rising*), I know not why I should not say my friends, I have to some extent deceived you. I was like Timon, tired of the hollowness of the world, sick of its tinsel show, and I came here hoping to find more simple joys, and sincere, though humble friendship. I have not been deceived. I may mention as an instance the kind solicitude of Mrs. Cupps. She was quite unaware that it was in my power to repay her fully, she shall not go unrewarded. Mrs. Cupps—a little cheque ! (*Tears it from book and hands it.*) I am about to return to the position to which I am by birth entitled ; my daughters are about to take their place in society among the noblest and the best !

Jenkins (*a little tipsy, enters quickly with a badly folded parcel*). Here's the dry sherry, and here are the kicksies. They'll suit you. (*Displays a pair of light trousers and a white waistcoat.*)

Grant (*taken a little aback*). My worthy friend, I was in jest. Our Mr. Jenkins, a much esteemed though humble friend, has a good heart. I have on various occasions noticed that he has under the disguise of disburdening his sample-case, left various things for my daughters, such as—as shall be nameless. He cannot be expected to possess the refinement which would have made it clear to him that even if we required such aid our pride would not have allowed us to accept it. But he meant well, and I ask him to accept—a little cheque! Mr. Deecie, with whom I deeply sympathize, lent my daughters a piano—he did not mean to offend—I thank him with—a little cheque! As for that young man Wyatt, though a plebeian, he would, had I found him worthy, have formed an alliance with me; but he is not—but a few moments back, to test him, I asked him to lend me 10*l.* He would have been repaid in thousands, but he had the worst vice of the vulgar—no faith, no confidence. I will have no more to do with him. (LOTTY *goes to* JACK. GRANT *takes her hand and crosses her in front of the table, where she sinks in grief.* IDA *goes behind and consoles her.*) I am indebted to him in some small sums, 20*l.*, 30*l.* I wish never to see him again. I clear the score—a little cheque! (*Tears out cheque and offers it. The curtain falls.*)

In these scenes the character of Grant and Mr. Albery's method of developing it are sufficiently indicated. Taken by itself as a piece of character-drawing, his figure is far above the average of modern comedy. But it is not brought well into relation with the other characters of the play. The attitude of his daughters towards him, for instance, is never clearly or consistently defined. There is a vague attempt to indicate that Ida has inherited some of his pride, or rather arrogance, and for that very reason she now and then comes into conflict with him, but the conflict is never dramatic, it never leads to anything. In the design of the situation which concludes the second act there seems to be some trace of what might have formed the true drama of the play. By very elaborate, not to say impossible, contrivances, both daughters are present, concealed, when a scene occurs between Wyatt and Grant, in which the latter's meanness, dishonesty, and arrogance of character are brought out in unmistakable colours. If this came as a startling revelation to the daughters, altering their whole attitude to their father and with it the course of the action, it would be a really fine piece of drama. As it is, we scarcely know whether or not any new light is thrown upon Grant's character in his daughters' eyes; their emotions are left altogether undetermined; and whatever they may be they produce not the smallest effect upon the course of the play. One can scarcely imagine an elaborate situation more hopelessly thrown away.

The young men of the play are a rather colourless pair, though the blindness of Caleb Deecie gives him character and renders him effective on the stage. Jack Wyatt's poetry and philosophy are, as a rule, of a very commonplace type indeed. "Our Mr. Jenkins," on the other hand, is an original and really amusing figure both in his unregenerate condition of the first act, and as a "shining light" in the second and third. It is a pity that he has nothing to do with the action.

There are delicate touches of wit and poetry scattered throughout the play, and Mr. Albery has a happy knack now and then of putting his poetry into action in the form of pieces of pretty and fanciful stage-business. These, with the characters of Digby Grant, Caleb Deecie, and Our Mr. Jenkins, account for the popularity of "Two Roses," and entirely justify it. "In the kingdom of the blind, the one-eyed is king"—among comedies of the day "Two Roses," with all its faults, stands prominent in the front rank.

For one reason or another, the rest of Mr. Albery's original plays have lately fallen into neglect, in London at any rate. The fact is difficult to account for. In my own vague recollection, as I have said, and in the report of "old playgoers," "Forgiven" is noted as the ablest of all his works; "Tweedie's Rights," I believe, has many points to recommend it; and of the merits of "Apple Blossoms" circumstances enable me to speak with more certainty.

With all its faults, to use the unavoidable formula, it is a charming and delicate idyl. Perhaps it would be wiser to avoid that much-disputed and much-abused word, and call it a garden-comedy. Its scene, its atmosphere, and its aroma, disarm criticism. We do not look for realism under the apple-blossoms, in the garden of a village inn in Devonshire, or in the inn-parlour at Christmas-tide, with the holly, to use Tom Penryn's phrase, "speckling the dull corners with quaint lights." The English country inn has a prescriptive, half-legendary charm, of which not even its unfortunate relationship to the public-house can entirely deprive it. Indeed the gin-palace is not really of the same family. It is an upstart by-blow of city commerce which has taken the name, and sometimes even the arms, of the village aristocrats. The aristocrats are dying out along with the modes of life of which they formed part, but a few specimens still remain, their charm doubled by their rarity. Mr. Albery's inn is one of these: it is called the Apple-Tree Inn: it is placed in Devonshire, "the chosen home of chivalry, the garden of romance." Under these circumstances, what churl so wooden-headed as to demand realism and truth? We want sentiment, we want humour, we want flowers and sunshine, and red firelight and deep shadows. If we are to have any realism at all let it be of the real pump order, and take the form of real cider and real clotted-cream. It is not every day we are at a village inn in Devonshire. *Dulce est desipere in loco.*

"Apple Blossoms" tells a simple story, so slight that it almost falls to pieces on analysis. Tom Penryn has fallen in love with Jennie Prout of the Apple-Tree Inn. Her uncle and aunt, with whom she lives, not believing that his intentions can be honourable, send to his father, Captain Penryn, to ask him to get Tom out of the way. Captain Penryn, without even inquiring who the girl is whose happiness Tom is supposed to be endangering, commands him to leave the village. Tom refuses, and the choleric and obstinate old father promptly disinherits him and casts him off. In the second act we find that Tom has entered the navy as a common sailor, and Captain Penryn has been seized with an illness, through which he has been nursed by

Jennie Prout. He has become very much attached to her, and has practically adopted her. It is Christmas Eve, and in the midst of the preparations for the festivities Tom arrives in his sailor's dress. He steals in unnoticed by Jennie, who has just hung up the mistletoe and, sitting under it, takes out Tom's portrait in a locket.

Jennie. I wish you a merry Christmas, and all happiness, and give you the first kiss under the mistletoe. (*As she is stooping,* TOM *takes her hands from behind, and kisses her cheek over her shoulder, then keeps his chin over her head so that she cannot see him.*)

Jennie. Oh, Mr. Temple! what a shame! (*Pause.*) Isn't it you?

Tom (*gruffly*). No!

Jennie. Then it's Mr. Baggs?

Tom. No!

Jennie. Oh, who is it?

Tom (*sings*). "He was there, and I was there—"

Jennie (*drops her hands, and pauses a moment in a kind of dreamy wonder, then puts her arms round him*). Oh, Tom!

Tom (*looking round*). How pleasant it is to get back to the place you love!

Jennie (*thinking of him*). Yes, it is.

Tom. You had my letter?

Jennie. Yes.

Tom. And no one knows of this but ourselves?

Jennie. Only our Kittie.

Tom. Ah, you should not have told.

Jennie. I was obliged to tell her. *Another* one wanted to marry me.

Tom. Who was that?

Jennie. Mr. Trebit, the captain at Wheal George. Oh, he

is such a funny little man, with a great forehead on a very small nose—

Tom. Like a very large entablature on a very little column, eh?

Jennie. Yes; his nose looks as though it was a temporary nose put there to support his forehead, while his real nose was in course of erection.

Tom. Or as if it only marked the proposed site for a nose?

Jennie. But he's plenty of money.

Tom. And I'm so poor, *now.*

Jennie. What am I worth?

Tom. Yes, I'm rich. I wouldn't take worlds for you, though I might go out and pick a dozen on any star-light night.

Jennie. Ah, Tom, stars do nicely to speckle one's talk with, don't they?

But Tom has come not so much to see Jennie as to get news of his father, of whose illness he had heard. In doing so he has exceeded his leave by three days, and a corporal's squad of sailors is out searching for him as a deserter. At the end of the act, in a scene very cleverly arranged so as to get picturesque effects from the changes of light on the stage and over the snowy landscape outside, Captain Penryn refuses to conceal Tom and gives him up to the sailors who are in search of him. In the third act, Captain Penryn is gradually wasting away under ill-concealed remorse for his harshness, and longing for the return of his only son. The arrival of Tom's ship has been announced, and Bob Prout, Jennie's uncle, has gone to London to try if he can find Tom. On his return, of course unsuccessful, his wife Kittie, Jennie, and the lawyer, Mr. Temple, are sitting in the apple orchard.

Kittie. What did you see in London, Bob?

Bob. Well, I don't know where to begin. I saw sich a sight o' things. But the first thing I noticed was, that everybody sticks them gashly labels like Mr. Baggs do, awnly they are much beggerer, and they're all over the walls an' pailin's, and among um I see waun, a gurt picture of Mr. Baggs, and under et, et said, "Where are you going?" Then et said, "I'm goin' to see the gurt Baggs at the Gipsey Hall, Pickledilly."

Kittie. Why, isn't he dead?

Bob. Naw, he warn't this morning.

Jennie. Ah, his tricks again.

Kittie. Did you see un, then?

Bob. Iss, I did; and I axed un to tell me a good inn to stop at, and he said Furnivall's Inn was the cheapest and best, and axed me to meet un for a game of cricket in Lincoln's Inn Fields in the morning. But it was all es gammuts, agen; the Inn wasn't a inn, and the Fields was a gurt square.

Kittie. Ah, you ought to have taken me with you.

Bob. So I ought. But a wors very kind, and a said he knew the man that kipt the British Museum and the Natural Gallery, and he'd get me in for nawthin!

Temple. Baggs took you in nicely.

Bob. Aw, that ee did, very nicely, for we went to the Museum and a jist nodded to the man, and a let us in without payin' nawthin', and we saw everything there is all over the world. Then we went to the Natural Gallery.

Temple (*laughing*). And did he just nod his head again?

Jennie. And you had to pay nawthin'?

Bob. No, nawthin'; and they took our stecks. A told me that was cos the Prince of Wales had lost es steck, and they were lookin' to every one's to find it. . . . And then he said he'd take me to a theaatre to see a lady and lions, and a ded, and I see the lady . . . .

Kittie. Did ee see the lions, Bob?

Bob. Naw. I says to Mr. Baggs, "Where's the lions?" and a ses, ef ee doant caall for un they won't come; so I called out for un, and what do you think Mr. Baggs ded?

Kittie. I don't know.

Bob. Why, a pretended a dedn't knaw me, and says, "Turn un out;" and a gashly policeman came and took me away, and Mr. Baggs he helped un, and when we goat outside I thogt he'd a ben ill with laffin, and he took me and gave me a pint of beer!

Meanwhile, more practical efforts than those of Bob Prout have been made to find Tom and bring him home again. He arrives, is reconciled to his father, and the curtain falls upon him and Jennie singing under the apple-laden branches:—

He was there, and I was there;
  All that I remember now
Is the stillness of the air,
  And the blossom on the bough,
And the prudish beads I strung:
That was when the year was young.

He was true, and I was true;
  All that now comes back to me
Is the yellow autumn hue,
  And the ripe fruit on the tree;
Nothing said, yet all was told,
When the year was growing old.

It is impossible to examine this piece critically from any point of view without finding it full of faults. The plot is ludicrously slight, highly improbable, and turns on a series of almost inconceivable misunderstandings. The best situation in the piece, that which concludes the second act, is episodic and worked in almost entirely for its own sake, though it is not quite so glaringly useless as the analogous situation in "Two Roses," for it may be supposed to influence Captain Penryn's disposition towards Tom, and so to facilitate the happy winding-up of matters in the third act. Then the dialogue, as may be seen from the extracts I have given, is more bright than true, more pretty than natural. In its sentimental portions it is so "speckled with stars," and strewn with apple-blossoms, and laden with ruddy apples, that Mr. Albery might have borrowed a second title from Jean Paul and called the play a "Flower, Fruit, and Thorn Piece." Moreover there is a good deal of strained and incongruous matter in the humorous scenes dealing with "the great Baggs," Mr. Temple, and Mrs. Page. But in spite of all this, I should like extremely to see the comedy revived with an elaborate *mise-en-scène*, like that of "L'Ami Fritz" at the Théâtre-Français, and a hero and heroine who could give its full grace and charm to the sentiment of the play. In the characters, too, of Bob Prout and Handsome Bill, there is admirable scope for effective character-acting, and a comedian of taste and originality might make a very amusing figure of "the great Baggs." Perhaps the comedy would be more certain of success if Mr. Albery would slightly modify this part and that of Mr. Temple, especially with reference to the rather farcical compact between the latter and Captain Penryn as to Tom. I am convinced, however, that no very material change would be required in order that the comedy, properly placed on the stage and acted, should deserve, and even command, success, though the two things are no more synonymous on the stage than in the outer world.

Of late years Mr. Albery has made only one effort in the way of original comedy, the unhappy "Jacks and Jills" at the Vaudeville. From the title to the last line the comedy was unfortunate. Why "Jacks and Jills"? The phrase has no discoverable relevance to the matter in hand, for which such a name as "Brandy and Soda" would have been infinitely more appropriate. Every dramatist knows that there is a great deal in a name. "Give a play a bad name, and damn it," should be the playwright's first lesson in proverbial philosophy. But even a worse name than "Jacks and Jills" could scarcely have obtained for the comedy a lower place in the limbo of still-born plays than it claimed in virtue of its inherent defects. The first act was dull but inoffensive. True, the two old maids, Miss Cecilia and Miss Alice McGullup, were more unpleasant than amusing, and there was a notable lack of Mr. Albery's usual ease and polish of dialogue, but at the fall of the curtain there was still some hope that genuine ability in the succeeding acts might retrieve the day. The hope quickly vanished when it was found that the whole "fun" of the play was to be got out of drinking. Drunkenness is the first resort of the amateur playwright. When his maiden farce is becoming dull, and plot and puns are beginning to run short, he forthwith makes half his characters drunk. It is the cheapest way of raising a laugh ever invented, but, unfortunately, the laugh does not always come in at the right place, especially if the thing is overdone. Now Mr. Albery positively deluged us with drink, in Zola-esque profusion. Brandy-and-soda was produced early in the first act, and Major McGullup indulged in it liberally. Then in the second act, Edward Irwin came into the drawing-room after dinner in a maudlin condition. More brandy-and-soda was produced—in the drawing-room, be it noted. Miss Cecilia McGullup remarked sweetly that "she would just take a sip from Mr. Edward's glass"—surely an unnecessarily nasty idea—and then drank off half a tumblerful of brandy neat—surely a gratuitously offensive act. Then Samuel Irwin got drunk, Edward Irwin got drunker, and the two concocted a drunken letter in a drunken fashion, which was drunkenly delivered to the wrong person by the butler Pawle, who had not been drinking on the stage, but must evidently have been indulging in his pantry. The tableau at the close of the act showed Pawle carrying the helplessly intoxicated Edward upstairs in his arms. In the third act ale and champagne were substituted for brandy-and-soda; and, in short, one was reminded throughout of Mr. Leland's immortal verse which describes Hans Breitmann,

A–vorkin' out life's mission here
Soobyectifly und grand :
Some beoples runs de peautiful,

> Some vorks philosophy ;
> Der Breitmann solf de infinite
> Ash von eternal shpree.

Mr. Albery's characters were one and all "a-vorking out life's mission here soobyectifly und grand," and he himself had certainly "solfed de infinite" in the matter of bad comedy-writing.

Yet Mr. Albery's hand was not entirely unrecognizable even in this unhappy blunder of a play. There were little touches of charming poetic fancy in the dialogue, most of them placed, strangely enough, in the mouth of Major McGullup. Once or twice there was a touch of genuine wit and character, and the plot was not so utterly feeble as might at first sight be imagined. The complications in the third act were really ingenious, though so clumsily introduced and elaborated that it took some thought to separate them from their surroundings and judge of their intrinsic merit. One might even go so far as to say that there were the bones of a good play in the piece, but the flesh in which they were clothed was so flabby and unhealthy as entirely to hide their structure. It was a comedy in the last stage of alcoholism.

Though the fact is almost forgotten by the general public, Mr. Albery has done other original work besides his prose comedies. He has made at least two efforts in what may be called poetic extravaganza. "Oriana," produced at the Globe and "The Will of Wise King Kino," produced at the Princess's, both belong to a class of work in which Mr. Albery's qualities of fancy and wit should enable him to excel. Neither, unfortunately, can be considered quite successful, but both have such merits as to lead one to hope that the author may one day make another effort in the same direction.

"Oriana," like so much of Mr. Albery's work, is full of admirable ideas set forth in a fashion which can only be described as higgledy-piggledy. The cause of its failure—apart from possible defects of representation, of which I know nothing—clearly lies in the fact that the construction lacks symmetry and consequently dramatic force and clearness. King Raymond, monarch of the Happy Isles, has ceased to love his consort, Queen Oriana, and is given up to idleness and riotous living. In the first act the queen meets a little fairy, Peep, whom she at first takes for a lame beggar-child. Peep, however, convinces her of her over-earthly nature, and continues,—

> My home is in yon golden regions where
> The dying day garners his sunset clouds,
> Mid which the fairies sport. My work was but
> To speckle eggs that birds might know their own,
> Dot lady-birds, and make the little harps
> Grasshoppers play on all the summer-time.
> I painted butterflies and shrieking birds
> With radiant colours. Well, one day I went
> To hang some fern up—you call maiden-hair,
> And on my way home I lay down and slept.
> There, as I lay, our king's great hounds came by,
> And one, called "Glitter," the king's favourite,
> Lifted me up and dropped me from a rock!
> Down, down I fell, and broke my hand and foot.

Oriana. Poor little creature!
Peep. Slowly I crawled back
And I was very angry.
Solon. I should think so.
Peep.—
I took some deadly berries, whose dark juice
I used for blacking beetles, and I put them
In Glitter's food. I then went to the king,
That he might touch my limbs and make them sound.
His hand was raised—when came a messenger
To say the dog was dead. Then our king rose
And bade them take me from his golden land,
And said I never should come back again
Or move with perfect limbs till—here he stopped
To think of something that could never be.
Then, turning to his court, he clipped his oath
With "Till King Raymond loves his queen again."

Thus it becomes the object of Peep to help Oriana to win back the king's love. By means of certain spells, Peep procures a ring, the wearer of which will be ardently loved by whoever first beholds him or her with it on. This magic property, however, is unknown to all but Peep; and the rest of the play consists of the ring passing from hand to hand and the love at cross-purposes which of course results. And this it is that renders the play formless. There is no meaning or principle discoverable in the various changes of the ring. That the right person gets it at last is the merest chance, and it might have gone on changing hands through ten acts instead of two. Some of the complications are ingenious and original, especially that by which King Raymond, immediately after putting on the ring, sees his own face in a looking-glass, and falls passionately in love with it. But our interest is languid. The tale is clever and pleasant and pleasantly told, but it does not grasp our attention in virtue of either its action, its characters, or its diction. Oriana herself is a colourless character, and there is not much force or life even in the comic parts, such as Oxeye, a democrat, whom Mr. Albery makes the vehicle of a great deal of satire—for Mr. Albery, be it known, is a staunch Conservative. Here is an example:—

Oxeye. Why is King Raymond superior?

Cloe. He is a king.

Oxeye. Ah! thou hast hit it, Cloe. Now, hear me speak. A prince once called his lord high butler to bring him some brandy. He brought it him in a fine crystal bottle, with a shabby little cork at the top. "What a shabby little cork," said the prince, "for such a beautiful bottle." "I am a fine stopper," said the cork. "You're a shabby little cork," said the prince. "You're a shabby little prince," said the cork. "I am a great monarch," said the prince. "Prove it," said the cork. "I am the prince of a great people." "I am a splendid stopper," said the cork. "Prove it," said the prince. "I am the stopper of a great bottle."

Cloe. And what did the prince say?

Oxeye. He grew very angry, and threw the cork in the fire. That is the way with princes. Now, Cloe, what do you make of the fable. Do not answer. Hear me speak—King Raymond is the cork! I am the beautiful bottle.

Cloe. You mean the bottle represents the people?

Oxeye. 'Tis too commonly the case. I represent the bottle.

Cloe. So I've heard.

Another unfortunate circumstance which must have militated against the success of the play is the fact that both the comic and the serious portions unavoidably evoke reminiscences of "A Midsummer Night's Dream" and "Comus"—reminiscences which suggest odious comparisons, and almost force upon us a quite unfair standard of criticism.

I confess my inability to give any rational and comprehensible account of the action of Mr. Albery's second fantastic play, "The Will of Wise King Kino;" and in this confession is implied the first and last word of criticism with reference to it. Its motive is vague, intangible, probably trivial. It is mainly a satire upon the levelling tendencies of the age—for Mr. Albery, I repeat, is a Tory of the Tories—mixed with hits at the "veneering" tendencies of modern life, and other commonplaces of the social satirist. In the realm of Clencantia, says the Lady Baume,—

> Government was quite hard up for liberal measures,
> And as last year the crops were very bad
> They laid it all to inequality,
> And said if all distinctions were removed
> The weather would improve, the earth be fruitful,
> The people would work harder and be happy.
> And so they did away with names and titles
> And everyone is numbered like a cab.
> Our sweet Princess is Number One, the Regent
> Is Number Two, and had you had your number
> You'd be about—Three Millions, I should think.

*   *   *   *   *   *

Trottoir.—

How has this numbering of the people answered?
Has all distinction vanished with the measure?

Lady B.—

Oh, no. Indeed, I think it's rather worse.
The tens of thousands won't mix with the hundreds,
The hundreds with the millions will not mix,
And in our sphere if one is Forty-Six
His great desire is to be Forty-Five,
And then he'll plot and lie and scheme and cheat
To get his number changed to Forty-Four.

It is scarcely necessary to point out the logical feebleness of this line of satire. To show the absurdities of a measure, which, instead of levelling, emphasizes, formulates, and multiplies a millionfold the distinctions of society, is scarcely a happy method of satirizing the theory of equality. It is much more important to note that the fantasy is an amusing one, and leads to some clever dialogue with many touches of wit and tenderness. Take as examples the following little epigrams:—

Pride's like a pelican, so lovingly
It feeds its little sins upon itself.

***

And surely one who holds so high a place
Should know what's right.
'Tis true enough he should,
But he is not the only man in power
Who fills his place as gravel fills a well.

If Mr. Albery had only mounted his dialogue upon a consistent and intelligible framework of plot, "The

Will of Wise King Kino" would have been a piece of real literary merit. As it is, the allegory is strained and confused; whereas in this species of work the action may or may not be simple, but must above all things be clear and comprehensible. The author's philosophy may be as mystic as the night, but his plot must be clear as the day. The surface of his mirror must be smooth and flawless, whether it is to reflect the furthest constellations or only the opposite side of the room.

If Mr. Albery has narrowly escaped being *facile princeps* among original dramatists, he has entirely attained that distinction among adapters. His adaptations—those which he has acknowledged at least—have not been many, but they have been the best in their respective kinds. Two of them, unfortunately, have been executed for the Criterion Theatre, and these I shall deal with first, leaving "The Crisis" and "Duty" until afterwards. I feel so grateful to Mr. Albery for much of his work, that I wish my last words on him to be words of appreciation.

I am not going either to attack or to defend "The Pink Dominos," Mr. Albery's adaptation of "Les Dominos Roses." My own mind is quite undecided on the question whether such work is admissible on the stage. I confess to having seen it several times both in London and the provinces, and I am quite ready to go and see it again should it be revived. For it is certainly the cleverest play of its kind the English stage has ever seen; only "The Snowball" can compare with it in point of ingenuity of construction and finish of dialogue.

The first act and the third are masterpieces of comedy-of-intrigue. The French plot is extremely ingenious and the English dialogue is just what light-comedy dialogue should be. There is not a strained point in it, scarcely a word-play. Every speech developes the plot, not a line is thrown away. The second act is not so masterly, for its humour depends on the simple expedient of half a dozen doors, through which the characters pop in and out at perpetual cross-purposes. Still even here the dialogue is excellent, and the Cremorne waiter is a slightly caricatured character-sketch of great value. In point of ability the piece entirely deserved its phenomenal success. Did its humour compensate for its immorality? That is the question; or rather, to put it more generally, can humour, on the stage, ever compensate for immorality? If there is any meaning at all in "The Pink Dominos," it is a shallow and vulgar sneer at conjugal faith and ordinary honesty of speech and conduct between man and wife. A play which should seriously satirize the institution of marriage as at present understood, would be at once tabooed by the Lord Chamberlain. Not so "The Pink Dominos," which does not attack the principle of marriage, but flippantly and cynically derides and desecrates its practice. Which of these two courses is the more immoral? The former, says the Lord Chamberlain, and he is an authority from whom there is no appeal. It may be urged, however, that such an inquiry is beside the question, and that "The Pink Dominos" need have no more moral or immoral meaning for us than a story of Boccaccio or a comedy of Macchiavelli. The argument is a questionable one, seeing the characters speak our language, wear our dress, are in every way calculated to excite vivid personal sympathy or antipathy. Still, I accept it in a measure. I salve my conscience with it when I see and enjoy "The Pink Dominos" or a work of its type. But I would no more take ladies to see it than I would choose the Decameron for family reading; and the stage in England is and must be a family institution. That the Criterion has not long ago become forbidden ground for ladies is a strange commentary upon our boasted English propriety. The key-note struck in "The Pink Dominos" has been maintained through a series of plays which have followed it. Some one—I think it was Goethe—had a pet idea of a theatre to which only a picked audience, principally masculine of course, should be admitted, so that works unsuitable for a mixed public might be represented in their entirety. Mr. Charles Wyndham has done his best to realize this ideal on the Criterion stage, though he has taken no measures to pick his audience. His house might be re-christened the Club-Smoking-Room Theatre, so far as the plays presented in it are concerned. From the date of "The Pink Dominos" onwards Mr. Albery has been his faithful and earnest coadjutor in this great work; and if he has not always been as successful as in "The Pink Dominos," his second avowed effort—"Where's the Cat?"—proves that it was not because of any lack of enthusiasm for the great cause, or of boldness in furthering it.

When Mr. Bronson Howard's "Truth" was produced at the Criterion, the audience was severely blamed for a prurient insistence on discovering double meanings where none were intended. The blame was by no means undeserved. The audience had made up its mind to discover another "Pink Dominos," and would have scented equivoques even if the play had been written by a bishop and the Church and Stage Guild in solemn conclave had pronounced it free of offence. With fine tact and thoughtfulness Mr. Albery determined in "Where's the Cat?" to save his audience from all risk of a similar accusation. It needed no prurient quickness of apprehension to see the double meanings. The audience saw them and remained blameless, for it could not possibly help seeing them. They were as plain as the footlights, and a great deal plainer than the plot of the piece. But it is a misnomer to call many of them double meanings. The phrase applies to speeches which have an innocent surface interpretation as well as a questionable suggestion. This was not the case with a great deal of the wit of "Where's the Cat?" It either meant nothing at all, or else it meant something of which the less said the better. To take a very mild instance: when a young lady, supposed to be wandering in Westmoreland, marches jauntily upon the stage, and cheerfully remarks, "I've heard of lost women, and now I'm one myself," is there any wit, humour, point, or meaning in the remark, except in so far as it contains an allusion to a subject not generally discussed by young ladies in mixed society? To be sure, it may be alleged that the young lady in question is supposed to be soliloquizing; but if young ladies do make such brilliant jokes to themselves in private, which I hope is not generally the case, that is no reason why they should speak them openly on the stage.

This coarseness, for that is the only word, was to my mind the less excusable, as the plot of "Where's the Cat?" so far as it had a discoverable plot, was comparatively inoffensive, and might quite well have been worked out without it. To be sure it would have been a rather dull piece, but then no one was under any obligation to adapt it at all. The framework of the German original "Sodoma und Gomorrah" had been retained, and was so excessively clumsy as to remind one of the old query of the French Abbé so much ridiculed by Mr. Carlyle, who wrote an essay to inquire "Si un Allemand peut avoir de l'esprit?" The *esprit* of the plot was decidedly ultra-Rhenish, which perhaps necessitated an extra infusion of Gallic salt into the dialogue. But it was dispiriting to see the talent of the author of "Two Roses," "Apple Blossoms," and "Oriana" applied to such work. Morality apart, it is trivial, vulgar, unworthy of an artist and a thinking man. That Mr. Albery should have condescended to take even his leading position among the chosen band of adapters-in-ordinary to the Criterion Theatre, seems to prove a radical defect in his nature, and in a measure to explain some of the shortcomings of his worthier work.

To some of this worthier work let us now turn. By a fortunate chance two of the strongest of modern French plays have fallen to the lot of the ablest of English adapters. "The Crisis" and "Duty" are both excellent plays, and perhaps for that reason, the former met with dubious success, the latter proved a distinct failure. I cannot believe, however, that their story has yet been told to the end. Two such plays will surely not be allowed to sink into oblivion.

I have never seen "Les Bourgeois de Pont-Arcy," but from the *à priori* point of view I should guess that "Les Fourchambault" is a better play, simply because the latter is by Augier and the former by Sardou. "Duty," on the contrary, is a better play than "The Crisis," which suffered from the strange insistance of the British public, or at any rate the British manager, on having the scene of every French play transferred to England. The motive of "Duty," though at least equally strong, fits itself to English life with less strain and loss of probability. It lacks, indeed, the fine character-drawing of "The Crisis," and the more delicate touches of Augier's genius. Augier is a poet, Sardou only a skilful playwright. But translation has a tendency to level distinctions of manner, and leave only the broad differences of theme and matter. Moreover, the very failure of "Duty" renders it more interesting than "The Crisis," for it enables one to point an important moral. Consequently, I shall examine the former more minutely, merely saying of the latter that the adaptation was done with excellent wit and taste. I cannot praise Mr. Albery's dialogue more highly than by saying that I was often in doubt as to which points were his own and which Augier's;

and that on referring to "Les Fourchambault" I found that several of the best points were not in the French.

"Duty" has one great fault of construction, arising from the fact that Mr. Albery has too closely adopted Sardou's habit of going about the exposition of his theme in a very leisurely and diffuse fashion. While the play is proceeding we scarcely notice it, so skilfully has Mr. Albery done his work; but as soon as the curtain falls upon the second act, we become alive to the fact that the real action of the drama has not yet begun. We have been listening to a great deal of amusing and graceful dialogue, and towards the close of the second act we are given a hint that something of importance is likely to occur in the course of the third. So far as the story is concerned, however, the first two acts could quite well be run into one, and even then it would not be too full of action. Indeed, the sole practical use of the second act is to arrange the meeting between Sir Geoffrey Deene and Marcelle. This could be done almost as easily at the end of the first act—indeed, there is no necessity that it should be arranged beforehand at all—in which case the second act might be dropped from the piece altogether, and, so far as the action is concerned, no one would miss it. Thus in respect of construction "Duty" is by no means a masterpiece.

Critics, both French and English, have taken far graver exception to the motive of the piece than to its construction—in my opinion most unjustly. The motive is this: Sir Geoffrey Deene is on the point of marrying Mabel Holne, when he learns that his father, who has recently died, idolized by all who knew him, has in the last years of his life been carrying on an intrigue with a French lady, whom he has cruelly and disgracefully wronged. This woman, Marcelle Aubry, comes to tell Sir Geoffrey that, unless a sum of 800*l.* is forthcoming, a creditor of the late baronet has threatened to reveal the whole scandal. Marcelle's presence in the house is discovered by chance; it is found that Sir Geoffrey has given her a large sum of money, and the only way in which he can prevent the truth from becoming known to his mother is to take the guilt upon himself. This he thinks his "duty," and does; and this, say the critics, no one either could, would, or should do. For a trumpery matter of sentiment, they say, he sacrifices his own happiness and good name, and the happiness of his betrothed, and at the same time inflicts upon his mother a sorrow almost, if not quite, as poignant as the truth would cause. In real life, it is said, no one would have done it, and no one would have had a right to do it. But let us look at the matter a little more closely. Sir Geoffrey's mother had been accustomed to regard her husband with a love which merged into reverence. His life had seemed spotless, his character exalted, his love for her boundless. Since his death she had literally worshipped his memory. Such a state of mind may be uncommon, but I should be sorry to believe it impossible. Granting, then, the mental condition of Lady Deene as postulated by the dramatist, what would be the effect on her of a sudden revelation that her dead husband's love had been estranged from her, and his character sullied by the basest of crimes? It must be remembered that there is no opportunity of breaking these terrible ideas to her by degrees. She holds in her hand a letter from her husband to his mistress. Her son must either let the truth burst upon her with a suddenness which might almost be fatal, or he must claim the letter, and the sin it involves, as his own. There is no time for reflection as to what he "has a right" to do. Devoted to his mother as he is, and knowing what a shock the revelation has been to himself, he simply has no choice. That he immensely alleviates the shock cannot be doubted. In the first place, the crime loses half its gravity when removed from his father's shoulders to his. It is bad enough for his mother to think him profligate, but it would be fifty times worse for her to know her dead husband faithless, heartless, and profligate in a much less excusable way. In the second place, the mere fact that he is alive takes half the sting from his mother's sorrow. The living are within reach of repentance, reform, reconciliation. While there is life there is hope. But what can be more terrible than to learn that the dead have deceived us, that their love was a lie, their purity corruption? King Harold Fairhair, in the old Saga, had a beloved wife named Snæfrid. She died, and for three years the bereaved king sat beside the body with his eyes fixed on it, and by some miracle of the gods it decayed not, but remained life-like and beautiful. At last he touched it and tried to move it, and in a single moment it all dissolved into fetid carrion. Would Lady Deene have been able to endure either in body or mind the sudden crumbling to loathsome corruption of her fair-seeming idol, like the body in this old legend or in Edgar Poe's ghastly tale? Her life, or at least her reason, was in danger. Was not her son justified in sacrificing anything and everything to save her? Others he could undeceive afterwards, and her he might reconcile and comfort. He took a comparatively slight and effaceable stain on himself rather than cast a hideous and indelible stigma upon his father. The action was noble, but it was neither irrational nor Quixotic. It was *splendide mendax.*

A much more debateable point, it seems to me, is whether Lady Deene should in the end be allowed to learn the truth. It would be quite possible for the dramatist to unravel the skein and leave her in ignorance—to clear the son's character, without disturbing her worship of the father. A thorough-paced cynic would have wound up with a venomous sarcasm, by making the curtain fall upon Lady Deene clasping her son to her breast, and at the same time giving a glance of mute and reverential invocation to the portrait of his sainted father. Sardou, writing for popular audiences, has eschewed this effect. By an ingeniously devised chance, Mr. Hammond, Lady Deene's brother, learns the truth, and thinks it his "duty" to break it to her. And here, in the changed condition of things, the dramatist's art is clearly shown. The shock which yesterday would have come upon her like a flash of lightning, now finds her in a measure prepared. Nay, more—the same hand which shatters her hollow idol, raises a new and worthier object of worship for her woman's heart. The glory taken from her dead husband falls upon her living son. The same breath which tells her of the one's unimagined baseness, assures her of the other's unimagined nobleness. The shock is terrible, but to-day it is not without alleviation, as it would have been yesterday. "I can still bless my husband," she says, "for giving me such a son."

Thus I believe the motive of the piece to be as true and natural as its development is ingenious and effective. One short passage might have been omitted—that in which Lady Deene urges Sir Geoffrey to make reparation to his supposed mistress by marrying her. The ideas are repulsive and the scene is unnecessary. This I regard as the only grave fault of the serious portion of the play.

And now what is the moral to be drawn from the failure of "Duty"? It is this, that those who underrate the influence of newspaper criticism in England make an enormous mistake. "Duty" was literally killed by unappreciative criticism. It presented a moral problem, and that is the one thing the critics cannot away with. It had the further disadvantage of attempting the solution in a sense opposite to that which commended itself to the critical intellect. One and all decided that it was Sir Geoffrey's duty not to take his father's sin upon himself. As Mr. Burnand ably put it in that moral paper *Punch*,—"Sir Geoffrey looks up at the portrait of his 'awful dad,' and exclaims that what he has heard is 'too horrible to be true.' There is nothing whatever 'horrible' about it. It is a disillusion—a painful disillusion perhaps—but nothing to scream and pant and tear one's hair about. 'Fancy the poor old governor having gone in for this sort of thing,' would have been a far more natural remark." Now, this view of the case may or may not be justified. I hope I have succeeded in showing that there is at least something to be said on the opposite side. And in this lies, for me, the charm of the play. I do not want to assert that Sir Geoffrey acted absolutely rightly. All I maintain is that he acted conceivably, and that his conduct presents an extremely interesting problem in moral casuistry. Even if we grant that it was a piece of irrational Quixotism, I cannot see in that any reason to condemn the play. In reading "Don Quixote," the sympathies of every well-regulated British critic of course go entirely with Sancho Panza; but that is surely no reason why he should throw away the book and pronounce it a failure. Of its own accord the public would never have done so with "Duty." I can assert from personal observation on more than one occasion, that, with all its supposed "unpleasantness," the piece interested and amused to the top of their bent those audiences who came to see it in spite of the critics.

I should like, in conclusion, to sum up Mr. Albery's literary character in a neatly-rounded paragraph, but it somehow does not lend itself readily to neatly-rounded treatment. It is too full of contradictions and paradoxes. His mind has so many different veins and strata that a whole case-full of specimens would be necessary to present an adequate sample of it. I can only hope that he will continue to work the "Two Roses" or the "Oriana" vein, and leave unworked and forgotten the layer from which was extracted that jewel "Where's the Cat?"

MR. FREDERICK W. BROUGHTON.

As a writer of smart dialogue—I use the word "smart" advisedly—Mr. F. W. Broughton has few rivals on the English stage. His work belongs to the school of Mr. Theyre Smith, whose style Mr. Sydney Grundy and Mr. Herman Merivale have also adopted in some of their minor plays. None of these writers, however, has been more successful than Mr. Broughton in handling this particular manner. "Ruth's Romance" and "Withered Leaves" are among the brightest comediettas our stage can show.

In Mr. Albery's "Apple Blossoms" the great Baggs, on hearing some repartee by Tom Penryn, pulls out his note-book and says, "If you don't mind, I'll put that into my entertainment; it's just the sort of joke I like; it's so rude." This is a palpable hit at the comedy of no manners and it goes home to its mark. But at the same time the defects of the school, when restrained within reasonable limits, are not without their palliation. The stage which holds as 'twere the mirror up to nineteenth-century human nature, would reflect very incompletely if it failed to show a tendency to good-humoured rudeness in modern conversation. I do not know the origin of the word "chaff," but strongly suspect that the name and the thing alike are products of the last fifty years. The "quizzing" of last century was akin but different. "Chaff" at the present day is often a sign of friendship. When the intimacy of two men, or even of a man and woman, has reached a certain point, it often manifests itself in elaborately humorous impertinences. This phenomenon may be a sign of modern degeneracy, or of modern progress, or of neither one nor the other; I merely state it as a fact which is within the observation of every one. As Mr. Gilbert has remarked, "Chivalry is an ingredient sadly lacking in our land," so far at least as conversation is concerned. This is, perhaps, the result of a reaction from the effusiveness of a century ago, or even less, which in present-day slang we should denominate "gush." Be this as it may, it is the tendency of the age to veil its feelings in "chaff" rather than to flaunt them in "gush," and the stage could not be blamed for reflecting that tendency, but that it often grossly exaggerates it. Of a modern "verray parfit gentil knight" it could not be recorded that he "never yit no villeiny ne said in all his lyf unto no manir wight;" that is if we take "villeiny" in the modified sense of jocular impertinence, which may sometimes cover affectionate confidence and true feeling. We often laugh where our grandfathers and grandmothers would have wept.

Mr. Broughton is a master of the art of "chaff." He elaborates it with a great deal of wit, and sometimes with a touch of genuine humour. Moreover, in the two pieces I have referred to, he uses it in its right place—that is between friends, people who are on such terms that we can see the kindness, or at any rate inoffensiveness of intention in the rapid thrust and parry of playful fun. Some other writers use rudeness to produce their comic effects on every possible occasion. In many modern comedies, from those of Mr. T. W. Robertson downwards, the merest acquaintances habitually address each other in terms which in real life would lead to the use of canes or horsewhips even in this pacific age. Mr. Broughton does not carry the comedy of no manners to this extreme, in his two best-known works at least. Their main faults are an occasional touch of puerility, into which he is betrayed by his dread of allowing a single speech to be dull, and an occasional touch of vulgarity which is much less excusable. All the misunderstanding with reference to the baby in "Ruth's Romance" is jarring and out of place. That such grossly injurious suspicions should interrupt the felicity of a newly betrothed couple produces a painful impression even in a fanciful "summer's evening sketch," and the imbroglio would be just as amusing without the introduction of the terrible infant. "Chaff" on such subjects is not in good taste even in a comedy of no manners. Still more offensive are certain passages in "Withered Leaves." There may be spheres of society in which "flirtation" is carried on as it is between Tom Conyers and the lady who turns out to be his step-mother, but if so, the practice is neither amusing nor edifying. The said Tom Conyers, who is the son of a baronet and supposed to be a gentleman, on his second meeting with a lady whose name he does not even know, calmly "puts his arm around her waist," upon which she only remarks, "How very dreadful!" adding aside, "And yet not so very dreadful for a man to squeeze his mother." The same elevated tone of thought reappears in the scene where Sir Conyers Conyers, not recognizing his son, remonstrates with him for his conduct towards the said lady, and Tom retorts, "Well, I'm not a bad-looking fellow, and I thought she'd like it. Surely there's no harm in a platonic cuddle." An east-end shop-boy on Hampstead Heath might conceive such a thought, but I doubt if even he would express it in such an offensive fashion.

Here let me say a word generally as to the vulgarity which seems to me such a prominent characteristic of the modern English drama. It requires some moral courage in these days to use the word "vulgar," for one is apt to be met with an accusation of superfineness, not to say snobbishness. And indeed the term should be applied sparingly, since every one of any delicacy of feeling may have small personal susceptibilities on this point, peculiar to himself and incomprehensible to others who are, in the main, equally sensitive. Vulgarity, in short, is to some extent a matter of convention, and one cannot expect to impose upon other people the precise conventional code one happens to have adopted. As to the use of slang, for instance, there is the greatest discrepancy of opinion. I may taboo one expression and admit another, while persons of whose general refinement there can be no doubt may precisely reverse my judgment, or rather my prejudice. In one of Mr. Pinero's plays a young man says to a young lady, "If you were a fellow, I should slap you on the back." This use of the word "fellow" jars upon my ear so much that I unhesitatingly call it vulgar. Yet I grant that it would be difficult to give my reasons, and that to others whose opinion on the point I must respect, the expression may perhaps seem quite permissible. Again, in "Ruth's Romance," Ruth, who is supposed to be a young lady of the utmost refinement, makes use of the word "sweethearts" in speaking of herself and Jack Dudley, whom she has just promised to marry. Now I admit that "sweetheart" is a good old English word, even a pretty and poetical word; yet I think the custom of the language has confined its use to children and to bucolic couples of the Jenny and Jessamy type. More unquestionably objectionable is the phrase "That's his young woman" used by the irrepressible Tom Conyers in "Withered Leaves." The said Tom introduces his friend Arthur Middleton to his father and step-mother in the following terms:—"A very average Christian, a rattling good scholar, and the perfection of a gentleman"—a thorough proof, I think, that Tom is *not* "the perfection of a gentleman." In all these cases, however, except perhaps the last, one must admit that the objection one feels to the phrases is a matter of sentiment and convention. I am so accustomed to hear people, of whose delicate taste I have not the slightest doubt, occasionally using a phrase which jars on my ear, that I fully admit my own particular standard, especially in matters of language, to be conventional and now and then irrational. But there is another side to the question. However large may be the debateable land, it has its limits, beyond which expressions, thoughts, and acts are undoubtedly vulgar, and bear their patent of tastelessness on their very face. This border-line many English playwrights are only too fond of overstepping. Vulgarity, of course, is the very fairest butt of the satirist, but in many English comedies it is difficult to tell whether the "gentleman" or the *roturier* is the more vulgar—whether the baronet or the butterman is the greater cad, to use a word which I fear may be charged with vulgarity. Not to mention the bloated aristocrats of melodrama, who have a sort of prescriptive right to be ludicrously vulgar, we too often find that even in "society" comedies for which "the west-end of town books its stalls in advance," the noble hero and his military *fidus Achates* are snobs of the most pronounced description. In "Caste," for instance, not to come nearer our own time, I have often wondered whether Captain Hawtree, old Eccles, or the Marchioness was the most vulgar personage, and have finally come to the conclusion that the Marchioness bears off the palm. In these cases, in which the vulgarity is not a question of temporary fashion in the use of words, but is proved by the application of the most ordinary standards of good feeling, good taste, and good manners, I have not the slightest hesitation in using the term. Here we are not upon the ground of convention but of fundamental principle. No one, I think, will question the gross vulgarity of the passages from "Withered Leaves" given above. They conflict with the most rudimentary ideas of manly courtesy and womanly modesty. Thus, too, in "Ruth's Romance," the conduct of Ruth on the discovery of Jack Dudley's misunderstanding is that of a coarse-minded woman. She has just promised to marry him, when he happens to overhear a conversation between her and Captain Wilton, in which he misapprehends some allusions to the latter's child, Ruth's nephew, and conceives the most injurious suspicions as to the relation between them. I have already said that the introduction of the baby at all seems to me an error in taste, but much worse is Ruth's subsequent conduct, when she finds out the misconception under which Jack is labouring. A girl with any delicacy of mind could not fail to be painfully impressed by the very awkward mistake, and would surely explain it as quickly and as gravely as possible, or, more properly still, leave it to her brother-in-law to explain. Not so Ruth. She regards it as a capital joke, purposely keeps Jack in the dark for some minutes and asks him whether "he's quite sure he wouldn't like to have a peep at the baby." One is almost ashamed to discuss such gross solecisms, as though there could be two opinions as to their vulgarity. As a matter of fact, however, I have no doubt the author considers his work eminently refined, while it has been played before hundreds of audiences not one of which has protested against its tastelessness.

With several of Mr. Broughton's works I am, unfortunately, unacquainted, among them being "Years Ago," "A Debt of Honour," "A Labour of Love," "Eyes and Hearts," and "The Finger of Fate." His three-act comedy "Light and Shade" had many of the merits of his shorter plays, but lacked constructive skill. The first act was excellent, though its concluding situation was quite irrelevant, the second act was fair, though the dialogue in the love-scenes degenerated into puerility, and the third act contained one amusing scene brought about by wildly absurd methods. Nor was "Glass Houses," another three-act play produced in the provinces, by any means a step in advance. Mr. Broughton is essentially a dialogue-writer, and does not appear to have the strength for sustained efforts. In collaboration I should think his talent would prove very effective; but it seems useless to commend collaboration to English authors, who will jump and jump ineffectually after the high-hung fruit of success, rather than attain it with ease and certainty by the simple means of "giving each other a back."

MR. F. C. BURNAND.

THE present age is an age of parody, and Mr. Burnand is the leading parodist of the day. He has parodied every thing and every one, including himself. His position on the staff, and now at the head, of our much-abused but still much-loved *Punch*, has strengthened in him the natural bent towards parody. He has a peculiar manner of his own which is quite inimitable, and often very amusing. And as parody is essentially a thing of mannerism, the more his manner has grown upon him, the funnier he has become. His work of the last few years is his best. Who can ever forget his inimitable burlesque of "Weeder," for which the world at large owes him a debt of gratitude? In the theatrical comments too, which he regularly supplies to *Punch*, his peculiar faculty is often exercised with such admirable effect that I am sure a carefully edited collection of these trifles, with the characteristic illustrations which often accompany them, would meet with much appreciation. The amount of work which he does—for he is one of the most indefatigable workers we have—of course renders his production unequal. But his humour, such as it is, seems practically inexhaustible. I say such as it is, for it is not humour of the first order. Not to go beyond contemporary literature, it has not the depth, originality, or spontaneity of some American humour. It is more of a manufactured product, and not so much a necessary outcome of the writer's temperament. Moreover, the fact that it almost always partakes of the nature of parody detracts from its independent value and relegates it to a subordinate rank. Still it cannot be denied that Mr. Burnand is the leading English journalistic humorist. What Mr. G. A. Sala said with peculiar inappropriateness of Oliver Wendell Holmes might be said with peculiar appropriateness of Mr. Burnand—he is "essentially a funny fellow."

But this distinction does not satisfy Mr. Burnand's ambition. He is not content with making the jokes of a nation; he aspires to make its dramas. Some years ago, in one of the perpetually recurring newspaper controversies on dramatic matters, he unhesitatingly stated his profound conviction of the existence of at least one "competent dramatist" in England. This competent dramatist, he explained, was only prevented from developing into an Augier by the adverse conditions under which he laboured. Managers besieged him with French farces to be adapted, and paid him for such trifles, which occupied three weeks, much more than they would pay him for original work which cost him the labour of three months. Thus, as even a competent dramatist must live, and as he cannot live upon happy thoughts alone, he is compelled to waste his genius upon pot-boilers, and only at rare intervals indulges in the luxury of showing himself in his true colours as an original, inventive, witty, moral, and generally "competent" playwright.

Mr. Burnand may have excellent reasons for the faith that is in him, but the evidence actually before the court is far from conclusive. We may take it for granted at the outset that he does not found his claims to competency upon his burlesques, though, as he himself would say, his "competency" is probably founded upon them. Adaptations from the French, too, may be put out of court, for originality is an indispensable element in the received definition of competency. There remain, then, some eleven farces, one or two dramas of the Adelphi school, and—one comedy. The farces—such as "Romance Under Difficulties," "B.B.," "Carte-de-Visite," and "Easy Shaving," —most of which were written in collaboration with Mr. Montague Williams, prove his possession of the unflagging animal spirits which are the first requisite of the farce-writer, but which go a very short way towards the outfit of a competent dramatist. The dramas again—"The Deal Boatman," "Dead Man's Point," "The Turn of the Tide,"—prove nothing, save that at the date of their composition unsophisticated audiences accepted very unsophisticated work, which would now-a-days have small chance of success in the West End, unless supplemented by very elaborate scenic and spectacular accessories. "The Deal Boatman" had been known long before Mr. Burnand's day, as a Yarmouth boatman, under the name of Peggotty. "Dead Man's Point, or the Lighthouse on the Carn Ruth," after a well-conceived opening act, degenerates into the conventional and improbable. Of "The Turn of the Tide" I cannot speak from personal knowledge, but I am given to understand that, whatever may have been its merits, it did not rise into the sphere of literature in which the great works of a competent dramatist should surely find their place. I have sometimes wondered whether it was as a grim retribution for his burlesque of "Black Eyed Susan" that the fates led Mr. Burnand to devote himself exclusively to nautical subjects in his attempts at original drama.

His one original comedy, "Our Club," remains to be considered. Of it, unfortunately, I have a very vague recollection, much less vivid than one would naturally expect to retain of the work upon which a competent dramatist expended three months' labour, with the settled purpose of proving his competency. It struck me, I remember, as a clever parody of French comedy of intrigue—the work of a writer who, having closely studied the French "intriguists," if I may coin a word, had caught their manner, or rather their mannerisms, and very little else. It was a feat of dexterity, curious, but of no independent worth. A schoolboy's hexameters, looked at as so many dactyls and spondees, may be more or less Virgilian, but that does not make them good poetry. At the time of the production of

"Our Club," a critic compared it to a game of "cat's cradle," in which the players twine a string into a series of elaborate figures, for the sole purpose of untwining it again. The comparison was far from inapt.

Among Mr. Burnand's adaptations, however, there is one in which he claims, with some justice, to have so far remodelled the work adapted as to have produced a play which may fairly be called original. M. Labiche's "Moi," though far from being one of the masterpieces of that great humorist, is a remarkable study of selfishness. On it Mr. Burnand founded "Ourselves." He had at his command a fair field and no favour. He had chosen a moral theme of perennial interest and importance. Some of the greatest triumphs of all literature have been made in studies of selfishness. We need only look at George Eliot's Tito Melema and Rosamond Vincy to see what dramatic developments and effects can be obtained from the study of this vice. Moreover, he had an excellent company to interpret his work, in a theatre of very respectable, if not very lofty, traditions. Here, one would have thought, was an opportunity for a competent dramatist to give us a genuine English comedy, apart from punning repartee and cup-and-saucer banality. The opportunity was there, but the competent dramatist apparently was not.

Upon the failure of the comedy, Mr. Burnand himself assured us several times that it possessed "touches of nature and strong contrasts of character," and that its composition had occupied him six months. Unfortunately the only conclusion to be drawn from this assurance is that the merits of a play are not always directly proportionate to the time spent upon it.

Not that "Ourselves," was an essentially bad piece; it was only hopelessly feeble. Its merits and faults were alike entirely negative. There was nothing ludicrously wrong in the construction, it was only thin. The characters were unobjectionable and undefined. The dialogue was inoffensive and flat. It had good points, but they were not many. Mr. Burnand was commendably sparing in strained word-plays, but he failed as a rule to attain genuine wit, or that still higher species of dialogue whose interest arises from brilliant development of character or action, quite apart from wit. In short, his comedy lacked colour, interest, character. Its intrigue was poor in itself, and was developed with little ingenuity. There was a certain flaccidity about the play throughout—a want of firmness of touch and clearness of intention. It was full of those saddest of sublunary things—lost opportunities. Let us take an instance. Norman Fane, in the first act, relates how, in Central Africa, he saved the life of a young Englishman at the extreme risk of his own. John Peddington, one of the two types of selfishness in the comedy, argues that such acts of self-devotion are mere folly and Quixotism, until it appears by chance that the young man whose life was saved was his own son. Then his better nature breaks through, and he cannot help giving the lie to his own cynicism. Now, here is a good motive, which might have been elaborated into a powerful dramatic scene. But Mr. Burnand did not do so. The scene passed tamely, and it is only on analyzing the situation, apart from Mr. Burnand's treatment of it, that one sees its possibilities. This is where the difference between the competent dramatist and the only semi-competent comes in. Many playwrights have good ideas, but not many can work them out clearly and firmly, or weld them together into a strong and compact whole.

Mr. Burnand, as we have seen, complains that managerial tyranny forces him to devote to paltry adaptations the genius which might otherwise prove itself in original plays. Let us now look at some of these adaptations Some years ago Mr. Burnand, writing of the "Pink Dominos" and other similar pieces, suggested as a title for them the phrase "An Immorality in Three Acts," and played the champion of injured British innocence with much effect. This was in *Punch*, and *Punch* is nothing if not moral. But because *Punch* is virtuous, says Mr. Burnand, shall there be no more cakes and ale? Yes, by St. Anne, and "Niniche" shall be hot i' the mouth too, and "Bébé" piquant to the taste. A competent dramatist can easily smuggle his manuscript past the unsuspicious Lord Chamberlain, and then leave the public to read between the lines for itself, which it has been admirably trained to do. We need not even compromise our virtue by inventing double meanings. For the immorality of the plot we are not responsible; and as for the dialogue we may make it pure as driven snow, spotless as the pages of

Punch, yet the audience will scent an allusion from afar off, and neigh like the old war-horse it is at the sound of the mildest innuendo.

It must be admitted that Mr. Burnand is singularly skilful in toning down the works he takes in hand. Plays which, in their original form, the Licenser would not touch with the tongs, become, when fumigated by Mr. Burnand, quite grateful to his nostrils. They are apt to lose their colour along with their too Parisian aroma, but that is quite unavoidable. They remain frivolous, empty, and degrading to human nature, but they are not openly indecent, though many of their scenes are rather motiveless, unless we mentally reconstruct them in their French form, which it is generally very easy to do. Indeed, the Bowdlerizing process is carried on by means of a sort of cipher to which every one has the key. When Mr. Burnand introduces us to a variety actress or a female acrobat, we all know what was the lady's profession in the original French; and that elastic and convenient term "flirtation" covers a multitude of sins, but covers them in a very gauzy fashion. In short, the Augean stables, though externally they are made to look very spick and span, retain a lingering trace of their original aroma, which sometimes seems to me more sickly and oppressive than the pungent and undisguised effluvium of their unpurified state.

"Boulogne" and "Betsy" are Mr. Burnand's best known works in this manner. Both are good specimens of what may be called the Theban type of comedies—not because it takes a learned Theban to write them, but because they have each at least a hundred doors. The plots which depend upon a room having doors in every panel, so that the characters can play hide-and-seek in a rough-and-tumble fashion to any given extent, are rather mechanical, it is true, but never fail to be amusing. The situations which can be evolved from these materials are practically endless. Given eight characters and eight doors, it is a simple mathematical problem in permutations and combinations to find out how many situations can be worked up. The patience of the audience is in effect the only limit, and Mr. Burnand is generally skilful in gauging the patience of his audiences. "Betsy," however, afforded a good instance of the way in which English "moralization" spoils the logic and symmetry of French work. In "Bébé" the plot turned upon the pleasant little philosophic theory of Kernanigous (Mr. Burnand's Captain McManus) as to the three lunar phases of development through which a young man should pass in his relations to the other sex. The theory was not of a nature to be reproduced, but as it gave the comedy its main cynical meaning, we lose in point of art what we gain in point of morals by its excision. The design and symmetry of the play was also injured by the elevation of the chambermaid into a leading character, indeed the title-part. Some such title as "Innocence" would have suited the play better, being more consistent with the relative importance of the characters. Besides, it would have been of a piece with the fine spirit of satire which reigns at the Criterion. "Truth" was a panegyric upon lying:

why should not the name of "Innocence" have been given to an encomium upon—its opposite?

Mr. Burnand's latest and greatest success is also an adaptation from the French, though in this case his special skill in deodorization was not called for. Indeed, "The Colonel," though described as an adaptation of "Un Mari à la Campagne," might quite as fitly be called "a dramatic version of *Punch*." That time-honoured publication—I use the phrase with no satiric intention, for "with all its faults I love it still"—has of late been little more than a record of the doings of Messrs. Maudle and Postlethwaite and the Cimabue Browns, with occasional interludes, in which are set forth the humours of Grigsby, Mrs. Ponsonby de Tomkins, and Sir Gorgius Midas. As Hogarth gave us the Rake's Progress, Mr. Du Maurier has devoted himself to depicting the Prig's Progress. A modern Don Quixote, he has set pencil in rest against the shams of latter-day art culture, with Mr. Burnand as his Sancho Panza supplying a comic commentary on his feats. The Don having demolished the puppet-show, Sancho now pieces the mannikins together again, and puts them through their antics after his own fashion. Very amusing antics they are, all the more so as the figures have some slight resemblance to real men and women.

All the characters, many of the incidents, and much of the dialogue are taken direct from *Punch*, though the plot is that of "Un Mari à la Campagne," or "The Serious Family." And here we find one of the most prominent defects of the play. The two elements do not mix well, if I may use the expression. The plot does not harmonize with the characters and the dialogue. It is a putting of new wine into old bottles. We feel that it is a parody rather than a play, for the essence of parody is telling a story in an incongruous form, originally designed for some totally different matter. It is perhaps all the more amusing on this account, for Mr. Burnand is the master parodist of the day, but as a work of art it suffers. If Mr. Burnand had been a satirist instead of a parodist, he would have seen that he was overshooting his mark in adopting the framework of "Un Mari à la Campagne." Such people as Maudle and Postlethwaite may exist outside the columns of *Punch*. I am inclined to believe they do, though in such small numbers that it really seems as if the satire levelled at them, even in that journal, were quite disproportionate. But when we come to "The Colonel" the disproportion becomes glaring. Has Mr. Burnand any ground whatever for accusing the votaries of high art not only of affectation and vanity, but of dishonesty and all sorts of baseness down to gluttony and drunkenness? In "The Serious Family" the case was different. There it was actual religious hypocrisy which was satirized, and of the existence of religious hypocrisy there can be, alas! no question. Cantwell and Mawworm, Stiggins and Chadband, are everyday characters. But high art is not religion, and does not lead even mothers-in-law to such excesses. In "The Serious Family" there was some ground for the domestic misery of the husband. His wife and her mother, in their narrow-minded way, were sincerely anxious for his temporal and eternal welfare, and sincerely alarmed when the godless Irish officer made his appearance upon the scene. Pitiful as all this was, it was not so odious and ridiculous as the conduct of Lady Tompkins and Olive, who are only actuated by an æsthetic "fad." This fact, too, destroys all possible sympathy with the husband. We do not despise a man who respects his wife's religious convictions, however little he may share them. If he lets his house become "his mother-in-law's castle" through that lady's religious influence over his wife, he no doubt acts weakly, but not quite contemptibly. But when he fails to exert his legitimate authority in opposition to mere sham æstheticism, he becomes simply despicable, and even the meagre excuse he would otherwise have for his lapse in conjugal duty vanishes entirely. Thus Forrester, his wife, and Lady Tompkins are all more thoroughly despicable than their prototypes, while Lambert Streyke and Basil Giorgione become, not types observed from the life, but odious figments of the imagination, which cannot be said to caricature, but rather to libel, a section of society whose foibles are surely quite innocuous.

There is, certainly, no reason why æsthetic cant should not be satirized on the stage, though to devote a three-act comedy to that end alone seems like cracking a walnut with a steam-hammer. But gross caricature is not satire, which should always be just if not actually generous. Yet it must be admitted that the breadth of its caricature is what saves Mr. Burnand's comedy from absolute offensiveness. We can laugh at it with a good conscience, because we are sure that such wild-flying shafts will not inflict deadly injury upon any one.

To apply criticism to the construction of the piece would be useless. It is a mere framework for Mr. Burnand's satire, and, as I have tried to show, not a very well-chosen framework. It is Mr. Burnand's dialogue which saves the piece. Though it belongs to the verbal pyrotechny school throughout, it is masterly in its kind. Whenever something is said utterly unlike what any sane man or woman would say under the circumstances, the audience pricks up its ears, for it knows that a "point" cannot be far off. Sometimes it is a good way off, but we sit and watch with patience, and our faith is always rewarded. Thus when Olive, on hearing the name "Fisher" mentioned, rises, and with perfect irrelevance, remarks, "Three fishers went sailing out into the west," no one imagines for a moment that she is temporarily insane, which would be the most obvious explanation of the phenomenon. On the contrary, we feel that it is a hint to get our risible muscles cleared for action; and, sure enough, after a comparatively short pause, there comes a pun about "the *bar* and its moaning," at which we all laugh consumedly. The finest and most successful instance of this style of wit is the point where Olive calls her husband "the unhatched bird of art," so that Colonel Woodd may remark, "Ah! that's why Lady Tompkins is always sitting on him." But Mr. Burnand has so much of this spontaneous humour at command, that he surely need not descend to such tricks as calling his hero "Woottweell W. Woodd," so that he may get a laugh out of the spelling of the name:—"W, double o, double t, &c." One great disadvantage of this species of dialogue is that after the first hearing its attraction has entirely vanished. When we know what is coming the humour begins to pall. On the first hearing, when we find the author laying the train for a flash—and a pretty long train it sometimes is—we feel a sort of languid interest as to what the flash will be. But when we are perfectly prepared for the explosion beforehand, what at first seemed a very nitro-glycerine bomb of humour, is apt to assume the proportions of the merest cracker. In short, the wit of "The Colonel" is of such a quality that at the first draught we may mistake it for champagne, but on a second taste we discover it to be only zoedone. Mr. Burnand's humour is a thing of beauty and a joy for once in a way.

I have now to speak of the works which constitute the great bulk of Mr. Burnand's dramatic production, that is to say his burlesques. Before doing so I wish to say a few words on the subject of burlesque in general, or rather to quote a few words in which a great writer has touched upon the point with admirable force, directness, and conviction.

One of the essays in "Theophrastus Such" is entitled "Debasing the Moral Currency." It has as a motto the following passage from La Bruyère:—"Il ne faut pas mettre un ridicule où il n'y en a point: c'est se gâter le goût, c'est corrompre son jugement et celui des autres. Mais le ridicule qui est quelque part, il faut l'y voir, l'en tirer avec grâce, et d'une manière qui plaise et qui instruise." George Eliot then goes on to say :—

. . . I wish he had added that the habit of dragging the ludicrous into topics where the chief interest is of a different or even opposite kind is a sign not of endowment, but of deficiency. The art of spoiling is within the reach of the dullest faculty; the coarsest clown with a hammer in his hand might chip the nose of every statue and bust in the Vatican, and stand grinning at the effect of his work. Because wit is an exquisite product of high powers, we are not therefore forced to admit the sadly confused inference of the monotonous jester, that he is establishing his superiority over every less facetious person, and over every topic on which he is ignorant and insensible, by being uneasy until he has distorted it in the small cracked mirror which he carries about with him as a joking apparatus. Some high authority is needed to give many worthy and timid persons the freedom of muscular repose under the growing demand on them to laugh when they have no other reason than the peril of being taken for dullards; still more to inspire them with the courage to say that they object to the theatrical spoiling for themselves and their children of all affecting themes, all the grander deeds and aims of men, by burlesque associations adapted to the taste of rich fishmongers in the stalls and their assistants in the gallery. . . . The world seems to me well supplied with what is genuinely ridiculous; wit and humour may play as harmlessly or beneficently round the changing facets of egoism, absurdity, and vice, as the sunshine over the rippling sea or the dewy meadows. Why should we make our delicious sense of the ludicrous, with its invigorating shocks of laughter, and its irrepressible smiles which are the outglow of an inward radiation as gentle and cheering as the warmth of morning, flourish like a brigand on the robbery of our mental wealth? or let it take its exercise as a madman might, if allowed a free nightly promenade, by drawing the populace with bonfires which leave some venerable structure a blackened ruin, or send a scorching smoke across the portraits of the past, at which we once looked with a loving recognition of fellowship, and disfigure them into butts of mockery? nay, worse, use it to degrade the healthy appetites and affections of our nature, as they are seen to be degraded in insane patients whose system, all out of joint, finds matter for screaming laughter in mere topsy-turvy, makes every passion preposterous or obscene, and turns the hard-won order of life into a second chaos hideous enough to make one wail that the first was ever thrilled with light?

This is what I call debasing the moral currency. . . . And yet, it seems, parents will put into the hands of their children ridiculous parodies (perhaps with more ridiculous "illustrations") of the poems which stirred their own tenderness or filial piety, and carry them to make their first acquaintance with great men, great works, or solemn crises through the medium of some miscellaneous burlesque which, with its idiotic puns and farcical attitudes, will remain among their primary associations, and reduce them throughout their time of studious preparation for life to the moral imbecility of an inward giggle at what might have stimulated their high emulation or fed the fountains of compassion, trust, and constancy. One wonders where these parents have deposited that stock of morally educating stimuli which is to be independent of poetic tradition, and to subsist in spite of the finest images being degraded, and the finest words of genius being poisoned as with some befooling drug.

It is probable that even in the midst of the noble indignation which inspired this passage, George Eliot scarcely knew the full extent to which the evil she denounced had gone. She knew the irreverence of our *cacoëthes ridendi*—our itch for laughter—but not being a habitual theatre-goer, she can scarcely have realized its inanity and imbecility. She could see from her lofty point of observation the moral obtuseness it involved, but not the literary and artistic degradation. I shall not speak here of the material immorality which clusters round the burlesque stage. It is not my business to describe the young and old patrons of art who gather in the stalls of a burlesque theatre about ten every evening, to applaud and throw bouquets to the "actresses" who gabble through their halting lines with a lofty disregard of metre, meaning, punctuation, and H's. I only refer to this point at all because it is a mystery to me how men of character and principle can be found to contribute in any way to this form of modern vice. However liberal may be one's code of ethics, there can surely be no excuse for the species of immorality which characterizes the burlesque stage. It is "worse than wicked, it is vulgar." The gentlemen who write burlesques no doubt salve their consciences with the theory that they are not responsible for the morals of their actors and their patrons, that the immorality does not lie in their work, but in an accident beyond their control, and that if they did not write the burlesques some one else would, and would perhaps write them worse. The same sophistry can be used to prove murder an act of self-sacrifice. Since there is a yearly average of murders, if A kills B, he saves C from killing D, and thus does a most benevolent action to C and D at the expense of a trifling and temporary inconvenience to B. There may be no immorality in the actual words of their burlesques—

much virtue in a "may"—and it may not be absolutely necessary that the costumiers, "actors" and "actresses," and audience should introduce immorality into the chaste framework. But it is always done, and the author constructs the said chaste framework well knowing that it will be done. This is what I call being an accessory before the fact; and it astonishes me that men who in their private life and in their ordinary sentiments and conversation are doubtless well-living and "respectable" citizens, should lend themselves to the supply of this degrading demand. If they were all hack-writers driven by necessity to prostitute their pens, the wonder would be less. As it is one can only fall back on the old "explanation" that man is an inexplicable animal.

But let us forget the inseparable concomitants of burlesque and look only at works themselves. To all of these, of course, George Eliot's indignation does not apply. There are many quite legitimate subjects for burlesque, both literary and dramatic. When Thackeray and Bret Harte parody Lord Lytton and Lord Beaconsfield, or even Charles Dickens and Charlotte Brontë, there is no harm done. In the former two instances a positive service is rendered to art, in the latter a little good-natured laughter at a great writer's mannerisms leaves intact our admiration for his or her merits and beauties. In the same way every one must thank Mr Burnand for his burlesque of Ouida, and I do not think that even Mr. Swinburne can be very indignant at his travesty of Victor Hugo. But even where burlesque deals with the most legitimate object possible, it can become illegitimate by being childish or vulgar. For the last twenty years this has been the case with English dramatic burlesque almost without exception. It often deals with subjects which good taste and reverence for historic worth and poetic beauty would have left untouched; and it is always characterized by an almost incredible puerility of wit and vulgarity of tone. The exceptions are to be found in Mr. Gilbert's popular extravaganzas, which have always genuine wit and literary finish, though even they would often fall under George Eliot's ban by reason of their persistent ridicule of the loftiest human sentiments.

Let us now return to Mr. Burnand, in whose works these characteristics are amply exemplified. The following is a list of a few of his burlesques, which will show how wide is the range of subjects with which he has dealt:—"Dido;" "Fair Rosamond;" "Robin Hood, or the Forester's Fête;" "Acis and Galatea;" "Ixion, or the Man at the Wheel;" "Pirithous, or like Father Like Son;" "Snowdrop, or the Seven Mannikins;" "Rumplestiltskin, or the Woman at the Wheel;" "Cupid and Psyche;" Venus and Adonis;" "Dido (second edition);" "Faust and Marguerite;" "Ulysses, or the Ironclad Warrior, and the Little Tug of War;" "Patient Penelope;" "Paris, or Vive L'Emprière;" "Sappho, or Look before you Leap;" "Antony and Cleopatra, or History and Her-story;" "Black-Eyed Susan, or the Little Bill that was Taken Up;" "Elizabeth." Here we have Greek mythology and legend, Homer and Virgil, Shakespeare and Goethe, English history and romance, and finally two of the most graceful themes of nursery lore laid under contribution as food for laughter. And how? With graceful humour and playful fancy? In polished verse, full of wit and epigram? I have waded through several of these productions to see whether they contain any really clever writing which had been lost upon me in the theatre owing to the way in which burlesque dialogue is always gabbled by the "artists" who deliver it; and when I had done this penitential study, I no longer wondered at the artists' gabbling, for it is the only way in which to treat the lame metres, cockney rhymes, inane puns and senseless "topical" allusions of which the dialogue consists. As for examples, I am embarrassed by their profusion. My hand happens to fall on "Ixion," and opening it I find in the very playbill the following gems of humour:—

Venus (the Goddess of Beauty; still a spinster, although it has been said by a great authority that *Venus orta mari*, which, being translated is *Venus ought to marry*). . . . *Miss Ada Cavendish.*

Ganymede (Jupiter's beautiful "Buttons;" a nice active lad, the original fat boy, who may be described as a Gany-*mede* and Gany-*pursey'un*, too). . . . *Mr. Joseph Robins.*

Minerva (Goddess of Wisdom; a very studious and quiet lady, though generally appearing with an *'owl*). . . . *Mr. Felix Rogers.*

Minerva is of course played by a man, nothing being held more humorous on the English stage than for men to flourish about in female dress. No burlesque is complete without one or two such characters, which are only less degrading to the actors who represent them than to the audiences who tolerate and even demand them. Further, let me quote the following single page from "Ixion:"—

Enter JUNO *and* IXION *walking lovingly together*, L.

Ixion. Juno, my love increases every hour.
I am drawn to you by some mighty pow'r.

Juno. Ixion!

(*He kisses her hand, and puts his arm round her waist*—GANYMEDE *and* MERCURY *look out* L. *and* R. *in flat—look at one another—telegraph—retire.*)

Ixion. I ne'er thought, till that last action,
You "heavenly bodies" had so much "attraction."

(VENUS *appears* C., *listening.*)

Juno. You don't love Venus, then?

Ixion. That painted fright!
The "Tinted Venus!" '*Tint* a pretty sight.

(VENUS, C., *clenches her fist and retires.*)

Juno. Am I to mortal women much superior?

Ixion. The loveliest is immensely your inferior.

Juno. Mine was a stupid simple question, dear;
But we're not "women of the world" up here.

Ixion (*walking to* R. *and* L.). There's not one girl in mortal form encased
Can *hold a candle* to your *taper waist*,
The finest lady has not such an arm!
Show me your *hand:* Ah! there you *bear* the *palm!*
As brightest poetry to dullest prose,
As Tennyson's above the poet Close,
As Crystal Palace fountains high in air
Are to the squirts that grace Trafalgar Square,
So you are far above each mortal fair.

Juno. Such love as this I never heard Jove make.

Ixion. I would I were a god, dear, for your sake.
(*Aside.*) Now to aim high shall be my first endeavour.
Juno. Wouldst have me make you "beautiful for ever"?
I fear I can't: refusal is distressing—
Ixion. But let's talk on it, come!
(*Putting his arm round her waist as if about to lead her away*, L.)
Juno (*bashfully*). Oh! you're so *pressing.*

Duet: Air, "The Tank."

Ixion. Ju-no,
You know
What I mean by saying,
Fol de riddle lol de riddle lol lol lay.
Juno. Ix-i-
on, I
Am the meaning weighing,
Of fol de riddle,& c.

I choose this passage since it exhibits the empty vulgarity of tone which characterizes the whole. In the matter of puns and versification it is decidedly above the average. "Palm" and "arm" are not an immaculate rhyme, but the poet who makes "torn" rhyme with "Colleen Bawn," "fervour" with "Minerva," "Ixion" with "iron," "reporter" with "water," and "saw" with "shore," is capable of any enormity. Of the insane pieces of "business" of which these burlesques are full, I shall say nothing except that they probably come to a climax in Queen Elizabeth riding round the stage on the shoulders of one of her courtiers—Lord Burleigh, if I remember aright.

Yet the inventor of this "business," the writer of

these rhymes, this caricaturer of history, vulgarizer of mythology, and desecrator of poetry, is a man of university education, of some pretensions to culture, and, upon occasion, possessed of genuine humour. It is a standing enigma to me how he can find it in his heart thus to serve up so much that is worthy and beautiful, "butchered to make a cockney holiday." Voltaire had as much excuse in writing "La Pucelle."

Of late years there has been an improvement in Mr. Burnand's style, even in burlesque. When he has some definite object to parody he is often inspired with really humorous ideas. His travesties of "Diplomacy" and of his own translation of "Une Cause Célèbre"—"Dip-lunacy" and "Over-Proof"—were extremely funny and quite unobjectionable. There were even one or two funny ideas in "Robbing Roy" and "The Hunchback back Again," though "Balloonacy" was a direful fiasco. Last of all he has contributed to the newest development of burlesque—the enormity known as a "three-act burlesque drama." He himself is of opinion that "Like the 'Forty Thieves,' 'Whittington' is the sort of piece to which you might take your children, if you have any; or anybody else's if you haven't. You can't go wrong, *because the story is clear*. That is a great point, in fact, one of the greatest points in the piece. It is on the old lines, with lots of new ones thrown in, and not generally thrown away." The italics are Mr. Burnand's, not mine, and are explicable when we remember that Mr. Burnand wrote a dispassionate article in the *Theatre* to prove that the story of "Ourselves" was clear, and that it was the intellect of the audience which was befogged. I paid the greatest attention to "Whittington," but if I had not known the story beforehand, I should not to this day have had an idea what it was all about. Perhaps the juvenile mind for which Mr. Burnand professes to have written—and indeed there is plenty of puerility in the piece—may be better at following out a plot in which there were certainly more new lines than old. But if the juvenile mind can appreciate the "topical hits" of which most of the dialogue consisted, it must be an extremely well school-boarded juvenile mind, and extremely well read in *Punch* and the daily papers. On the other hand, there were many strokes of such humour as must be apparent to the meanest intellect—or to none at all. One of the hits of the piece was a song with the chorus, "Where did you get your trousers from, and did they cost you much?" If I wanted to encourage in any children an appreciation of this refined style of humour, it should certainly be in other people's children and not my own.

MR. HENRY J. BYRON.

In dedicating "Cyril's Success" to Mr. Shirley Brooks, Mr. Byron gives as his reason for ushering in that play with a special flourish of trumpets, the fact that he is "somewhat tired of being termed a 'droll,' a 'punster,' and so on." As it is "original, and a comedy, and in five acts," he thinks that "Cyril's Success" should finally put to silence the unappreciative or mis-appreciative critics who have applied to him these derogatory epithets. I fear that the publication of this masterpiece did not produce the desired effect. Since 1870, when the dedication was written, Mr. Byron has, I believe, been several times called a punster, and perhaps even a droll, though the former term is much the safer, as it does not commit to any judgment on the quality of the puns. But he has brought it upon himself. He has made and caused to be uttered upon the public stage several thousand puns and other distortions of the English language. If this does not constitute a punster, what does? Mr. Byron cannot be more tired of being termed a punster than I am of applying the term to him, mentally or verbally. Every time I have seen or read a play of his I have had to use the objectionable word, or think the objectionable thought, once every two minutes or so. It is a painful necessity. I should infinitely prefer to call him a "wit," or a "moralist," or a "dramatist," but punster is really the only term available—or if not the only term at least the mildest. When a man has punned himself into fame and fortune, and then protests against being called a punster, he is like one of Mr. Byron's own favourite buttermen who object to being reminded of the shop. And said buttermen have as a rule retired from business before they begin to despise it, whereas Mr. Byron continues to turn out puns at the rate of two or three comedies-full a year, and yet is tired of being called a punster! He deals with the English language as the gypsies in "L'Homme qui Rit" dealt with that unhappy nobleman Lord Linnæus Clancharlie, *alias* Gwynplaine: he distorts its fair face until it becomes an object one cannot look at without laughing—or weeping. In one of his latest comedies a character remarks, "I feel so desperate, I could perpetrate the most despicable quibble without a blush." Whether from desperation or not, Mr. Byron has long ago given up blushing. I almost fear that he has become callous since 1870, and that in 1882 not even the term punster will call the unwonted blood to his cheek. On the other hand I have blushed for him often enough, and still oftener for the audiences who accept his periodical exhibitions of word-torture as good, or even tolerable, dramatic writing.

Perhaps after this I need scarcely say that Mr. Byron is my *bête noire* in the dramatic world. I openly plead guilty to a rooted prejudice against his style, which may possibly render me unjust in details of my estimate. But of this I am sure, that he has done more than any other man to hinder the development of a worthy modern drama in England, by fostering a taste for frivolous and puerile work. I do not deny him what may be called the domestic virtues of the stage—that is, an avoidance of everything in matter and manner which can seriously offend the feminine portion of the great middle-class. His plays are full of conventional morality, and their vulgarity never trenches upon positive indecency. The curtain generally falls upon two or three engagements between his two or three heroines and the gentlemen whom they probably describe as their "young men." Than this nothing can be more moral and proper. If puns and propriety were the sole requisites of a good comedy, Mr. Byron would indeed be what an appreciative actor-manager has called him, "one of the best and purest dramatists of our time." Unfortunately a playwright may be chaste as ice, pure as snow, yet shall he not escape criticism.

To show that I do not exaggerate the influence Mr. Byron has exerted upon the stage, I quote from the title-page of one of his comedies an authorized list of his works up to the date of publication of that play ("Old Soldiers"):—

"Weak Woman;" "Old Sailors;" "War to the Knife;" "Cyril's Success;" "The Old Story;" "Dundreary Married and Done For;" "Cinderella;" "Blue Beard from a New Point of Hue;" "Robinson Crusoe;" "Little Don Giovanni;" "Mazeppa;" "The Maid and the Magpie, or the Fatal Spoon;" "The Babes in the Wood;" "Bride of Abydos;" "Fra Diavolo;" "Jack the Giant Killer;" "Very Latest Edition of the Lady of Lyons;" "The Nymph of the Lurleyberg;" "Pilgrim of Love;" "The Garibaldi Excursionists;" "Aladdin, or the Wonderful Scamp;" "Esmeralda, or the Sensation Goat;" "Goldenhair the Good;" "Ivanhoe in Accordance;" "Beauty and the Beast;" "Rival Othellos;" "Whittington and his Cat;" "Puss in a New Pair of Boots;" "Miss Eily O'Connor;" "George de Barnwell;" "Our Sea-side Lodgings;" "The Rosebud of Stinging-nettle Farm;" "The Sensation Fork;" "My Wife and I;" "Beautiful Haidee, or the Sea Nymph and the Sallee Rovers;" "Ill Treated Il Trovatore;" "The Motto: 'I *am* all there!'" "St. George and the Dragon;" "Lady Belle Belle;" "Orpheus and Eurydice, or the Young Gentleman who charmed the Rocks;" "1863, or the Sensations of the Past Year;" "Mazourka, or the Stick, the Pole, and the Tartar;" "The 'Grin' Bushes;" "Lion and the Unicorn;" "Sensation Dramas for the Back Drawing-Room;" "Princess Springtime, or the Envoy that Stole the King's Daughter;" "La Sonnambula! or the Supper, the Sleeper, and the Merry Swiss Boy;" "Pan;" "Lucia di Lammermoor;" "Pandora's Box;" "A Hundred Thousand Pounds;" "William Tell with a Vengeance; or the Pet, the Patriot, and the Pippin;" "Lucretia

Borgia, M.D.;" "The Lancashire Lass;" "Enchanted Wood;" "Not such a Fool as he Looks;" "Lord Bateman, or the Proud Young Porter and the Fair Sophia;" "The Corsican Brothers, or the Troublesome Twins;" "Eurydice, or Little Orpheus and his Lute;" "An English Gentleman;" "Daisy Farm;" "Prompter's Box;" "Orange Tree and the Humble Bee;" "Robert Macaire's Camaralzaman;" "Partners for Life;" "Tottles;" "Dearer than Life;" "Good News;" "Wait and Hope;" "Uncle Dick's Darling;" "Sour Grapes;" "Haunted Houses;" "Fine Feathers;" "Lady of the Lane;" "Old Chums;" "Bohemian Gyurl;" "Little Don Cæsar de Bazan;" "The Bull by the Horns;" "Married in Haste;" "Blow for Blow;" "Oil and Vinegar;" "An American Lady;" "Our Boys;" "Little Doctor Faust;" "Guinea Gold;" "A Fool and his Money;" &c., &c.

The "&c., &c." now includes, "The Girls;" "Courtship;" "Bow Bells;" "Punch;" "Michael Strogoff," and numerous farces and burlesques to which the memory of man runneth not. Thus it is clear that by sheer bulk, if in no other way, Mr. Byron has been a power in the dramatic world. He has filled a certain place, occupied a certain amount of room on the stage, if he has done nothing else. His wares have stocked, and occasionally glutted, the market. It may be said that he has only supplied an evident demand, and so no doubt he has. But appetite comes in eating, and supply begets, or rather fosters, demand, almost as inevitably as demand begets supply. The law of action and reaction reigns in the dramatic branch of economics, as it does everywhere else.

How to deal with this portentous list of works within the limits of a single essay! I thought of making an anthology of the wit and wisdom of Mr. Byron, and giving, without comment, a full selection of his puns and epigrams. But I found that this course would be at once unjust and inadequate, since on the one hand, the witticisms divorced from their context would often seem more inane than they actually are; while, on the other hand, their utter inappropriateness and incongruity could not be recognized without a full knowledge of the situation in which they occur. Consequently I have determined to take two or three of his works and analyze them more or less in detail, leaving the rest to be estimated from these samples. This course will be the less unfair as Mr. Byron's manner is always the same.

First let us look at the play on which Mr. Byron seems content to found his reputation, namely, "Cyril's Success." It is certainly the most carefully written of his works, and puns, in the strict sense of the word, are carefully excluded from the dialogue. But what is the matter of this "comedy in five acts"? Cyril Cuthbert, a young and very successful author, has shown a trifling coldness towards his wife. A certain Major Treherne happens to drop a letter in the Cuthberts' drawing-room one evening. Mrs. Cuthbert picks it up and reads as follows, "I have been expecting you all day. Heartless one, come and see me.—Your own Clara." She at once jumps at the conclusion that this letter has been addressed to her husband by a rival; and without even letting him know what she suspects, she leaves him, and goes to live with a misanthropic old schoolmistress. Where, except on the stage, do people act with such inconceivable, nay, criminal, foolishness? But next day, to make matters worse, Mrs. Cuthbert and her friend the schoolmistress conceive the extraordinary idea of going to call upon the lady who wrote the fatal note—a widow rejoicing in the name of Mrs. Singleton Bliss. As is usual in making an afternoon call, they enter her drawing-room without their names being announced, and the consequence is that Mrs. Bliss, on being challenged with having written the letter to her mysterious visitor's husband, jumps at the conclusion that Major Treherne, to whom she is engaged, is already married. If any one were sane enough to find out anybody else's name, the whole fabric of the play would fall to pieces. As it is, they are all ready to adopt the most grossly injurious theories about each other rather than attempt the smallest explanation, or even make the most natural inquiries. Cyril Cuthbert never thinks of asking why his wife has left him. Major Treherne, on being told by Mrs. Bliss to "go to his wife," never thinks of assuring her that he has not got one. Cyril and Treherne, for no reason whatever, except that it is such an eminently natural and usual thing for two Englishmen to do, fight a duel, in which Treherne is shot through the arm. Cyril at once jumps at the conclusion that a wound in the arm is necessarily mortal, and for months suffers agonies of remorse, under the belief that Treherne is dead. At last, in the fifth act, after every one has been thoroughly miserable for about a year, the explanations which only an epidemic of insanity prevented in the third act, are exchanged on all sides, and this original comedy is brought to an end. "Jumping at Conclusions" would be a much better name for it than "Cyril's Success."

And now let me give a short specimen of Mr. Byron's dialogue at its very best. It is a little passage between Mrs. Singleton Bliss, Matthew Pincher, "a literary hack," and the Hon. Frederick Titeboy, "a musical amateur:"—

Mrs. B. Can you tell me the time, Freddy? My watch here is elegant, but useless. (*Hands it to* TITEBOY.)

Tite. A good one to look at. (*Sits.*)

Pinch. But a "bad 'un to go."

Mrs. B. Just so.

Tite. (*looking at his own watch*). Really I—I can't say to a quarter of an hour, but as far as I can be certain, I should say it was—

Pinch. (*pulling out fat silver watch*). Twenty-five minutes and three-quarters past two, Greenwich time.

Mrs. B. Thanks.

Tite. (*looking at* PINCHER'S *watch through eye-glass*). That's an elegant horological article, that is.

Pinch. Yes, sir, an heir-loom. Tells the time to a second. Bad complexion but well-regulated interior.

Tite. A good weight I should say. I say, Pincher, when you pull that enormous watch out, don't you—Ha!—don't you find your time hangs rather heavy?

Mrs. B. Ha, ha, ha!—Freddy, don't be a fool.

Pinch. Perhaps I do, sir—perhaps I do. (*Takes* MRS. BLISS'S *watch.*) This is quite a different style of thing. Eh?

Modern watches remind me somewhat of modern ladies do you know, Mrs. Bliss.

Mrs. B. Do they, oh railer against the sex; why?

Pinch. Well, this elegant toy for instance. Hem! Well enamelled—nice back—delicate hands—plenty of jewels—and —a—*remarkably incorrect.*

Tite. Shameful! Any one could tell you were a bachelor. (PINCHER *looks hard at him and snuffs.*)

This is, in all seriousness, a quite favourable specimen of Mr. Byron's dialogue. It has nothing whatever to do with the play, but that is the general characteristic of Mr. Byron's good things. The analogy between watches and women, and the fact that a man with a big watch may be said to find time hang heavy, clearly presented themselves to Mr. Byron's mind as inspirations, and the result is an interlude of fifteen speeches specially devoted to their elaboration. I need scarcely comment on the refinement of the lady who says to a casual male acquaintance, "Freddy, don't be a fool." She must have been brought up at the boarding-school of Mrs. Cuthbert's protectress, Miss Grannett, who, among other amenities of language, makes use of the phrases, "Deuce take his kindness;" and, "It doesn't gammon *me.*"

If "Cyril's Success" is Mr. Byron's literary masterpiece, the phenomenal run of "Our Boys" has made it *the* play with which Mr. Byron's name will always be connected. And indeed it is in the matter of plot one of his least objectionable works, mainly because its plot may be called a minus quantity. It is marvellous to observe how faithfully Mr. Byron relies upon the old stock-in-trade of threadbare theatrical devices in composing even the small framework of action upon which he strings his quips and quiddities. There is scarcely one of his plays in which the stage uncle is not made use of in one or other of his various forms: the *oncle d'Amérique* who leaves the hero a fortune just in the nick of time, the philosophic uncle who has made an imbecile will upon the conditions of which the plot hinges, the hard-hearted uncle who objects to the marriage of the hero and heroine, the nabob uncle who was supposed to have died of liver-complaint, but turns up in robust health just at the wrong moment, and so forth through all the time-honoured developments of stage-avuncular eccentricity. Then we have lost wills, and unexpected codicils, and rash investments, and forgeries, and pretended losses to test sincerity of friends, and remarkable likenesses between twin sisters, and husbands and wives rising Enoch-Arden-like from the grave at peculiarly inconvenient junctures, and, in short, every attenuated ficelle that has been handed down from generation to generation of play-manufacturers. Considering how little plot Mr. Byron requires at all, one cannot but wonder that he should not be able to do without this antiquated frippery, and make his plots as simple as they are trivial.

To return to "Our Boys." Its plot, I repeat, so far as it can be said to have a plot, is less absurd than those which Mr. Byron generally evolves. Its dialogue, on the other hand, carries to an extreme pitch the style which Mr. Byron has made his own. It is curious in reading any of Mr. Byron's plays, to note what a large proportion of words is italicized so as to draw attention to the distortion of spelling or sense to which they have been subjected. I should like to reprint "Our Boys," verbatim and literatim, with a few marginal comments and queries perhaps, but in the main leaving it to the reader's unprompted judgment to decide whether every second speech is not unnatural, or impossible, or a breach of good taste, or an offence against good manners—the last defect being quite as often observable in the part of the baronet as in that of the butterman. As I cannot, however, lay the whole case before the court, I must content myself with quoting one or two of the most admired passages, some of them points which may be said to have made the fame and fortune of the play. Here is the famous scene between old Middlewick and his son, after the latter's return from abroad:—

Mid. Paris now—nice place, ain't it?

Char. Glorious!

Mid. 'Ow about the 'orse flesh?

Char. A myth.

Mid. Railly though! And I suppose frogs is fallacies. Only to think.

Char. Paris is a paradise. But Italy—well, there!

Mid. But ain't it a mass of lazeyroneys?

Char. A mere libel. A land of romance, beauty, tradition, poetry! Milan! Venice! Verona! Florence!

Mid. Where the *ile* comes from.

Char. Rome! Naples!

Mid. That's where Vesoovius is, ain't it?

Char. Yes.

Mid. Was it "fizzin'" when you was there, Charley?

Char. No. There was no eruption when I was there.

Mid. That's wrong, you know, that's wrong. I didn't limit you, Charley; I said, "See everything," and I certainly expected as you'd insist upon an eruption.

Char. But, my dear dad, I saw everything else—Pompeii and Herculaneum.

Mid. Eh?

Char. Pompeii and Herculaneum—they were *ruined*, you know.

Mid. Two unfortnit Italian warehousemen, I suppose.

Char. Nonsense! They were buried, you remember.

Mid. And why *not?* It'd be a pretty thing to refuse an unlucky firm as went broke a decent—

Char. You don't understand.

Mid. (*bluntly*). No, I *don't.*

The youth who comes back from Italy to vent his transports in the classic phrase, "Well, there!" is a worthy son of the father who does not know what a volcano is. The latter point, which I have often heard quoted with admiration as a gem of humour, has the additional disadvantage of being impossible. A man who has made a fortune in London commerce may be ignorant, but can scarcely be imbecile. As for the point about Pompeii and Herculaneum, I need scarcely remark that it is secured by making the son rather more imbecile than the father. If, "in a lucid interval," as Mr. Byron would say, he had thought of mentioning that they were cities, the misunderstanding would have vanished—but then the humour would have vanished with it. Let me now quote one of the elegant love-scenes of the comedy—that between Talbot Champneys and Mary Melrose :—

Tal. Who's that talking about old maids?

Mary. I was.

Tal. Why, you're all alone.

Mary. Yes, I like to be alone.

Tal. That means I'm to—

Mary. Oh, *no*, you're—

Tal. Nobody. Don't count. Thanks.

Mary. I didn't *say* that.

Tal. No, but you *meant* it.

Mary. Why?

Tal. Because you didn't *say* it. (*Pause.*)

Mary. What do you mean.

Tal. What I say.

Mary. What's that.

Tal. Nothing.

Mary. Then you mean nothing.

Tal. On the contrary, I mean a lot, but I can't say it.

Mary. Then I wouldn't try.

Tal. I won't. (*Slight pause.*) I say, Miss Melrose, do you know I'm dreadfully afraid of you.

Mary. Am I so very terrible?

Tal. You're so fearfully sensible, you know—so satirical and cutting, and "awfully clever," and I'm *not*, you know.

Mary. Not *what*, you know?

Tal. None of *that*, you know. I'm a—a—muff, that's what *I* am. I haven't got a second idea. I don't believe I've got a *first*, but I'll *swear* I haven't a second.

Mary. Well, at all events you're not conceited.

Tal. What on earth have *I* got to be conceited about? What are *my* accomplishments? I can play a fair game of billiards, though I'm too short-sighted for cricket. I can stick on the maddest horse that ever gladdened a coroner, and I can smoke like—like *Sheffield.* Not much to recommend oneself to a woman, eh?

Mary. I don't know. Miss Melrose, for instance, my rich and handsome cousin, has a great admiration for the Guy Livingstone virtues.

Tal. Don't like her—at least, don't *admire* her.

Mary. Why not?

Tal. Because I've been commanded to. Private feelings ain't private soldiers—you can't order them about and drill them like dolls. Human nature's obstinate as a rule. Do you know how they get the pigs on board?

Mary. No.

Tal. Put their noses towards the vessel and then try and pull them away, *backwards.* The result is that they run up the plank into the vessel *immediately. I'm* a pig.

Mary. You don't say so?

Tal. And *my* sentiments are *pig-headed*, my governor's are *pig-tailed*—that's to say, old-fashioned—the old "school" strict obedience, marry according to *orders*, you know, eh? (*Nudges her.*) Ha! ha! Some of us know a trick worth two of that, eh?

Mary. Ha! ha! ha!

Tal. (*laughs with her*). You're a *sharp* one, *you* are. (*Nudges her.*)

Mary. So are *you.*

Tal. *Am* I, though?

Mary. Only in the *elbow.* Suppose you sit a little further off; you never crowd up so closely to Violet.

Tal. No, I'm not given to *poaching.*

Mary. Poaching! *Eggs?*

Tal. Eggs be—*hatched!* Haven't you seen Charley Middlewick loves her as much as—as—(*aside*) I'll *go* it now—I'm wound up *to* go it, and go it I *will.*

Mary. As much as *what?*

Tal. As I love *you.*

Comment is here quite unnecessary. A love-scene which opens with such witty and original badinage and culminates in the lovers "nudging" each other, may be left to speak for itself. There may possibly be certain classes of society in which such a scene, minus a few individual inanities, might be conceivable. If Mr. Byron had meant it as a satiric picture of the decline of courtesy and growth of vulgarity in modern life, it might have had some relevance. But nothing was further from his intention. The young gentleman who "nudges," and the young lady who protests by saying, "You never crowd up so closely to Violet," are intended to command our sympathy and esteem.

I do not deny that there are many really funny touches in the play. In writing it Mr. Byron drew with unwonted liberality upon that commonplace-book of witticisms which I cannot but see in my mind's eye lying ever at his elbow as he writes. It would be easy to make a collection of sayings from "Our Boys" which would be genuinely funny if only they fitted the characters who utter them, and the situations in which they occur. The last act especially contains a good deal of real humour with few passages that are notably bad. The "slavey" Belinda, perhaps comes as near being a possible and consistently-drawn character-sketch as any figure in the play. Mr. Byron has made a science of cockneyism. He carries its phonetic principles to their logical extreme, and has thus evolved a dialect which no one ever spoke in London or elsewhere, but which is often irresistibly funny. This dialect Belinda and Perkyn Middlewick speak to perfection, and to this fact, I believe, the success of the comedy was largely due. If there were no H's in the English language to drop and to misplace, Mr. Byron's occupation would be gone.

Let us now glance at one of his failures—"Wrinkles," produced with disastrous effect at the Prince of Wales's. It is decidedly a solider and better play than many of his great successes. There is actually a conceivable plot in it, which was probably the cause of its failure; for Mr. Byron is so unaccustomed to handling a plot that the moment he allows, anything to depend upon it the whole fabric breaks down. The plot of "Wrinkles" is not more feebly treated than those of many others of his plays, but he has not taken the precaution to bury it in dialogue. His audiences are accustomed to ignore his plots and think only of his word-plays. In this case he did not allow them to do so. The plot forced itself upon their notice, and they could not help recognizing its looseness of structure. Even the attempt at serious character-drawing was unlucky. Harold Carre, though vividly described in the stage-directions as "the sort of man one would never tell a funny story to, or take into one's confidence," does not come out with equal vividness in the play; and the relation between Winifred Piper and Bob Blewitt, probably intended to be pathetic, merely succeeds in being painful. Nor must it be supposed that because the dialogue is not brilliant enough to conceal the plot, it is therefore good or natural. Mr. Blewitt, when reflecting whether he will ask Graham Carre to lend him money, remarks to himself, "He's a most indulgent father—yes, as a *pater* he's inestimable, but as a 'parter' he's certainly open to improvement." Need I give further specimens of the humour of the play?

"Blow for Blow," "Daisy Farm," and "100,000*l*." are among Mr. Byron's other plays of serious or melo-dramatic interest. The first turns on a conventional intrigue, conventionally treated and filled in with comic episodes so irrelevant to the plot that they deserve to be called by the Elizabethan name of interludes. "Daisy Farm," dealing with a similar subject, contains in the person of Mr. Craven one of those busy-body characters of whom Mr. Byron is particularly fond. Mr. Craven's sole function is to utter funny sayings and drop in as a *deus ex machina* whenever he is least expected. He has no organic connexion with the plot, but wanders through it aimlessly until, in the end he brings about a startling catastrophe as conventional as it is arbitrary and inartistic. Mr. Byron's absolute inability to repress a small joke even in his most serious situations is well exemplified in this play. Bridget Armstrong has just heard her only son accused of a murder, and is being gradually brought to the belief that some further and more terrible calamity is hanging over the family. Craven, as usual, is on the spot, and observing Mrs. Armstrong's very natural excitement, tenders the following advice:—

Craven. Now, my dear Mrs. Armstrong, do go and lie down

or something—your nerves are overstrung. Now, pray take my advice; remember, I was going to be a doctor, only—

Bridget (*with womanly malevolence*). Only you couldn't pass the examination.

Craven. Just so. (*Aside.*) I lost myself among the muscles; they're very confusing—a sort of anatomical Clapham Junction.

Bridget's speech, uttered "with womanly malevolence," and Craven's aside, at the height of a situation described in the author's own stage-direction as "one of quiet, sustained intensity," have always struck me as the acme of dramatic inappropriateness. In "100,000*l*." again, the whole action turns upon the errors of a lawyer whose imbecility is so preternatural as to remind one of Mr. Burnand's tragic reflection in "Happy Thoughts"—"What a dreadful thing it must be to have an idiot solicitor!" A plot so constructed cannot be expected to grasp our interest very strongly. Fortunately Mr. Byron has not placed any dependence upon his plot, but has tortured the English and French languages so perseveringly that idiocy of character is quite swallowed up in—ingenuity of dialogue.

Three very characteristic examples of Mr. Byron's manner are the lighter comedies, "Old Soldiers," "Old Sailors," and "Weak Woman," produced at the Strand in 1873, 1874, and 1875 respectively. The action of the first two consists of a "shuffling and dealing" among several pairs of lovers, which brings into strong prominence one of the characteristics of feminine human nature as conceived by Mr. Byron—namely, a perfect willingness to marry the wrong man at five minutes' notice, if for any reason the right man is not available. For with all Mr. Byron's care to write *virginibus puerisque*, I know few comedies which would be more repulsively cynical than his, if the slightest serious meaning were to be attached to them. Mr. Gilbert's wildest burlesques are not more lowering to human nature. After a course of Mr. Byron one begins to doubt whether fine sensibility, serious thought, and worthy emotion exist anywhere in the world. In so far as his comedies are full of marrying and giving in marriage, they are conventionally moral; but in so far as they represent a little punning flirtation intermingled with "chaff" as the only necessary prelude to putting up the banns, they seem to me little short of immoral. Few writers have done more than he to "soil with all ignoble use" the name of love. "Soil" is perhaps too strong a word, or rather suggests inaccurate associations. "Vulgarize" is more exact, but even it does not convey the precise idea. In Mr. Byron's eyes love is synonymous with flirtation and flirtation with more or less impertinent banter. Passion, chivalry, even the commonest sober respect are all equally foreign to his conception of love. He regards it in all good faith as a sort of mental measles—a disease too slight to be treated seriously, whose external symptom is a ridiculous rash eminently available for the purposes of the caricaturist. He is not the first, nor perhaps the worst, offender in this respect. I do not know that in any of his comedies he goes quite so far as Mr. T. W. Robertson, for example, has gone in "School," where two young men are introduced to two school-girls at lunch-time and are satisfactorily engaged to them the same evening. The immorality of this arrangement—I can use no other expression—is rendered more insidious by an infusion of watery sentiment, which, to do Mr. Byron justice, he usually spares us. His lovers are so perfectly unaffecting and undeceptive, that a good deal of the harm their vulgar triviality might do is obviated. Still it cannot be called edifying to find love systematically regarded from the point of view of Mr. Gilbert's "Engaged" only without Mr. Gilbert's irony of intention.

The "hero" of "Old Soldiers" is a certain Lionel Leveret with whom it may be supposed that Mr. Byron feels a certain sympathy, since he played the part himself. Here is the dialogue in which he is introduced to us. Captain Mactavish and his daughter Kate are on the stage, discussing her former lover, Gordon Lockhart:—

Kate. Not a word *against* him! I won't hear it. Not a syllable. Poor dear boy—*where* is he now?

McT. Poor dear boy—there's a *rich* dear boy ready to your hand—that's better—Mr. Leveret, who—

Kate. Compared with Gordon he is—

McT. No more of this. I forbid you ever to mention him again—a scamp—an adventurer, an upstart!

(*Enter at gate,* LIONEL LEVERET.)

Lev. Halloa! Scamp! adventurer! and upstart! Why, McTavish, are you talking to yourself?

McT. Well, a—a—

Lev. You can't have been addressing Miss Kate, here. (*To Kate.*) How are you? (*Shakes hands.*)

McT. I was simply abusing a man I know.

Kate. Yes. Behind his back.

Lev. Behind his back! Best way, too; for in case of kicking, the *man* is certainly at a disadvantage.

McT. (*aside*). What a son-in-law he'd make. This place would suit me to a T.

Lev. (*to Kate*). I thought you'd come here to-day.

Kate. No, really?

Lev. Yes, I was dreaming of you last night.

Kate. No, *were* you?

Lev. Yes, I always dream after Welsh rabbits.

Kate. Really, I—ha! ha!

Lev. I wonder who invented Welsh rabbits.

McT. Some Welshman, I suppose.

Lev. Ah! or some rabbit. Rubbish! I was thinking of something else.

After this no one will be surprised to learn that Mr. Leveret is described as being "rather weak-minded." The only wonder is that any writer should have thought it worth while to depict such weak-mindedness, or any audience to listen to it. Again, in "Old Sailors," the chief character is a Lieutenant Lamb described in the stage-direction as "a mild elderly gentleman, gentle, *but with a sense of humour.*" This sense of humour he exhibits by carefully abstaining, during three long acts, from saying anything that can by courtesy be called funny. The most amusing remark he makes is his retort to his servant Joe, when the latter boasts of making both ends meet, "Aye, aye, Joe, you're too extravagant. *Why* make both ends meet; why not make one meat and the other *bread?*" It is said that a sense of humour is the great distinction between man and the brute creation ; if this remark be the result of a sense of humour, the distinction is certainly not without its drawbacks. In "Weak Woman" there is a touch of ingenuity in the plot, though it of course turns upon one of those eccentric "uncle's wills" which are much better known on the stage than at Somerset House. If the intrigue had been carefully and gracefully worked out it might have made a pretty fantastic comedy. As it is, its word-plays are neither above nor below Mr. Byron's average.

It would be useless and tedious to attempt even the most cursory glance at all Mr. Byron's comedies. The one or two specimens given above are, I believe, genuinely and fairly representative. If I could find in his whole works one truly dramatic, truly witty, or truly fanciful scene, I should quote it at length. But they are all on a dead-level of H. J. Byronism. If there be any irregularities, it is that he descends to the depths, not that he rises to the heights. It can scarcely even be said that he has degenerated of late years, or written himself out. Even "Bow Bells" is scarcely more absurd than some comparatively early works, such as "Not such a Fool as he Looks;" and "Courtship," one of his latest comedies, would be one of his best were it not that the action finishes satisfactorily at the end of the second act, and the third is tagged on without an appearance of rhyme or reason. As a specimen of his very latest manner I may give a sketch of the comedy of "Punch," which was to have revived the fortunes of the theatre rendered illustrious by "Our Boys," but somehow or other failed to do so.

Professor Mistletoe is a Punch-and-Judy man, who has a long-lost brother and an adopted daughter. The latter he has educated at a fashionable boarding-school, where there are apparently no holidays, since her room in the Professor's house has been waiting for her for six years. At the end of the six years she returns, announces to her adopted father that she has accepted a situation as companion in a wealthy family, and starts for the said situation before she has been ten minutes in the house. This is the first act of "Punch." Six months elapse. The step-son of the self-made man, in whose house the Professor's adopted daughter is domiciled, falls in love with her. The Professor comes to exhibit his moral "drayma" at a children's party. The adopted daughter reveals to the step-son her quasi-relationship to the Professor. The step-son is no respecter of persons and doesn't care. The self-made man, however, does, and is in the act of turning the Professor and the adopted daughter out of his house, when the Professor, without even the intervention of a strawberry-mark, recognizes in the self-made man his long-lost brother. He has not seen him for fifty years, and probably recognizes him through a family peculiarity in the matter of aspirates. This is the second act of "Punch." Twelve months elapse. The step-son has mysteriously disappeared, and is supposed to be faithless, The adopted daughter has been ill, and the long-lost brother has disowned the Professor. The step-son suddenly turns up and explains matters to the

Professor, though not to the audience, the long-lost brother is humiliated through the opportune breaking of a bank, and all ends merry as a marriage bell. This is the third act of "Punch."

It must be evident to the meanest capacity that this ingenious and complex intrigue offers vast opportunities for distortion of the Queen's English. In the first act there are exactly five flashes of wit at which the audience screamed with delight. They consist of Professor Mistletoe's substitution of "preformance" for performance, "juneviles" for juveniles, "philophizer" for philosopher, "innywindows" for innuendoes, and "parential" for parental. This is the wit of the first act. In the second act the humour is even more unforced and overflowing. The Professor says "burgular" for burglar, "dramatis personibus" for dramatis personæ, and "bacheldoors" for bachelors. The long-lost brother says "libery" for library, "magisteeral" for magisterial, "espinach" for espionage, and "prestidigipotator" for prestidigitateur —which reminds one of the immortal "ultipomatum" of "Our Boys." But it must not be imagined that the wit is confined to coruscations like this. No! there are numerous puns of the most "mirth-provoking" description. Trevanion, the self-made man, remarks that he has got several good names among the directors of his new brass-polishing company, because a brass-polishing company always needs "nobs." Then there is a conversation between Trevanion and Dr. Lattimer, which positively sparkles with humour. Here it is, or something like it:—

Dr. Lattimer. Your dinners and you suffer from the same complaint—you're both too *rich.*

Trevanion. But what if my dinners were *plain?*

Dr. Lattimer. Even then there would be a marked resemblance. (*Pause for a laugh.*) Look at old So-and-so. He's eighty and looks fifty. Yet he only eats one lean chop a day. *Toojoor perdree,* as the French say.

Trevanion. Come, you said *one* first, and now you say two. . . . But we've established baths in the town.

Dr. Lattimer. Baths are excellent things. *Mens sana in corpore sano,* as the Romans say.

Trevanion. Oh, but we've *women's* baths, too.

The last piece of wit was familiar to our remote ancestors in the tale of the shoemaker who inscribed over his door "Mens conscia recti," upon which the owner of the opposition establishment, determined not to be outdone, painted beneath his sign "Men's and women's conscia recti." Again, we seem to recognize an old friend when Percy Trevor, in a fit of quite meaningless rage against the Trevanion family, says, "And then the son! There will soon be an eclipse of that sun;" and the climax is reached when, in answer to Dr. Lattimer's offer of a glass of dry sherry, the Professor remarks that he prefers his sherry wet. This is the wit of the second act. The third is mainly given over to pathos with a comparatively moderate intermixture of humour. Mr. Byron seems to adopt as his motto this parody of the popular couplet :—

When puns are done and quibbles spent,
Then pathos is most excellent.

And indeed the sentimental dialogue throughout is full of poetry and grace. The love-scene between the step-son and the adopted daughter, is ingeniously introduced by his handing her a piece of music, saying, "I couldn't get you Chopin's Mazurka, but I got you this instead—the title seemed to me so suggestive—'Dreams of Hope!'" Could there be anything more delicately poetical? Next to carrying on a love-scene by means of conversation lozenges, this seems to me the most charmingly idyllic style of thing imaginable. It is the same romantic step-son who, when the girl he is supposed to be in love with testifies her very natural joy on finding that he isn't, remarks to himself, "I shouldn't like to say it to a third party (*sic*), but I believe Lydia's lunched." Mr. Gilbert might truly say of Mr. Byron's heroes that they are—

> Waterloo-House young men,
> Steady and stolidy,
> Jolly Bank-Holiday,
> Threepenny-'bus young men.

These extracts, be it remembered, are chosen not for their badness but for their comparative goodness. They include all the points which "took" best in representation. But some members of a London audience will laugh at anything Mr. Byron chooses to write. In "Bow Bells," Fred Latham, to introduce the subject of his intended marriage, says to Mr. Twinklehorn, "Now you, sir, are, I presume, an anti-Malthusian," whereupon Twinklehorn retorts, "I'm not an *anti*-anything. I'm an uncle." Again, in "Michael Strogoff," when the Emir of Bokhara dictates to John Blunt a message to the English people, that gallant "special"—played by Mr. Byron himself—notes it down with a red pencil, so that when the Emir asks the reason he may reply, "I like what I write to be *read*." I believe some people were actually found who could summon up a smile at these two brilliant and eminently typical coruscations of Mr. Byron's humour.

Of Mr. Byron as a burlesque writer I shall say nothing. To those who are anxious to obtain in short compasss an insight into the depths and graces of his genius in this department, I can recommend a publication entitled "Bits of Burlesque," in which for the trifling sum of one shilling is given a selection of gems from his innumerable parodies and extravaganzas. If my readers will study this work, will solve the problems of humour in which it abounds (they will always know where a joke is to be looked for by the fact of several words being italicized), will admire the elegance of the versification, the refinement of the ideas, and the purity of the English in which they are expressed—if my readers will do all this, they will understand why, before Mr. Byron's burlesques, like Postlethwaite before a Botticelli, "I am dumb." They are not worse than the general run of burlesques—some of the earlier ones, indeed, are probably better. But as I confess to a prejudice against modern English burlesque in general and Mr. Byron's style in particular, I feel that it is wiser to pass over a subject which is not at the best a fruitful one.

It will be said that my whole estimate of Mr. Byron is coloured by violent prejudice, and I am willing to admit that my personal distaste for cockneyism in language, ideas, manners, and morals, is perhaps stronger than strict reason would sanction. On this account I may underestimate Mr. Byron as a humorist, though I fully admit that his works contain many funny sayings and quaint and ingenious distortions of language. My main contention is, however, that a humorist does not of necessity constitute a dramatist, and that of Mr. Byron's three dozen comedies and dramas there is not one whose construction is skilful, whose characters are possible, or whose dialogue is natural. His plays are a carnival of cockneyism. They do not contain a thought worth thinking, a lesson worth learning, a scene worth remembering, or a character worth loving or hating. Their pathos savours of the theatre, their humour of the minor comic papers, their wit and wisdom of the theatrical clubs. Mr. Byron has been described as a man of the world, but his world does not extend beyond the West Central postal district. That such plays, at any rate the best of them, should find a public, is natural enough, since every class of people likes to see itself mirrored on the stage, and the lower their culture the less are they particular about the absolute faithfulness of the portraiture. Thus there is a natural demand in London for works which reproduce with a good deal of caricature the manners and language, ideas, prejudices, and morals of the lower-middle classes. On the same principle the lucubrations of "Mrs. Brown" have, I believe, met with a large sale. But we have a higher literature alongside of the brochures of "Mrs. Brown"—have we a higher drama alongside of the plays of Mr. Byron and his school? Fortunately we have, but the proportion of the former to the latter in quantity is miserably small; and when we look at the amount of popularity accorded to each, the comparison is still more dispiriting.

MR. W. S. GILBERT.

BY right of success, if for no other reason, Mr. W. S. Gilbert stands foremost among present-day dramatists. Few, if any, contemporary writers for the stage have made so much money from that source alone, none has acquired so wide a fame. The name of Gilbert, coupled generally with that of Sullivan, it is true, is known throughout Greater Britain. Mr. Gladstone is not, Lord Beaconsfield was not, more famous. They have only made the laws of a people—Mr. Gilbert has written the songs, and, better still, invented the popular catch-words not of one but of two great nations.

Far be it from me to deny that he has other claims besides that of success, to a leading place on the roll of our dramatists. On the contrary, I wish to emphasize at the outset my respect for him as the most striking individuality, the most original character our theatre of to-day can boast. He is not a mere spinner of verbal humour. He is not a mere constructor or adapter of comic or pathetic situations. Other dramatists have qualities which he has not, or has only in a minor degree; but in all his work we feel that there is an "awakened" intellect, a thinking brain behind it. He impresses us as a man who has looked at life with his own eyes, and has looked below the surface. There is a certain irony in his treatment of it, and that not only, nor even mainly, when he is professedly ironical. His so-called cynicism is shallow enough, but even it is genuine in so far as it proceeds from a genuine temperament. In short, he is not merely *l'homme sensuel moyen*, to use Mr. Matthew Arnold's phrase, who has more or less turn for making jokes, and more or less eye for superficial eccentricities of character, which he looks at through spectacles borrowed from Charles Dickens. This is the ordinary English dramatist, but this is not Mr. Gilbert, and therefore in my opinion he is the most interesting figure in our dramatic literature. The very fact that he is personally by no means popular in the theatrical world is not without its significance. This may arise partly from adventitious circumstances, such as his severity as a stage-manager—a severity which produces admirable results—and may be partly due to absolute faults of character. Of this I have no means of judging, nor does it affect my argument, which is, that in such a world as that of the London theatres no one can be thoroughly popular who is not either an accomplished Philistine or an accomplished hypocrite. That Mr. Gilbert is not thoroughly popular, and holds himself more or less aloof from theatrical society, is at least a negative indication of some depth of character. And, after all, even in that peculiar form of literature the modern English drama, a man's works should receive their main interest from his character. This is why so few contemporary English plays can claim to rank as literature—they give but slight indications of character, and what they do indicate is absolutely uninteresting. Mr. Gilbert's, on the other hand, manifest a strong and interesting individuality, and this, it seems to me, is their chief distinction.

The mention of the word literature suggests another of Mr. Gilbert's peculiar merits. He is almost alone in the attempt to give literary grace and finish to his work. His attempt is not always successful, so far at least as the grace is concerned, but any effort in that direction is a thing to be grateful for. I shall have some criticisms to make on his literary workmanship, in the course of this paper; but it would be ungracious not to admit at the outset that its faults seldom or never arise from mere slovenliness, which is in itself a rare distinction in these latter days, when three-act comedies are written in three nights and re-written at rehearsal.

Here let me admit that the word "Dramatists," in the title of this work requires qualification. A certain shade of contempt attaches to the word "playwright," otherwise I should have used it. Were "dramatist" to be taken in its strict sense, this series would be reduced to two, or at most three, papers, none of which should deal with Mr. Gilbert. For he is not a dramatist. He is essentially a humorist whom circumstances have led to write for the stage. Long habit, and no doubt a certain natural bent, have given him a mastery of stage technique, but he has never created a character or written a drama. In two or three instances he has chanced upon a truly dramatic subject, and has treated it seriously, and in a measure successfully. But in none of his plays is there the growth and development, the action and reaction of character and incident, in short, the creative and inventive force which go to make a true drama.

In the category of serious plays,[1] I reckon "Dan'l Druce," "Sweethearts," "Charity," and, shall I say, "Gretchen"? As it is not fantastic and still less amusing, this seems to be the only head under which it can come.

"Dan'l Druce" is Mr. Gilbert's nearest approach to a drama. Its motive, taken from "Silas Marner," is exquisitely conceived, but it remains a play of lost opportunities. It consists of two dramatic incidents, the one occupying the first act, the other the second and third. The first act is a little play in itself, and should have been called a prologue, to use a word often abused, but precisely fitted for the present case. Its chief fault lies in the letter which Sir Jasper Combe leaves with the infant Dorothy.—"Be kind to the child, and it shall profit thee. Grieve not for thy gold, it hath taken this

[1] I do not mention "Randall's Thumb," as it is an early work of crude construction, which Mr. Gilbert has not included in the collected edition of his plays. It possesses, however, especially in the humorous part, which is almost wholly unconnected with the serious action, some distinct touches of the peculiar manner which its author has since developed. "The Ne'er-do-Well," too, has been in a measure disowned by its author, who has probably recognized that the merits of its opening are insufficient to redeem the absurdities of its development and close.

form." Sir Jasper had evidently been reading "Silas Marner" in the course of his flight from the Roundheads, or such an idea would never have occurred to him. The British public certainly requires to have an idea shoved down its throat, but this is ramming it home with a ramrod. The prologue over, there remains matter for a full and rounded drama, in three or even more acts, not merely for the incident in two acts which Mr. Gilbert gives us. The true drama surely lies in the struggle in Dan'l Druce's mind after he has discovered Sir Jasper Combe to be Dorothy's father—the struggle between love and duty, the doubt as to what course of action duty really claims, perhaps the adoption of a wrong course and its punishment. In Mr. Gilbert's play Dan'l is entirely passive. Time after time chance takes choice out of his hands. At the end of the second act the curtain falls upon a trumpery and utterly illogical misunderstanding with Geoffrey Wynyard, which has even not the excuse of theatrical effectiveness, since it breaks the sympathy with Dan'l. This is a badly arranged episode, not an organic portion of the drama. The scene with Reuben Haynes in the third act is a little better, for it is at least rational. Indeed, the drama might be made to lie in some such temptation as that to which Dan'l here momentarily yields, better motived and more fully developed. On the other hand, the turn of affairs which shows Dan'l to be Dorothy's father after all, and Sir Jasper the betrayer of Dan'l's wife, is extremely bad. It is a violent and improbable *coup de théâtre* which produces no effect, and if anything spoils the motive. It is as hard to swallow as a camel, and as unsatisfactory as a gnat. The result is in the inverse ratio of the effort, which is precisely the wrong proportion.

The love-scene in "Dan'l Druce" is one of the prettiest bits of writing Mr. Gilbert has done, and Dorothy is a theatrically effective character; yet it is perhaps she who proves most plainly how far Mr. Gilbert's mechanical skill falls short of the true dramatic gift. The fact that her dialect is precisely that of the Bible may be passed over, though I see no reason to suppose that a village girl in the reign of Charles II. would speak exactly as certain divines wrote in the reign of his grandfather. But if one were seeking an example of theatrical effectiveness as opposed to dramatic truth, it would be difficult to find a better than the following soliloquy:—

Dor. Geoffrey returned! and Geoffrey a stalwart mariner, and grown to man's estate! I can scarce believe it. Of a truth I could weep for very joy! I was but a child when he left, and now—I am seventeen! Geoffrey loved children—it may be that he will be displeased with me now that I am a woman. I am rejoiced that I am decked in my new gown—it is more seemly than the russet, in which methinks I did look pale. Geoffrey a man!—my old playmate a man! Pity that I have not my new shoes, for they are comely; but they compress my feet, and so pain me sorely. Nevertheless, I will put them on, for it behoveth a maiden to be neatly apparelled at all seasons.

No doubt Miss Marion Terry delivered this speech very charmingly, but it is none the less untrue to nature.

Even worse is her appeal to Sir Jasper in the last scene, where she winds up a pathetic speech with the words "Oh, sir, if thou hast no care for him, yet *for the love of my mother* have pity upon me." This invocation is under the circumstances one of theatrical convention, not of dramatic truth. Worst of all is her intervention between her father and Sir Jasper, on the revelation of the latter's crime: "Father, spare him—be merciful—be just. He is an old man now—thou art an old man—is it in the winter of your lives, that the heartburnings of hot youth are to be avenged?" &c. &c. These words might come well from the "Colonial Bishop-elect" of "Charity"—Dorothy's intervention should have been silent or almost so. The fact that he does not appreciate the value of silence is one evidence of the undramatic quality of Mr. Gilbert's talent. He leaves nothing to divination or even to action. He never gets into those depths of human nature where words are useless, or if he ever gets there he does not know it.

I have dwelt on "Dan'l Druce," because it seems to me a typical play. It illustrates admirably the limitations of Mr. Gilbert's talent on its serious side. He might have given its action the beautiful, natural curve of a rocket—the resultant between the impetus of dramatic circumstance and gravitation in the shape of the universal forces of human nature. He has chosen instead to make it a cracker—its course an arbitrary zigzag, accentuated by irrelevant explosions.

"Sweethearts" is a pleasant little piece, rather mechanical in its humour now and then, but full of healthy, human feeling, and on the whole the most satisfactory of Mr. Gilbert's serious plays. There is, indeed, an almost French grace about its conception which gives it a place apart in the modern English drama.

As "Charity" was a failure, and is consequently less known than the majority of Mr. Gilbert's plays, I may give a short account of its plot. Frederick Smailey, son of Mr. Jonas Smailey, is engaged to Eve, the daughter of a certain Mrs. Van Brugh. This lady's property all comes from her godfather, to whom Smailey is next-of-kin. Mrs. Van Brugh, who is an extremely charitable lady, has rescued from the streets and taken into her service a tramp named Ruth Tredgett, thereby exciting the unqualified disapproval of Smailey, who holds that "Society has decided that a woman who has once forfeited her moral position shall never regain it." A detective employed by Smailey discovers that at the time of Mrs. Van Brugh's marriage her husband had another wife alive; and as her godfather's will describes her as "wife of Richard Van Brugh, Esq.," all the property reverts to Smailey as next-of-kin. He forces her to confess that she never even went through the ceremony of marriage with Captain Van Brugh, and then refuses to believe this, and tries to get up a case against her for bigamy. To this end he advertises for the burial certificate of the first Mrs. Van Brugh. Unfortunately for him, Ruth Tredgett proves to be a girl whom he himself seduced in Melbourne many years previously, and who has in her possession a burial certificate of a certain Martha

Vane, which was forged by Smailey about that time in order to defraud a burial society. This Martha Vane was the wife of Captain Van Brugh, separated from him and going by her maiden name. Smailey is thus caught in his own trap, and is arrested at the end of the piece. His son has, of course, meanly broken off his engagement with Eve as soon as the troubles of the family commenced, and the Van Brughs, as the curtain fails, determine to sail to a new land with their friend, Dr. Athelney, a "Colonial Bishop-elect."

One cause of the failure of this play is clear enough even from the above sketch. The plot is unpleasant and extremely involved, while the unravelling of it is effected by means of a series of coincidences which quite transcend the bounds of probability. But the main cause of failure lay in the character of Smailey. Intended as a satirical portrait of the modern Pharisee and hypocrite, he is in reality a repulsive and self-contradictory caricature. Mr. Gilbert has failed to repress his bias towards burlesque. "The Smaileys are a very old and very famous family," says Mr. Smailey; "Caius Smaileius came over with Julius Cæsar." And again, in a serious scene with his son, "If Caius Smaileius heard that one of his race was about to marry into a tainted family, I believe the doughty old Roman would turn in his tumulus." The extravagance of these speeches might be amusing in the mouth of Sir Joseph Porter or of Major-General Stanley: in that of Mr. Smailey it merely destroys all illusion. Worse, if possible, is his speech to Ruth Tredgett, "In my case allowance should, in common charity, be made for follies that arise from extreme youth and—and inexperience. I was barely forty then." The relation, too, between the father and son is absolutely impossible. That two such "anointed scoundrels" should live together for twenty-five years, each believing the other to be an honest man, is a simple absurdity. But Mr. Gilbert does not make it clear whether or not Smailey is conscious of his own villainy. He occasionally keeps up his hypocrisy even in his soliloquies, especially if an amusing effect is to be got by so doing. It is a truism, of course, that many great rogues believe themselves highly respectable people; but Smailey is not consistently conceived as one of this type. One moment he seems a conscious scoundrel, and the next unconscious, his speeches being dictated, not by the necessity of his character, but by the exigencies of momentary effect. If Mr. Gilbert had any distinct conception of the character he wished to draw, it was probably something after the fashion of Bulstrode in "Middlemarch,"—

> But frequently he rather fatally misses
> Who ventures to shoot with the bow of Ulysses.

This remark applies with double force to "Gretchen." Mr. Gilbert is of opinion that Goethe's "Faust" is not a stage play, but a philosophical treatise upon human nature written in dramatic form. "It is scarcely going too far to say," he adds, "that in those versions of 'Faust,' which are current on the English, French, and Italian stages, the great master would hardly recognize his own handiwork. Whether it is allowable so to trim, patch, lop, mutilate, and disfigure an immortal work in order to adapt it to an arena for which its creator never designed it, is a point upon which the reader will form his own opinion. I trust, however, that in preferring to re-model for purely dramatic purposes the entire story of Gretchen's downfall, I shall at least be absolved from a charge of intentional irreverence towards the grandest philosophical work of the century." The result is that he has transmuted the marvellous legend into a common-place and painful seduction-story. His plea for total reconstruction might have been relevant had he been under any compulsion to place "Faust" upon the English stage at all. He was not; and even if he had been, the necessity for total reconstruction in general would not have justified the particular form which his reconstruction has taken.

His Faustus is not the weary student who has "durchaus studirt" all the world's wisdom, and after all knows only that he can know nothing. He is a blasé young man whose mistress has played him false, and who has consequently turned monk. A more utterly shallow character was never conceived, unless perhaps it be that of Mephisto—for this is the name of Mr. Gilbert's fiend, shorn of his tail in more senses than one. He is a sort of long-winded Dick Deadeye, only that his cynicism is good-humoured instead of snarling. He reminds one of Macaulay's recommendation to Robert Montgomery, that he should alter a few lines in his poem of "Satan," and rechristen it "Gabriel." His influence on the character of Faustus is nil. Indeed, the whole effect he produces in the play is to show Faustus a vision of Gretchen, to make love to Martha, and to cause Faustus' hair to grow with preternatural rapidity. The whole tragedy lies in Faustus' tonsure. In the first act he has a shaven crown concealed by a skull-cap: in the second, the next day, he has a full crop of ambrosial curls. Hence Gretchen never suspects that he is a priest, and it is his unguarded revelation of this fact that suddenly drives her to despair and death. Her sorrow at the sacrilege she has committed—a perfectly conventional and factitious emotion—is the cause of the catastrophe. Indeed, it is his character of Gretchen that one can least forgive Mr. Gilbert. He may say that we have no right to compare her with Goethe's Margarete, but, right or no right, we cannot help it. If she were even the faintest reflex of that exquisite incarnation of "das Ewig-Weibliche," she would be tolerable. But her ingenuousness is modern throughout, and perfectly self-conscious. Mr. Gilbert is responsible for the paradox, not I. She is a moral—I mean a moralizing, Gretchen. She is tolerant, not ignorant, of evil. When the penitent Lisa returns to the village, she cries,—

> Oh, sisters, is it fit
> That we should judge our sister, or withhold
> The mercy that we pray for, day by day?

She is eminently religious; sometimes high-church, sometimes evangelical. In short, there is not a breath of freshness, not a throb of life about her. No drop of warm blood runs in her veins, no thought of nature's teaching grows, flower-like, in her mind. To make up for this she can put all her thoughts into words, very precise and well-chosen words, and plenty of them. Here is a specimen—one speech addressed to Faustus—

> Ah, Heaven is kind to me, for all my sin!
> For when my heart is more than common sad,
> I need but close my eyes—and all at once,
> I wander at my will amid the days
> When thou and I may face the world again.
> And yet I am no fitting mate for thee,
> Thou, a great lord—rich, honour'd, and beloved—
> I a poor simple, untaught, peasant girl!
> Yet bear with me—my love shall plague thee little,
> Though ever and anon I come to thee
> With faltering step and tearful downcast eyes,
> A timid suppliant for such alms of love
> As thou in thy good will mayst grant to me.
> So, when thou seest, kneeling at thy feet,
> Thy poor, mad, love-sick, trusting, trembling wife,
> Throw her in charity one little flower
> Out of the boundless garden of thy heart,
> That she may go rejoicing on her way.

Now listen to six lines of Margarete's :—

> Du lieber Gott! was so ein Mann
> Nicht alles alles denken kann!
> Beschämt nur steh 'ich vor ihm da,
> Und sag' zu allen Sachen ja.
> Bin doch ein arm unwissend Kind,
> Begreife nicht, was er an mir find't.

I seem to find more humanity in these lines than in

all "Gretchen" put together—and yet "Gretchen" is a drama and "Faust" is a "philosophical treatise!" The death-scene is as verbose and conventional as the rest of the play—epithets which are too often applicable to Mr. Gilbert's pathos. It leaves us unmoved and cold. St. Patrick is said to have lighted a fire with icicles, but the age of miracles is past.

"Gretchen" is written throughout in blank-verse, and so are the five fantastic plays of which I shall next have to speak. Supposing each play to contain on an average 1500 lines—a modest computation—we find that Mr. Gilbert has written at least 9000 lines of blank-verse. Of these 9000 I venture to assert that there is not one which has the smallest metrical beauty. As a rule they are correctly enough measured off into ten syllables, but there is not one whose cadence lingers in the memory. Occasionally, they are positively bad. Such lines as the following are inexcusable:—

> Who could look on that face and stifle love?

and

> Tell me more of her!
> Well—
> What did she say?

Here every emphasis falls in the wrong place with unerring precision. Could a more dragging line be imagined than

> Even though Heaven's armaments be ranged;

or

> While he sat all day fuddling at the ale-house.

Sometimes a very slight alteration in the order of words would make an extremely wooden line tolerably graceful.

> My heavy debt is multiplied tenfold

would surely have a better fall in this form,—

> My heavy debt is tenfold multiplied

and the line

> Sang once more in the great green waving trees,

might be transposed thus—

> Sang in the great green waving trees once more.

But it is the negative and not the positive defects of his verse which seem to me fatal—its absence of merits and not its faults. I said that not one line lingered in my memory, but that was not literally correct. After a pretty close study of the blank-verse plays on the stage and in book form, I remember one line, that in which he has called in apt alliteration's artful aid to produce this lingual masterpiece—

> Lapped in a lazy luxury of love.

A perusal of his six poetical plays recalls Lowell's remark about the moral Gower,—"As you slip to and fro on the frozen levels of his verse, which give no foothold to the mind . . . . you learn to dread, almost to respect, the powers of this indefatigable man." I omit the unkind quotation from Wordsworth, which the reader who has suffered from Gower or Gilbert may look up for himself in Lowell's essay on Chaucer. But Gower had more excuse than Mr. Gilbert for manufacturing wooden verse, since his had only to be read while Mr. Gilbert's was written to be spoken by a generation of actors, who, as a rule, are notoriously incapable of delivering any verse whatever. True, the old Haymarket company, for which several of the plays were written, was not so bad in this respect as the company which played "Gretchen." But, at best, why choose this hampering medium of expression? Even in the hands of a poet and a master of its mysteries, it is of questionable effect in dramatic work. Shakespeare himself seldom or never wrote a whole play in blank-verse. Mr. Gilbert is neither a poet nor a master of its mysteries, and in binding himself down to cut his thoughts into lengths of five feet, he has merely made their expression needlessly verbose. He has seldom been betrayed into positive errors of style, though even in this respect he is not immaculate. Galatea, for instance, remarks, looking at a mirror—

> How beautiful! I'm very glad to know
> That both our tastes agree so perfectly.

This solecism has evidently slipped in through the exigencies of the metre, but such cases are rare. The sole use of the verse, however, is to cloak poverty of dialogue, meagreness of thought and imagery—richness of thought and imagery, too great, if that be possible, for expression in prose, would have been its sole excuse.

In two instances also, the verse is useful in giving a

certain consistency to plays whose slightness of motive would, without it, be too apparent. "The Wicked World" and "Broken Hearts" are pretty fantasies which, developed in very much narrower compass, and by a true poet, might have taken an abiding place in literature. Mr. Gilbert's cold and mechanical fancy was quite inadequate to their treatment, and he marred them, the former especially, by touches of vulgarity, of which I shall have more to say when I come to deal with "Pygmalion and Galatea."

But first a few words as to "The Palace of Truth." In this play, the keynote of Mr. Gilbert's peculiar talent is struck, his style of satire in epitomized. His most successful works have all for their scene an imaginary Palace of Truth, where people naively reveal their inmost thoughts, unconscious of their egotism, vanity, baseness, or cruelty. Touches of this peculiar mannerism are apparent in earlier works, such as the two fantastic farces, "Creatures of Impulse" and "The Gentleman in Black;" but it was first consistently adopted in "The Palace of Truth." The comedy is constructed and written with a good deal of ingenuity. It is so thoroughly fantastic, both in motive and treatment, that its cynicism does not become repulsive. The spotless Lady Mirza is a well-conceived figure, and her downfall an extremely effective touch. Altogether, the play is in itself one of Mr. Gilbert's best pieces of work; but it acquires double importance from the fact that since he discovered "The Palace of Truth," he has hardly ever succeeded in freeing himself from its enchantment. He conceives the whole world as subject to the spell. He seldom cares to use the talisman which frees him from its influence, and when he wants to use it, he sometimes seems to have mislaid it. It was the magic of the "The Palace of Truth," for instance, that spoiled the semblance of nature in "Charity," and contributed largely to its failure.

That he has touched nothing which he has not adorned cannot, unfortunately, be said of Mr. Gilbert. As he vulgarized the legend of Faust, so he vulgarized in an even greater degree the legend of Pygmalion and Galatea. His initial mistake lay in giving the sculptor a wife, and introducing the element of jealousy in a very modern and commonplace form. But even if we accept this as a necessary device for giving the story interest and consistency on the stage, it is impossible to accept his development of the theme in detail. It is remarkable that Mr. Gilbert, whose peculiar form of humour is based upon a strong logical faculty, should work out the problem of psychology presented by a vivified statue in a peculiarly illogical form; and it is also remarkable that he, who as a librettist has so successfully steered clear of vulgarity, should have treated this theme in a peculiarly vulgar fashion.

As we have no scientific record of a statue coming to life, the probable moral and intellectual condition of a being so created is left to the widest conjecture. The playwright may assume for it any stage of development he pleases, and his audience will readily grant his assumption. But if his work is to have any claim to artistic value he must not assume all sorts of different stages of development at every second word his creation utters. He must not make her a child in one speech, a woman of the world in the next, and an idiot in the next again. Of course it would be an extremely difficult task clearly to define in all its bearings and details the particular intellectual condition assumed at the outset, and then gradually to indicate the natural growth of a fuller consciousness. Difficult it would be, but by no means impossible; nay, it would be this very problem which would tempt the true dramatist to adopt such a theme. Mr. Gilbert has not even essayed the task. He regulates Galatea's state of consciousness by the fluctuating exigencies of dialogue whose comedy is levelled straight at the heads of the old Haymarket pit—never in the least over them. Shortly after she comes to life occurs the following passage:—

Pyg. O woman—perfect in thy loveliness?
Gal. What is that word? Am I a woman?
Pyg. Yes.
Gal. Art thou a woman?
Pyg. No, I am a man.
Gal. What is a man?
Pyg. A being strongly framed,
To wait on woman and protect her from
All ills that strength and courage can avert;
To work and toil for her that she may rest;
To weep and mourn for her that she may laugh;
To fight and die for her that she may live!
Gal. (*after a pause*). I'm glad I am a woman.
Pyg. So am I.

Then, a little further on, the conversation takes this turn :—

Gal. I wish that I could look upon myself,
But that's impossible.
Pyg. Not so indeed.
This mirror will reflect thy face. Behold !
(*Hands her a mirror.*)
Gal. How beautiful ; I'm very glad to know
That both our tastes agree so perfectly ;
Why, my Pygmalion, I did not think
That aught could be more beautiful than thou,
Till I beheld myself. Believe me, love,
I could look in this mirror all day long.
So I'm a woman !
Pyg. There's no doubt of that !
Gal. Oh happy maid to be so passing fair !
And happier still Pygmalion, who can gaze,
At will upon so beautiful a face !
Pyg. Hush ! Galatea—in thine innocence
Thou sayest things that others would reprove.
Gal. Indeed, Pygmalion ; then it is wrong
To think that one is exquisitely fair ?
Pyg. Well, Galatea, it's a sentiment
That every other woman shares with thee ;
They *think* it—but they keep it to themselves.
Gal. And is thy wife as beautiful as I ?
Pyg. No, Galatea, for in forming thee
I took her features—lovely in themselves—
And in the marble made them lovelier still.
Gal. (*disappointed*). Oh ! then I'm not original ?

Thus Galatea does not know that she is a woman, but knows the possibility of disagreement in taste, though

Pygmalion is the only living creature she has seen; does not see the futility of self-praise any more than an inhabitant of the Palace of Truth, yet sees the distinction between an original and a copy. Next day occurs the following dialogue:—

Pyg. Leucippe comes,
And he shall comfort thee till I return;
I'll not be long!
Gal. Leucippe! Who is he?
Pyg. A valiant soldier.
Gal. What is that?
Pyg. A man
Who's hired to kill his country's enemies.
Gal. (*horrified*). A paid assassin!
Pyg. (*annoyed*). Well, that's rather strong.

Here we find that Galatea has got the length of knowing the enormity of taking life, and appreciating the fine distinction between taking it of one's own motive and taking it for money. Yet it appears the next moment, when Leucippe enters with a fawn he has killed, that she does not know the difference between man and the brute creation. To point out even the more glaring inconsistencies of this sort would be an interminable task, as there is not the smallest attempt at consistency. Nor, I need scarcely add, is there any attempt at local colour, or the reproduction of Greek habits and modes of thought. As the play is purely fantastic, this was scarcely to be demanded. Only, with modern forms of thought and expression, was it necessary to import into the action a strong flavouring of modern vulgarity? Even the extracts I have given above show tendencies in that direction, which come out still more strongly in certain other passages with Pygmalion. But it is in the following scene, and some others of a like nature, that the taint is strongest. The personages are Galatea and Chrysal, an old and ugly art patron:—

Gal. (*who has been examining him in great wonder*).
Tell me, what *are* you?
Chry. What *am* I?
Gal. Yes; I mean, are you a man?
Chry. Well, yes; I'm told so.
Gal. Then believe them not,
They've been deceiving you.
Chry. The deuce they have!
Gal. A man is very tall, and straight, and strong,
With big brave eyes, fair face, and tender voice.
I've seen one.
Chry. *Have* you?
Gal. Yes; you are no man.
Chry. Does the young person take me for a woman?
Gal. A woman? No; a woman's soft and weak,
And fair, and exquisitely beautiful.
I am a woman; you are not like me.
Chry. The gods forbid that I should be like you,
And farm my features at so much an hour!
Gal. And yet I like you, for you make me laugh;
You are so round and red, your eyes so small,
Your mouth so large, your face so seared with lines,
And then you are so little and so fat!
Chry. (*aside*). This is a most extraordinary girl.

Gal. Oh, stay—I understand—Pygmalion's skill
Is the result of long experience.
The individual who modelled you
Was a beginner very probably?
Chry. (*puzzled*). No. I have seven elder brothers. Strange
That one so young should be so very bold.
Gal. This is not boldness, it is innocence;
Pygmalion says so, and he ought to know.
Chry. No doubt, but I was not born yesterday. (*Sits.*)
Gal. Indeed!—I *was.* (*He beckons her to sit beside him.*)
How awkwardly you sit.
Chry. I'm not aware that there is anything
Extraordinary in my sitting down.
The nature of the seated attitude
Does not leave scope for much variety.
Gal. I never saw Pygmalion sit like that.
Chry. Don't he sit down like other men?
Gal. Of course!
He always puts his arm around my waist.
Chry. The deuce he does! Artistic reprobate!
Gal. But you do not. Perhaps you don't know how?
Chry. Oh, yes; I *do* know how!
Gal. Well, do it then!
Chry. It's a strange whim, but I will humour her.
You're sure it's innocence? (*Does so.*)
Gal. Of course it is.
I tell you I was born but yesterday.
Chry. Who is your mother?
Gal. Mother! what is that?
I never had one. I'm Pygmalion's child;
Have people usually mothers?
Chry. Well,
That is the rule.
Gal. But then Pygmalion
Is cleverer than most men.

Chry. Yes, I've heard
That he has powers denied to other men,
And I'm beginning to believe it!

It must be remembered, in excuse for Mr. Gilbert, that he was writing not only for the Haymarket audience, but for the Haymarket management, and that such parts as Chrysal, and, in the "Palace of Truth," King Phanor, were demanded by Mr. Buckstone. Nevertheless, it is painful to see such elements imported into the treatment of a theme like that of "Pygmalion and Galatea."

"The Princess," the only blank-verse play I have not yet mentioned, is a neat burlesque, good-humoured beyond Mr. Gilbert's wont. It is not free from a tinge of vulgarity, but is witty, lively, and on the whole a favourable specimen of the lighter order of his work.

Written in prose, and placed in modern England, "Engaged" and "Tom Cobb" are yet as purely fantastic as any of the blank-verse plays. They are among Mr. Gilbert's most original works, but are of very different merit. "Engaged" was a success, "Tom Cobb," if I remember rightly, a comparative failure—need I say that the latter is by far the better play? The scene of both is laid in Mr. Gilbert's patent Palace of Truth. The characters are presented, as it were, with their moral skins off, for the satire very seldom gets more than skin deep. They are divested of the wrappings and integuments which generally shield our vanities and meannesses from the common gaze. I say our vanities and meannesses, for it is to be noted that in no single instance, unless it be that of Zeolide in "The Palace of Truth" itself, does Mr. Gilbert's flaying process reveal any unexpected nobleness or generosity. It is this which, in a sense, takes the sting from his cynicism. It is so unrelieved, that we recognize it as a mere trick or mannerism, and not the result of genuine insight. The jester who railed at every one from king to scullion, offended no one. Had he made exceptions, and shown reverence to Lancelot, or even to Arthur himself, the rest of the court might have resented his jibes as being personal, and not merely professional.

"Engaged" is a repulsive, vulgar, and—extremely amusing play. It shows us eight personages all actuated by the most unblushingly mercenary motives, who confess these motives in the most unblushing way, and with the air of uttering the noblest sentiments. The intrigue is really ingenious in its absurdity. Turning upon a Scotch marriage, it involves the *dramatis personæ* in an amatory imbroglio of unparalleled complexity. Cheviot Hill—inimitably played by the late Mr. George Honey—is an extremely parsimonious and extremely erotic young man. The train in which he is travelling is thrown off the line by a virtuous Scotch peasant, Angus Macalister, who makes his living by wrecking trains. Emerging from the wreck "a moral pulp, a mash, a poultice," as he himself describes his condition, Cheviot meets Maggie Macfarlane, the sweetheart of the virtuous Angus. He forgets that he is engaged to Minnie Symperson, and at once proposes to her, when the following scene ensues:—

Mag. Ah, kind sir, I'm sairly grieved to wound sae true and tender a love as yours, but ye're ower late ; my love is nae my ain to give ye. It's given ower to the best and bravest lad in a' the bonnie Borderland !

Ch. Give me his address that I may go and curse him !

Mag. (*kneels to Cheviot*). Ah, ye must not curse him. Oh, spare him, spare him, for he is good and brave, and he loves me, oh, sae dearly ! and I love him, oh, sae dearly, too ! Oh, sir, kind sir, have mercy on him, and do not—do not curse him, or I shall die ! (*Throwing herself at his feet.*)

Ch. Will you, or will you not, oblige me by telling me where he is, that I may at once go and curse him ?

Ang. (*coming forward*). He is here, sir ; but dinna waste your curses on me. Maggie, my bairn (*raising her*), I heard the answer ye gave to this man, my true and gentle lassie ! Ye spoke well and bravely, Meg—well and bravely ! Dinna heed the water in my 'ee—it's a tear of joy and gratitude, Meg —a tear of joy and gratitude !

Ch. (*touched*). Poor fellow ! I will *not* curse him ! (*Aloud.*) Young man, I respect your honest emotion. I don't want to distress you, but I cannot help loving this most charming girl. Come, is it reasonable to quarrel with a man because he's of the same way of thinking as yourself ?

Ang. Nay, sir, I'm nae fasht, but it just seems to drive a' the bluid back into my hairt when I think that my Meg is loved by anither ! Oh, sir, she's a fair and winsome lassie, and I micht as justly be angry wi' ye for loving the blue heavens ! She's just as far above us as they are !

(*Wiping his eyes and kissing her.*)

Ch. (*with decision*). Pardon me, I cannot allow that.

Ang. Eh ?

Ch. I love that girl madly—passionately—and I cannot possibly allow you to do that—not before my eyes, I beg. You simply torture me.

Mag. (*to Angus*). Leave off, dear, till the poor gentleman's gone, and then you can begin again.

Ch. Angus, listen to me. You love this girl?

Ang. I love her, sir, a'most as weel as I love mysel'!

Ch. Then reflect how you are standing in the way of her prosperity. I am a rich man. I have money, position, and education. I am a much more intellectual and generally agreeable companion for her than you can ever hope to be. I am full of anecdote, and all my anecdotes are in the best possible taste. I will tell you some of them, some of these days, and you can judge for yourself. Maggie, if she married me, would live in a nice house in a good square. She would have wine—occasionally. She would be kept beautifully clean. Now, if you really love this girl almost as well as you love yourself, are you doing wisely or kindly in standing in the way of her getting all these good things? As to compensation—why, I've had heavy expenses of late—but if—yes, if thirty shillings—

Of course the bargain is struck, but comes to nothing, as Cheviot forthwith falls in love with another young lady. The second act takes place on the day appointed for the marriage of Cheviot and Minnie Symperson, and here is part of a love-scene between the bride and bridegroom:—

Ch. Dear me! To think that in half an hour this magnificent dress will be *my* property.

Min. Yes. Dear papa said that as you had offered to give the breakfast at your house, he would give me the best dress that money could procure.

Ch. Yes, I *did* offer to provide the breakfast in a reckless moment; that's so like me. It was a rash offer, but I've made it, and I've stuck to it. Oh, then there's the cake.

Min. Oh, tell me all about the cake.

(*Cheviot and Minnie sit on sofa.*)

Ch. It's a very pretty cake. Very little cake is eaten at a wedding breakfast, so I've ordered what's known in the trade as the three-quarter article.

Min. I see; three-quarters cake, and the rest wood.

Ch. No; three-quarters wood, the rest cake. Be sure, my dear, you don't cut into the wood, for it has to be returned to the pastry-cook to be filled up with cake for another occasion. I thought at first of ordering a seven-eighths article; but one isn't married every day, it's only once a year—I mean it's only now and then. So I said, "Hang the expense; let's do the thing well." And so it's a three-quarters.

Min. How good you are to me! We shall be very happy, shall we not?

. . . . .

Min. Then how shall we spend our evenings?

Ch. We'll have pleasant little fireside games. Are you fond of fireside games?

Min. Oh, they're great fun.

Ch. Then we'll play at tailoring.

Min. Tailoring? I don't think I know that game.

Ch. It's a very good game. You shall be the clever little jobbing tailor, and I'll be the particular customer who brings his own materials to be made up. You shall take my measure, cut out the cloth (real cloth, you know), stitch it together, and try it on; and then I'll find fault like a real customer, and you shall alter it until it fits, and when it fits beautifully that counts one to you.

Min. Delightful!

Ch. Then there's another little fireside game which is great fun. We each take a bit of paper and a pencil and try who can jot down the nicest dinner for ninepence, and the next day we have it.

Min. Oh, Cheviot, what a paradise you hold open to me.

I need go no further. These quotations sufficiently

indicate the tone of the play, and the style of its humour. That it is extremely funny cannot be denied, especially when it is played with the business-like earnestness which Mr. Gilbert manages to impart to his interpreters. But it leaves a bitter taste in the mouth. It is as unpleasant and degrading as "Gulliver's Travels," without their deep human truth. Its cynicism is as irrelevant as it is exaggerated.

A much pleasanter, if not much cleverer work, is "Tom Cobb." It is a delicious piece of absurdity, very neat in its conception, and without a dull scene in its short, crisp action. The satire now and then takes a deeper grasp than is usual with Mr. Gilbert, especially in the scene at the beginning of the third act, where the Effingham family, mistaking Tom Cobb for the poet-warrior Major-General Fielding, gush over his most commonplace remarks, and come to the conclusion that "Shakespeare never said anything like them." Perhaps my preference is exaggerated, but this play, trifling as it is, seems to me the happiest of all Mr. Gilbert's works,—that in which the maximum of effect is attained with the minimum of (apparent) effort. It will surely be revived before long.

"Foggarty's Fairy," on the other hand, though it contained much clever work, failed by reason of a lack of the very quality of logic which is generally Mr. Gllbert's strong point. The idea is that of a man, who, by supernatural aid, overcomes the irrevocableness of the past. To avoid unpleasant consequences he "obliterates" a part of his past life. But in the process another set of events is substituted for those which actually occurred. He finds himself hampered as much as ever by the consequences of this new past, and from these difficulties the action is evolved. Now it is clear that the new chain of events which is substituted is an entirely arbitrary invention of the dramatist, not growing out of any logical necessity in the idea. The natural, or rather the logical, effect of "obliterating" a certain portion of one's life would be to carry one back to the point at which the obliteration commenced. The device did not result in a paradox, but in a wild absurdity. This might have been tolerated had it been carried out with particular tact and skill; but, as a matter of fact, though many of the scenes were very funny, it was felt that others were vulgar, strained, and unpleasant, and that in one or two instances Mr. Gilbert was quite unwarrantably repeating himself. Hence the play met with scant approval.

Mr. Frederic Harrison is of opinion that the age which can tolerate "H.M.S. Pinafore" cannot read Homer. The obvious reply is that the age must be very one-sided. Such a remark coming from a man like Mr. Harrison, suggests an inquiry as to whether he has ever seen "Pinafore." Perhaps he has; but in that case he cannot have seen the opera-bouffes which "Pinafore" and its family have in a measure—a small measure, alas!—succeeded in supplanting. Had he seen "Les Cloches de Corneville," to take one of the least objectionable examples, and compared its inane and vulgar buffoonery with the crisp neatness and literary and musical finish of "Pinafore," he would have been too thankful for small mercies to breathe a word against the reputation of that most famous craft which ever hoisted the British flag. Truly the step from the Odyssey to "Pinafore" is scarcely a greater descent than from "Pinafore" to an average opera-bouffe in its English dress. The wall which divides the stage of the Opera Comique from that of the Globe for years divided humour from inanity, art from horse-play, refinement from vulgarity, literature from the lowest form of literary hack-work.

"Princess Toto" was Mr. Gilbert's first operatic effort of any importance. It was not successful, but both in idea and writing it was very clever. Its music was composed by Mr. Frederick Clay—Mr. Gilbert had not yet found the musical collaborator whose talent has shown itself so congenial with his own.

"Trial by Jury" was the first effort in a new field, and was so successful that the "pardners," as Bret Harte would call them, have since unremittingly "worked the claim," which has proved a very Tom Tiddler's ground, giving a larger yield at each stroke of the shovel. "The Sorcerer," "H.M.S. Pinafore," "The Pirates of Penzance," and "Patience," have followed in unbroken, though not in quick succession. They have been treated with contumely by other critics besides Mr. Frederic Harrison, but they have taken the popular ear, and, what is more, they have become part of the national life. In the healthiest if not the loftiest way, they have enhanced the gaiety of nations. In so far as they have prevented Mr. Gilbert from doing serious work, we may perhaps regret their success; but I, for one, do not refuse to be comforted even on this score. Only Mr. Gilbert could have written "The Pirates of Penzance," whereas we have several playwrights who could have written "Dan'l Druce," and one or two who might even have perpetrated "Gretchen." As for the farces we might have had in their stead, it seems to me that the operas are fully equal in point of quaint humour to anything Mr. Gilbert has done, while Mr. Sullivan's music appears to have the power of soothing his savage breast, and sweetening the gall and bitterness which flavour such a play as "Engaged."

The humour of the operas is a thing by itself—so much so, that I have known people with an otherwise well-developed sense of the ridiculous, whom it seemed completely to elude. There is a good deal of the Palace of Truth mannerism in it, but this is not the whole secret. Indeed the operas are more closely akin to the "Bab Ballads" than to "The Palace of Truth," Mr. Gilbert having actually, with the frugality of true genius, worked up several ideas from those early productions. A strong logical faculty is the basis of this humour. *Reductio ad absurdum* is its favourite method of procedure. Maxims of morality carried to their logical extreme and developed into paradoxes are its chosen playthings. In "Pinafore," for instance, much of the fun is extracted from the logical development of the modern idea of consideration for inferiors, or rather the broader principle of essential equality modified by accidental distinctions of rank and office. In "The Pirates," material is found in pushing to its logical extreme the idea of duty. In "Patience," much of the action turns upon the absurdities which may be deduced from a literal acceptance of common maxims on love and unselfishness.

> How quaint the ways of paradox !
> At common sense it gaily mocks,

might be the motto of the whole series. The "contrast yet kinship," to use Mr. Carlyle's phrase, between the every-day common-sense application of these principles and Mr. Gilbert's apparently logical deductions from them, forms the basis of our enjoyment. There is a general inclination to attribute to these operas, or at any rate to the last three, a serious satiric purpose. Nothing could be more mistaken. Not even "Patience" is to be taken as a satire. It is an extravaganza, pure and simple, and so are its predecessors. Genuinely satiric touches are no doubt interspersed, but we are no more meant to conclude from "Patience" that Mr. Gilbert believes "æstheticism" as a whole to be a sham and a craze, than we are to conclude from "The Pirates" that he believes our police as a body to be arrant cowards. That they are not satires in the true sense of the term is proved by the fact that they leave every one's "withers unwrung." Satire which meets with universal acquiescence is unworthy of the name. The only person I ever heard of who felt himself aggrieved by Mr. Gilbert's "satire" was a sailor at Portsmouth, who loudly resented the disparaging terms applied by Captain Corcoran to Ralph Rackstraw in "Pinafore."

I have no hesitation in calling these operas the most characteristic productions of our contemporary English stage. Their humour, as I have tried to show, is original if not profound, their literary workmanship is thorough, and they are, like Mr. Cheviot Hill's anecdotes, all in excellent taste. I do not mean to say that occasional speeches do not occur, which the most rigid fastidiousness might wish eliminated. A few of the sayings, for instance, placed in the mouth of the Lady Jane in "Patience," are in questionable taste. But such cases are very rare, and quite unimportant. They do not affect the broad fact that Mr. Gilbert, as author and stage-manager, has succeeded in producing a style of entertainment fitted *virginibus puerisque*, yet capable of affording to intelligent men amusement not altogether despicable in its intellectual quality. Mr. Sullivan's share in this result cannot be overrated. It is quite evident that composer and librettist have learned to work together in the most literal sense of the term, and this is one of the great advantages they possess over all competitors. It is impossible to appraise the precise amount of credit due to each, but Mr. Gilbert's humour is evidently the fecundating principle. His share, too, is the more important in so far as it is the greater advance upon previous and contemporary examples of work of the same class. Light French music may or may not be equal or superior to Mr. Sullivan's; the difference between Mr. Gilbert's librettos and those of the ordinary opera-bouffe adapters, is the difference between positively good and positively bad. Let us hope that Fortune and his Muse will continue to favour him in this sphere, though not to the exclusion of more ambitious work.

MR. SYDNEY GRUNDY.

AMONG Mr. Sydney Grundy's writings there are three which stand pre-eminent as being at once more ambitious and more successful than the rest. They are "Mammon," "The Snowball," and "In Honour Bound." Before proceeding to a general examination of Mr. Grundy's talent it will be well to give some account of these three plays in detail.

Octave Feuillet's "Montjoye" is one of the most loosely-strung, tedious, and sickly-sentimental of his plays. The character of Montjoye, however, is a piece of actuality both in France and England. The great financier has been frequently put on the stage in France, but in England he has generally been seen in an H'less and semi-imbecile condition in popular farces, three-act or otherwise. Mr. Grundy consequently took Feuillet's hint and resolved to present him in a more serious and truthful form. Beyond the hint he took little from his French original. His play is in three acts, Feuillet's in five. Every line of dialogue, every scene and situation is his own. Sir Geoffrey Heriott has some of the traits of Montjoye with this great difference that he is really and practically a financier plunged in the vortex of business, while Montjoye might just as well be a rich *rentier* for all we see of his supposed commercial capacity. The story of the copper-mine which led to the suicide of George Sorrell's father, is the same in both plays, and the idea of the violets belongs to Feuillet, but has been much developed by Mr. Grundy. The relation between Sir Geoffrey and Lady Heriott is quite different from that between Montjoye and Henriette, and in "Mammon" Mr. and Mrs. Chinnery have an organic connexion with the plot, which cannot be said of the Marquis and the Marquise in the French play. Montjoye's irrelevant and feebly drawn son disappears altogether in "Mammon" along with several other useless and cumbersome characters, and above all Mr. Grundy has invented and introduced with rare effect the admirable figure of Parker, Sir Geoffrey's factotum, a creation which evinces the true dramatist. In short, the English play is in every way an improvement upon the French, and is, in the best sense of the term, an independent and original work.

Yet some of the faults of "Montjoye" cling to it, Among them is this primary defect, that the play is not so much a drama as a catastrophe. There is no struggle, no growth in it. In the first act we see a social card-castle erect, in the second and third we watch it gradually toppling over story by story, until it lies a flattened heap of ruin. The moment we see the erection we recognize that its fall is only a matter of time. Sir Geoffrey from the first is walking straight towards the precipice; the drama really occurred when he stood at the parting of the ways and chose that which led to destruction. The same may of course be said of many of the greatest dramas of the world. They show us not the crime, but the punishment. They take Nemesis on the swoop, so that our interest is not that of doubt, but of certain expectation. This is perhaps not to be called a fault, but it is at least a peculiarity.

More important to note is the lack of definition in the character of Sir Geoffrey Heriott. His figure is drawn with a bold and vigorous hand and is full of life and motion. His relation to the outer world is admirably given, but his relation to himself is left very vague, and this is, after all, the nucleus round which the details of a well-constructed character must group themselves. What does he think of himself? How does his own character represent itself in his consciousness? These are the first questions our analysis must ask, and the answer given in this case is very undecided. It is not that Sir Geoffrey's cynicism is inconsistent, and breaks down in his relation to his daughter. This is not only a possible but a probable trait. It is rather that his whole attitude towards the fundamental concepts of ethics is left undefined. It appears as if the words right and wrong had for him not only no authority but no meaning, which in a man of his intellectual capacity is surely impossible. On the commonest criminal above the merely animal level, the moral law imposes itself.

The distinction between right and wrong is ever present to his mind. He may use sophisms, conscious or unconscious, in his definition of the two categories, and so mistake wrong for right, or he may openly rebel against the tyranny, and say, "Evil shall be my good;" but always and in every case he recognizes the distinction. Not so Sir Geoffrey. He lays to his soul no flattering unction of casuistry and jesuitism. Nor is he in open rebellion against society, taking revenge for some real or supposed injury. He seems to have been born, like Hawthorne's Donatello, without a moral sense, and such beings belong to romance and not to the Stock Exchange. Both in word and deed he seems a conscious hypocrite and scoundrel, and yet we somehow feel that hypocrisy and scoundrelism have no meaning for him. When he says, "These honest men! These dreadful honest men! How they upset one's calculations and derange society!" the words sound like the sneer of a moral Nihilist whose object it is to overthrow society from its very basis. But nothing is further from Sir Geoffrey's intention. He rather believes in society, and does not see that his principles, or more properly his practices, must, if carried to their logical extreme, render society impossible. This, it seems to me, he is much too clear-headed not to understand. It is quite conceivable that he should act as he does out of rebellion against the moral law, and with perfect recklessness as to the consequences towards society. But I repeat that there is no trace of any such rebellion. He simply ignores morality, and that is what no man in these latter days can do. Self-consciousness and the consciousness of our relation to a moral law has for centuries been permeating more and more every fibre of our tissue. So much we may take for certain, without entering into any vexed questions as to intuition, experience, utility, and heredity. A man without the rudiments of a moral sense, if he exist at all, is as much a *lusus naturæ* as a man without any hair, and is equally unavailable for purposes of serious drama. It cannot of course be said that Sir Geoffrey has not the rudiments of a moral sense, but the state of his ethical consciousness is left undefined or defined in mutually destructive inconsistencies. The result is that the conclusion is the weakest portion of the play. If we are to be impressed by an emotional crisis, ending in a strong revulsion of feeling, it is absolutely necessary that we should first clearly conceive the mental condition which precedes the crisis. This clearness of conception is not given us in "Mammon."

My analysis of Sir Geoffrey's character may be mistaken, but the fact that it suggests such an analysis at all, proves its immense superiority as compared with the general run of characters on the modern stage. Here there is bone and fibre for the dissecting-knife to work upon. In most other cases one might as well attempt to dissect blown bladders which collapse at the first puncture. "This is a grotesque, this a lay-figure, that a monstrosity, the other a shadow," is too often the only criticism which can be applied to the characters of even a more or less serious play. Sir Geoffrey Heriott, on the other hand, is a solid creation, though there may be faults in his organism.

The first act of "Mammon" is in every respect masterly, posing the characters with force and precision, and sufficiently suggesting the action. Here is part of the first scene between Sir Geoffrey and his secretary Parker, who subsequently outwits him at his own game:—

Sir G. Any news this morning?

Parker. Everything is doing well, sir.

Sir G. Good.

Parker. You just sold those Mount Vesuvians in time. There's been a heavy drop.

Sir G. Yes, we arranged that there should be a drop this month. We must buy in again. They're going up next week. We've settled that already. The committee sent out to inspect the property will have returned by then, and I have almost finished writing their report. It will be very favourable. What say the newspapers? Do they announce my acceptance of the chairmanship of the Association for the Protection of Widows and Orphans?

Parker. Three leading articles upon the subject.

Sir G. Very good. Of course you've taken care my name appears in all subscription lists that are now published?

(*All this time opening letters, &c.*)

Parker. Yes, sir; and in none that are not published. At the annual meeting of the Penny Tract Society, the Bishop of St. Dunstan highly eulogized your noble and disinterested philanthropy.

Sir G. Did he? Did he, now? Send him one of our prospectuses.

Parker. I have already done so, sir; one of those specially intended for the clergy.

Sir G. Parker, you are worth your weight in gold.

Parker. I do my duty, sir, that's all.

Sir G. I doubt if I subscribe enough to charities. They're the best investments going. Double the amounts of our subscriptions, Parker.

Parker. To them all, sir?

Sir G. To them all.

Parker. They're a queer lot just at present, sir.

Sir G. All the better. Nothing pays so well as alms to the undeserving. The world doesn't like your calculating philanthropist who inquires into the merits of distress. Your devil-may-care fellow is the fellow the world likes, and the more mischief he does the better it likes him.

Parker. They shall be doubled, sir.

Sir G. And put it down to advertising. By-the-bye, do they announce my appointment to the treasurership of the Society for the Propagation of Christianity among the Christians?

Parker. The religious papers all have paragraphs upon the circumstance.

Sir G. That's right. Send them all prospectuses.

Here again is a passage from a scene between Sir Geoffrey and Lady Heriott. I may note that George Sorrell's father, who is here discussed, was ruined by means of a piece of very sharp practice on the part of Sir Geoffrey himself.

Sir G. My daughter cannot possibly marry the son of—well, a ruined banker.

Lady H. He was much respected.

Sir G. But he failed, and it is not respectable to fail. Besides, you must forget the manner of his death.

Lady H. Misfortune drove him to it.

Sir G. Doubtless. I am not the man to be severe upon an

old friend, particularly when he is unfortunate; but after all you must admit that suicide is not respectable.

Lady H. At least you cannot hold the son accountable for what the father did when *he* was quite a child.

Sir G. It is not I—it is the world.

Lady H. The world respects the son.

Sir G. The world of Eastminster.

Lady H. Which knows him.

Sir G. My dear, a man's respectability depends on the opinion not of those who know him, but of those who don't, and nothing in the world has less to do with his reputation than his character.

Finally, let me quote a portion of the scene between Sir Geoffrey and his old school-fellow Wentworth, who has taken to journalism and gone very much to the wall.

Wentworth. Had I been less faithful to my principles, I should have been more successful.

Sir. G. Much depends on what your principles are. Something outrageous, I'll engage to say.

Went. Nothing outrageous. I believe in truth and liberty. Few things are certain in the moral world, but—

Sir G. (*aside*). Now we're going to have a leading article. (*Rises.*)

Went. Those are the two sure principles—

Sir G. I quite agree with you. Those are two sure principles (*aside*) to bring a man to ruin.

Went. But they have not succeeded in my case.

Sir G. Because you have not been content with asserting them, but have been so foolish as to act upon them. I shouldn't be surprised, now, if you were a red republican.

Went. I certainly do think— (*Rising.*)

Sir G. I knew you did. And I shouldn't wonder if you are a free-thinker.

Went. Well, it is true—

Sir G. I knew it was. Now, Wentworth, tell me: do you ever go to church?

Went. No, Geoffrey. I suppose you do.

Sir G. Twice every Sunday.

Went. Well, you do what you think is right.

Sir G. No, Wentworth; mark the difference between us. *You* do what you think right: *I* do what *other people* think right. Behold the consequence (*putting his hand on* WENTWORTH): a grand catastrophe; (*putting his hand on himself*) a great success.

Went. You jest, Geoffrey. You are not a hypocrite.

Sir G. But *I* go *with* the tide. You fight against it. It is idle, Wentworth, idle. The tide will run. When the moon changes it may set your way. Whichever way it sets, go with it. Take my advice and mend your ways.

Went. I am too old to mend.

Sir G. But you are not too old to go to church. That has not much to do with mending.

These extracts will suffice to show the crispness, vigour, and thoughtfulness of the dialogue. Its style could scarcely be better, for its effectiveness on the stage is equal to its literary poise and polish.

In the second act, the crucial scene between Sir Geoffrey and Lady Heriott—crucial in two senses, since it turns upon a diamond cross—seems to me introduced and developed with less than Mr. Grundy's usual skill. Sir Geoffrey appears to be seized with a fit first of maladroitness and then of brutality, both of which are inconsistent with his ordinary character. The remaining scenes, however, are without exception excellent, and the stage effect at the conclusion is a touch of genuine originality. The third act, with many excellent points, is altogether more faulty. Sir Geoffrey's insistence on Violet's remaining in the room during the series of accusations, insults, and humiliations which he has to encounter, is surely quite unmotived; and an extremely false note is struck in the working-out of the scene where Violet, placed between her father and her lover, chooses to cast in her lot with the latter. To the radical weakness of the conclusion I have already alluded. It is perhaps in the nature of plays which deal with such characters as that of Sir Geoffrey Heriott to wind up unsatisfactorily, since a "happy ending," and an entirely tragic one are equally inadmissible. We feel the same difficulty in "A Game of Speculation" (Mercadet) the only play on the English stage which is to be compared to "Mammon," in its treatment of modern commercial morality.

"The Snowball," like "Mammon," is partly suggested by a French play, but owes even less to "Oscar, ou un Mari qui trompe sa Femme," than its predecessor owes to "Montjoye." It is a piece of the lightest comedy, frivolous no doubt, but never offending against good taste or morality. Its construction is admirably ingenious and finished. It is as unflaggingly amusing as "The Pink Dominos," and has the technical advantage of simpler mechanism, its whole action passing in one scene without that elaborate arrangement of doors upon which half the ingenuity of so many French imbroglios depends. Its dialogue is admirable. There is scarcely a dull speech in the play, and yet there is not a single pun, scarcely a single "epigram" or clever saying.

The humour grows out of the situation, and forms an organic part of it. For this very reason it is inseparable from the context, and defies quotation. It is easy to quote puns, catch-words, cockneyisms, and malapropisms, which are funny or stupid, as the case may be, altogether apart from their context. This sort of wit is like spangles of gilt foil loosely tacked to the stuff of the play. Not so Mr. Grundy's. Its threads are skilfully woven into the very tissue of the work and cannot be extracted without injury to the whole fabric.

I have now to speak of Mr. Grundy's most powerful and original work—original, though it was suggested by a play of Scribe's, powerful, though it was passed over with bare mention by the critics at the time of its production. "Une Chaîne" is a drama in five acts, the one act of "In Honour Bound" plays for about half an hour; yet the whole matter of the former is compressed into the latter, and presented under a novel and very ingenious form. There are four characters in the piece, Sir George Carlyon, Q.C., M.P., Lady Carlyon, Philip Graham, and Kate Dalrymple, a niece of Sir George Carlyon's. The place is Sir George Carlyon's study, the time evening. The action opens with a scene between Sir George and Philip, which I quote almost at length, as it seems to me one of the most masterly expositions ever written. One must go to France to find its equal in ingenuity, and even there one will scarcely find its superior.

Philip. Lady Carlyon is quite well, I hope.
Sir. G. Perfectly, thank you.

Philip. It is two years since I saw her.

Sir G. So it is. We have seen nothing of you lately—you whom we used to see so much of. Where have you been?

Philip. Well, all over the world. The day I met you, when you were so kind as to invite me here, was the day of my arrival home.

Sir G. So kind as to invite you! My dear boy, you raised enough objections to my invitation.

Philip. I was afraid of trespassing upon your hospitality.

Sir. G. And so you have been round the world?

Philip. From Dan to Beersheba.

Sir G. And you found all barren?

Philip. Upon the contrary, I've had a very jolly time—especially upon the voyage home.

Sir G. You look the better for it.

Philip. I am a new man.

Sir G. You weren't well when you went away.

Philip. I was depressed and out of sorts.

Sir G. So I observed.

Philip. You noticed it?

Sir G. And I remember thinking at the time there was a woman in the case.

Philip. That is all over now. I am as happy as the sand-boy in the saying.

Sir G. Then there's another woman in the case.

Philip. My dear Sir George, according to your views, there is a woman in every case.

Sir G. (*pointing to table*). There are some twenty briefs. Open which one of them you please, and somewhere in the folds you'll find a petticoat.

Philip (*rises*). What, twenty women hidden in these briefs? (*Sits.*)

Sir G. At least. There never was a case without a woman in it, and I never leave one till I've found her; for I know well enough until I do I have not mastered it. There is a woman in your case, my friend.

Philip. To tell the truth, there is. A charming girl I met upon the voyage home.

Sir G. The jolly voyage home!

Philip. I am in love this time, Sir George.

Sir G. Oh, yes! we always are in love this time.

Philip. I thought I was before, but I was wrong.

Sir G. Of course, we never were before!

Philip. And, better still, I am engaged.

Sir G. What, to the charming girl?

Philip. The only girl in the wide world for me.

Sir G. Well, you've been round it, so you ought to know. I hope you will be happy. It's a toss-up, Philip.

Philip. I am afraid that your profession makes you cynical.

Sir G. Gad, it would make an angel cynical. (*Sits on lounge.*)

Philip. No doubt you meet with some extraordinary cases. (*Turning over briefs.*)

Sir G. Never. All ordinary. To a man who has had twenty years' experience, no possible case can appear extraordinary. There aren't three there of which I didn't know the end before I turned a page. No wonder we don't always read our briefs, for we know most of them by heart. (*Lies back.*)

Philip. Hallo! (*Smiling, surprised.*)

Sir G. What have you found?

Philip. A breach of promise case. This looks amusing.

Sir G. Very amusing for the judge and jury. Very amusing for the public, too. Very amusing for the new-made wife to read in all the newspapers her husband's past.

Philip. Is the defendant married, then?

Sir G. Of course he is. They always are. And of course he was on with the new love before he was off with the old. They always will be. The old love was no better than she need be, and no more was he. Very amusing for the new love, isn't it?

Philip. Of course the letters will be read in court? (*Takes letters.*)

Sir G. And published in the papers. "November, 1877—Your own loving devoted Harry. (Laughter.) November, 1878—Yours most affectionately, Henry. (Loud laughter.) November, 1879—Yours truly, Henry Horrocks. (Roars of laughter.) Oh, it's a most amusing case—for Mrs. Henry Horrocks.

Philip. Why don't you settle it? You are for the defendant.

Sir G. We've tried, but it's too late. Take warning by my client.

Philip. I?

Sir G. You be in time, it you are not too late already.

Philip. Excuse me, mine was quite a different case. Thank heaven, I have no reason to reproach myself. There was no love, at any rate on my side, in the matter you allude to.

Sir G. And yet you fled the country to avoid the lady. (*Sitting up.*)

Philip. I never said so.

Sir G. No, my boy; you never said that two and two makes four, but it does, doesn't it? (*Looking at* PHILIP *through his glasses.*)

Philip. No doubt. I felt that my position was— (*Hesitates.*)

Sir G. Equivocal.

Philip. That is the word I wanted.

Sir G. Useful word.

Philip. And feeling that, I thought the best course was to—

Sir G. Run away.

Philip. But as for promises of marriage, there was nothing of that sort. In fact, there couldn't be.

Sir G. Because the lady was already—

Philip. Hang it, Sir George, *you're* telling *me* my case!

Sir G. (*drops glasses*). You'll find it in the third brief on your right.

Philip (*looking at brief*). "Winter *v.* Winter and Hockheimer?"

Sir G. That's your case, as far as it has gone.

Philip. (*takes up brief and reads endorsement*). "In the High Court of Justice—Probate and—" But this a divorce case!

Sir G. Just so.

Philip. Oh, that's not my case. (*Puts brief back in its place.*)

Sir G. I said as far as it had gone. Hockheimer ran away. You ran away. But Hockheimer came back again. And I observe that *you've* come back again.

Philip. But I'm not Hockheimer.

Sir G. As far as you have gone. Hockheimer was a friend of Winter's—

Philip. But I'm *not!* I never saw the man in my life!

Sir G. No, but the other man?

Philip. What other man?

Sir G. The husband.

Philip. I never said he was my friend!

Sir G. Oh, yes, you did.

Philip. When did I say so?

Sir G. When you ran away. (*Puts glasses up.*)

Philip. Spare me, Sir George. You make me feel like a witness under cross-examination. I didn't mean to breathe a word of this, and somehow I have told you everything.

Sir G. (*rises*). Well, you have told me a good deal. (*Drops glasses.*) Now, will you let me give you my advice?

Philip. By all means.

Sir G. Keep those women apart.

Philip. Which women?

Sir G. (*smiling*). The charming girl and the neglected wife.

Philip. I never said she was neglected.

Sir G. But she is, isn't she? (*Putting up his eye-glasses.*)

Philip. Those glasses worry me.

Sir G. (*dropping the eye-glasses*). I beg your pardon; it's the force of habit. Off with the old love—friend, or what you will—and never let the new one see her. Off with her entirely! That's my advice: and many a hundred guineas have been paid for worse.

Philip. Oh, they will never meet. I mean to live abroad. The girl I am engaged to is a South Australian (SIR G. *lifts his head quickly*), and she has only come to England on a visit. Her parents are both dead, and she came over with a maiden aunt, with whom she is now stopping.

Sir G. Where?

Philip. At Bayswater. In a few weeks she will go back to Melbourne, and then all danger, if there be any, is over.

Sir G. So you have come from Melbourne in the *Kangaroo.*

Philip. Who told you what boat I came over in? (*Rises.*)

Sir G. I gathered it from what you said yourself.

Philip. I won't say a word more, or in two minutes you will guess the lady's name.

Sir G. I have already done so.

Philip. What!

Sir G. Kate Dalrymple.

Philip. This is astounding!

Sir G. Not at all.

Philip. I have told nobody!

Sir G. You have told *me.*

Philip. You know Miss Dalrymple?

Sir G. She is my niece. She is a South Australian. She came to England in the *Kangaroo,* and has been stopping with a maiden aunt at Bayswater.

Philip (*steps back*). Your niece!

Sir G. I am her guardian, since my sister died.

Philip. Then, she is your wife's—

Sir G. Niece by marriage.

As it happens, Sir George Carlyon's wife is the very person with whom Philip Graham has been entangled, and Sir George, as Kate Dalrymple's guardian, before giving his consent to Philip's marriage with her, demands proof in the "neglected wife's" own writing that the chain which has bound Philip to her is broken for ever. I cannot follow all the rapid developments through which the action passes. Suffice it to say that the play contains passages of thrilling dramatic suspense and almost tragic intensity of emotion, while its knot is untied in a manner as artistic as it is ingenious. The ethics of the piece are perhaps rather buried in the intrigue, for Mr. Grundy is a true disciple of Scribe. Nevertheless the moral problem presented is interesting, and the solution suggested is to my mind the right one, though that is a point of minor importance. I may note, as one of the boldest and most effective touches in the play, the method in which Mr. Grundy acknowledges his obligation to Scribe. Lady Carlyon and Kate Dalrymple have just returned from the theatre, where a French company has been playing "Une Chaîne." After Kate has given an account of the plot the following dialogue occurs :—

Sir G. (*to* LADY CARLYON). What did *you* think of it, my dear?

Lady C. It is a painful subject.

Kate. Aunt Bell didn't like it; but she took it all so seriously. If it were real it would be very sad, but after all, what is it but a play? Besides, it all takes place in Paris. Nobody pretends that such things happen here.

Lady C. Of course. (*Quickly.*)

Philip. Of course. (*Quickly.*)

Sir G. (*ironically*). Of course. (*Takes up the third brief on his right, and plays with it.*)

Kate. I read a notice of the piece this morning, and I quite agreed with it.

Sir G. What did the notice say?

Kate. It said it was "an admirable play, but an English version of it was impossible."

Sir G. Why so?

Kate. Because—how did it put it?—oh, "because these vivid but unwholesome pictures of French life have, happily, no—" something—I forget exactly what—" to the chaste beauty of our English homes."

In the conception of a passage like this one sees the talent of the true dramatist.

Besides the three plays here dwelt upon, Mr. Grundy has written several minor pieces with varying success. His first play, "A Little Change," was produced by Mr. and Mrs. Kendal at the Haymarket in 1872. It was a one-act trifle, written after the manner of Mr. Theyre Smith, and with all that clever writer's neatness and point of dialogue. Two comediettas by Mr. Grundy, called "All at Sea" and "A Bad Bargain," have been produced in the provinces, but have not yet been seen in town. A farce entitled "Reading for the Bar" was produced at the Strand in 1876, and a comedietta called "Man Proposes" at the Duke's Theatre in 1879. "After Long Years," produced at the Folly in 1879, was little more than a translation from the French of Scribe, and, with some pretty ideas, contained little of Mr.

Grundy's individuality. "Popsy Wopsy," a musical absurdity produced at the Royalty in 1880, was neatly and cleverly written, but lacked spontaneity. Two adaptations from the French of Labiche wind up the list of Mr. Grundy's works. "Over the Garden Wall" at the Folly was, despite its unfortunate title, a clever piece of work, but suffered from too much compression. "Dust" at the Royalty was evidently a piece of task-work, and its misfortunes arose largely from causes beyond Mr. Grundy's control. Another play of Mr. Grundy's has been heard of, but not seen. It is a comedy called "A Novel Reader," written in collaboration with Mr. Joseph Mackay, and founded upon "La Petite Marquise" of MM. Meilhac and Halèvy. The Licenser of Plays, in his infinite and irresponsible wisdom, decided that it was absolutely impossible for any play connected, however remotely, with "La Petite Marquise" to be otherwise than immoral, and put his veto upon its production. This called forth from Mr. Grundy a diatribe against the principle and practice of the censorship, which, in the fervour of its indignation, left the "Areopagitica" far in the rear. Its arguments were irrefragable, but were perhaps injudiciously stated.

Though the above list of plays is by no means a small one for a dramatist who is still on the right side of thirty-five, it cannot be denied that Mr. Grundy has not hitherto met with the appreciation he deserves. His is certainly one of the most remarkable talents at present applied to stage-work, and yet he is very far from being one of the popular dramatists of the day. An examination into the causes of this fact may throw some light not only upon the extent and limitations of Mr. Grundy's ability, but also upon the defective conditions of dramatic life in England.

Whatever else he may be, Mr. Grundy is certainly a dramatist in the exact sense of the term. He can weld action, character, and dialogue into a homogeneous whole, so that no one element preponderates over the others. More than this, he can develope and elaborate the possibilities of a given theme so as to extract from it its full dramatic value. He is an artist in his craft; he has studied its principles and can put them in practice. And this is the first disadvantage under which he labours. He is a dramatist, and not a humourist, and what the public demands is humour and not drama. Mr. Grundy has plenty of wit, and is by no means deficient in humour, but they are, as they should be in a writer of artistic plays, subordinate to his sense of dramatic fitness. Now dramatic fitness is the last thing the public thinks of demanding, appreciating, or even recognizing. It has entirely got out of the habit of asking itself "could this character conceivably say this thing under these circumstances?" "Is this funny?" or "pretty?" or "pathetic?" are the only questions it asks, and an affirmative answer covers a multitude of sins. Mr. Grundy will not—perhaps cannot—write plays in which probability, possibility, character, grammar, and the Queen's English are sacrificed to the immediate necessity of raising a laugh. Perhaps cannot, I say, for I am not sure that he possesses the requisite ability. Some of the popular playwrights of the day are men of great talent—men who last century would have been recognized as wits of the first water. It is not a question of amount of talent so much as of direction and balance. Mr. Grundy, I believe, has that "balance of power" which is requisite for the production of really artistic plays. If he has not the fatal gift of punning, he has the invention and observation, the inflexible logic and the correct taste which make a dramatist if they mar a buffoon. Two of his best plays are suggested by Eugène Scribe, and in a magazine article published some time ago he expressed the warmest admiration for that great playwright. This admiration is easily explicable, for there is a decided intellectual affinity between the two men. Mr. Grundy has many of Scribe's merits and some of his limitations. His inventive power is similar in quality though of course not equal in quantity. He is no more of a poet than Scribe was, and no less of a logician. He shows the same, perhaps exaggerated, determination to "get on with his story" at all hazards, and this I believe is what the public cannot forgive him. It loves to divagate and meander through a play. It has been so long accustomed to dialogue without plot in comedy, and plot without dialogue in drama that it resents the combination. Mr. T. W. Robertson has accustomed it to comedies in which there is no plot, Mr. Byron to comedies in which the plot does not matter, and Mr. Albery to comedies in which the plot is best forgotten. It could not help being interested in "Mammon" and

"In Honour Bound," but when the curtain had fallen it found that the net result was a moral question to reflect upon, not a store of puns to chuckle over. It went on its way, forgot the moral problem, and only remembered the absence of puns.

For this is Mr. Grundy's second great mistake—he dares to be moral. Not that in his acted plays he moralizes to the detriment of the action. His faith in Scribe is too great to permit of his falling into this error. An expository tirade, after the manner of Dumas *fils*, is quite foreign to his style. He will not even discuss in the abstract the question which his material presents in the concrete. This is erring on the safe side, if it be an error at all, which, to my mind, it sometimes is. I am not sure, for instance, that "In Honour Bound" might not have borne a more careful unravelling in the abstract of its ethical nodus. Be that as it may, the nodus is there in the concrete; and this, which constitutes the merit of the piece as a work of serious dramatic art, appears to the great public, I have no doubt, in the light of a defect. In short the moralist has no chance on our stage, and Mr. Grundy is, rightly or wrongly, a moralist. It lies in his temperament to regard a serious play as a thing which may conceivably affect human thought and action outside the theatre. This is heresy of the most condemnable order. We pay an official a handsome salary and give him unlimited powers to ensure that our stage shall on no account be moral. But with all its irresponsibility the censorship is practically under the jurisdiction of the public. It may be a little behind, or even a little in advance of public opinion, but it is as a rule merely an authoritative expression of the narrowest prejudices of omnipotent British Philistinism. Let the blame fall where it is due.

The moral bias of Mr. Grundy's talent is proved not only by "Mammon" and "In Honour Bound," but by two of his other productions as well. Nearly ten years ago he published a novel entitled "The Days of his Vanity." It was not a good novel, simply from the fact that in adopting the narrative form Mr. Grundy threw overboard his dramatic principles and preached to an inordinate degree. The motto—I had almost said the text—of every chapter was taken from Ecclesiastes, and the book was in fact a commentary upon the great preacher, illustrated by modern instances. It was very youthful in tone, not so much from lack of experience as from novelty of experience. It was clearly the work of a man whose eyes had been recently opened to the realities of life, and who had not yet got over the first ferment of wonder and indignation and contempt. But this only served to show in a clearer light the earnestness, the serious thought, in short, the essentially moral temperament of the author. In seeing or reading the works, dramatic or non-dramatic, of many other English playwrights, one wonders whether their eyes have ever been opened at all to the realities of life, and whether they may not be at fifty a great deal younger, not to say more puerile, than a man of Mr. Grundy's temperament at twenty-five.

The second production in which Mr. Grundy has

evinced his moral tendency is his prohibited play, "A Novel Reader." Of this work I know nothing, except what was incidentally stated at the time when its prohibition brought it under discussion. One of the facts then elicited was that it dealt with the influence of bad feminine fiction—the novels of Ouida and her school—upon the feminine mind. It would be difficult to name a more important social question of the day, or one which cries out more loudly for dramatic treatment. It is a subject of the very class which seems to me to come entirely within the province of the drama—serious, relevant to the life of every household, not too delicate in its nature, and capable of striking dramatic developments. Indeed it could probably be treated more effectively on the stage than in any other form. And it is a play on this subject of all others which our enlightened censorship sees fit to taboo! It may have been a bad play, but as the office of the Censor does not extend to æsthetics, that cannot have been the ground of its rejection. It cannot have been a frivolously immoral play, or it would have been promptly licensed with a few blue-pencil excisions merely for the sake of ornament. The cause upon which the Licenser condescended to ground his rejection was that it was remotely connected with "La Petite Marquise," which was an immoral work. For the same reason he should have tabooed "The Snowball," since "Oscar" is perhaps the most immoral, not to say disgusting, of Scribe's works. Yet I am sure that a young ladies' boarding-school—nay the Censor himself—might witness "The Snowball" without a blush.

Having stated several reasons for Mr. Grundy's lack of success in forcing himself to the front in public estimation, I must now confess that these reasons appear to me insufficient. If we place his abilities in the one scale and the "disabilities" I have enumerated in the other, the former seem as if they should still largely outweigh the latter. There must be some other defect in his character which I have no means of discovering —perhaps lack of energy, or lack of adroitness, or lack of self-assertion, or lack of skill in seizing opportunities. How is it, for instance, that after the success of "Mammon" he received no commission to adapt one or more of the serious French plays of which every season produces one or two? Surely he had proved himself eminently capable of doing such work artistically and with success. Was it entirely owing to the blindness of managers and the exclusiveness of the reigning dramatic ring? Perhaps so, but the dramatic ring is hedged by no divinity, and might have been broken into and taken by storm. The success of "The Snowball" secured him some pieces of task-work in the shape of adaptations of French farces, which he did cleverly enough but without the interest excited in his serious nature by a serious theme. Thus managerial stupidity and timidity have done their best to confine him to the class of work for which he has least special turn; but I cannot help suspecting that he might have made a better, or at any rate a more skilful, fight against these time-honoured attributes of the British manager. Perhaps he has the defects of his qualities, and thinks the laurel not worth having at the expense of the dust and sweat of the arena. If so, I, for one, cannot blame him. To a man who likes to draw his breath freely and uprightly the dust of the English theatrical arena has a peculiarly stifling quality.

But Mr. Grundy, I repeat, is as yet not far on the wrong side of thirty, and if, as some of us venture to hope, the tide of culture is setting slowly but surely towards the stage, his opportunity must ultimately arrive. I look forward with confidence to the time when he shall produce, under worthy circumstances, an original comedy or drama dealing seriously with some serious ethical problem or social question of the day. Original, I say, though its motive may be borrowed, as in the case of "Mammon," "The Snowball," and "In Honour Bound." For I regard these plays as in every sense original—as much so, at any rate, as it is possible to be in this old age of the world, when the kaleidoscope of life has been shaken so often and its patterns recorded with such minuteness by so great a host of witnesses. Let a dramatist invent motives as much as he pleases—he will find that some one else has used them, or something like them, long ago. The most he can hope is to invent new developments of old motives. Shakespeare, Molière, even Calderon himself, marvel of invention though he was, took their motives ready-made from history, legend, or tale, or even from some already existing play. Why should our modern dramatists be denied the same licence? Probably no one ever spun a drama entirely out of himself, as a spider, to use Heine's illustration, spins his web. Every play grows from some external germ—a piece of history, a passage in a book, an incident in real life, a paragraph in a newspaper. Sardou's "Fernande," for example, was suggested by a short tale of Diderot's, yet no one on that account denies its originality. The aid Sardou received from Diderot was of very much the same nature and amount as that which Mr. Grundy received from Scribe in writing "The Snowball" and "In Honour Bound." Is it reasonable to deny his work the epithet of "original," merely because "Oscar" and "Une Chaîne" happen to be in dramatic instead of narrative form?

MR. BRONSON HOWARD.

NOT many years ago critics used to devote much genius to explaining why America could not possibly produce good literature, whether in the shape of poetry, fiction, or the drama. We were told that the bustle and unrest, the lack of leisure and the lack of associations of a young and rising community, entirely prevented artistic development. Even after Longfellow, Hawthorne, Lowell, and Holmes—not to mention Ralph Waldo Emerson—had added to English literature some of the very best work of the nineteenth century, there were many critics who still held that the laws of nature utterly forbade that anything good should come out of America. Gradually, this prejudice has been breaking down, as concerns all spheres of art—except the drama. And it must be admitted that there is some ground on which it can maintain itself, when we remember the style of work which generally comes across the Atlantic. There is one exception, however, in the plays of Mr. Bronson Howard, and that exception does not prove, but destroys the rule. It shows that there is no reason in the nature of things why America should not produce artistic and solid dramatic work. Mr. Bronson Howard may be said to occupy a place among English dramatists somewhat similar to that occupied by Mr. Henry James among English novelists.

The play which first made Mr. Howard known as a dramatist in his own country was also the play which introduced his name to the English public. "Saratoga" was produced at the Fifth Avenue Theatre, New York, in December, 1870, and attained a remarkable success. "Diamonds" was the title of his next play, also produced at the Fifth Avenue Theatre, in the autumn of 1872. It has not yet been played in England. Two years later Mr. Howard met his first check, in "Moorcroft," a four-act comedy, produced at the Fifth Avenue Theatre, which failed to attract the public. But by this time Mr. Howard's fame had crossed the Atlantic, and in the same year (1874) "Saratoga," localized by Mr. Frank Marshall under the title of "Brighton," was produced by Mr. Charles Wyndham at the Court Theatre. Here, too, it secured immediate and enduring popularity. Mr. Howard's next appearance in his native country took place in 1878, when the Park Theatre, New York, was opened with two pieces from his pen, "Old Love Letters" and "Hurricanes." The former is a little one-act comedy, said to be full of charming humour and sentiment, but it has not found its way to the English stage. "Hurricanes" is a very different piece. If "Saratoga" took four years to cross the Atlantic "Hurricanes" naturally came quicker, and in 1879 was produced at the Criterion under the not very appropriate title of "Truth." But Mr. Howard's solidest and best work was yet to come. "The Banker's Daughter," produced at the Union Square Theatre, New York, in 1878, was localized under the title of "The Old Love and the New" by Mr. Howard himself in collaboration, with Mr. Albery, and produced by Mr. Wilson Barrett at the Court Theatre in December, 1879. Since then Mr. Howard has been strangely silent, having only produced a so-called "specialty" play for Mr. and Mrs. George S. Knight, entitled "Baron Rudolph." This, from the very nature of the case, may be presumed to be a work of small literary pretensions, whatever may be its dramatic merits.

It is perhaps unfortunate for Mr. Bronson Howard's artistic development that his fate brought him into such intimate contact with Mr. Charles Wyndham and the theatre he now manages. I have had a good deal to say about the Criterion and its style of art in dealing with Mr. Albery and Mr. Burnand. It has a special public which can only be allured by means of pieces which perpetually hover on the border-line of impropriety. This is generally effected by taking a French piece, re-arranging it so as to pass the Lord Chamberlain, and then leaving the audience to read between the lines, which it does with the utmost alacrity and penetration. In Mr. Howard's plays, on the other hand, open vulgarity is substituted for half-cloaked immorality, and I cannot tell which is the more objectionable. The knowledge that in "Brighton" and "Truth" we have to deal not with French frivolity but with home-made Anglo-

Saxon indelicacy, perhaps rather accentuates their unpleasantness. Without being distinctly immoral, they deal with a world in which the women have the manners of barmaids, and the men the morals and feelings of taproom loafers. There is not a gentleman or a lady in the two farces. "Brighton" is a saturnalia of vulgar watering-place flirtation. It should by rights have been called "Margate." "Truth," if we could attribute to it any meaning at all, would be a panegyric upon lying.

It is not the character of Bob Sackett with his amorous eccentricities that jars upon one in "Brighton." It is a creation of frank farce, ludicrously impossible, and therefore almost inoffensive. The worst point in the play is the conduct of the numerous so-called ladies who crowd the stage. Ordinary modesty, not to say delicacy of feeling, is apparently a thing unknown and undreamt of among them. "Give me a middle-age man," says one of them. "Well, I'm sure so-and-so is middle-aged," replies another. "I mean a man of the middle-ages" is the reply, "one of the men that always went about in armour—ate in his armour, drank in his armour, went to bed in his armour—" "A nice husband for cold weather," remarks Miss Effie Remington, the heroine of the play, in so far as it has a heroine—and the audience roars. I feel that an apology is due for even quoting such passages as this. I should be the last to do so, were it not that in bringing a charge of vulgarity one must cite chapter and verse on pain of meeting with the counter-charge of superfineness. In a previous paper I have admitted that this charge is often difficult, sometimes incapable, of disproof. But this, surely, is not one of these instances. Such mock-valentine wit as the above is of the kind which, even in the time of Charles II., Lord Roscommon declared to "admit of no defence." Yet in the refined age of Victoria it has been accepted without protest—nay, with loud appreciation, by hundreds of audiences. Further, it has either passed the Lord Chamberlain, the court official deputed to filter the wit-supply of the stage: or else it is a "gag," and has not passed him: in either case proving the futility of his office. The latter hypothesis reminds me that I am perhaps unjust in attributing such offensive puerilities as this to Mr. Howard, for both the plays in question have been revised and re-revised by other hands; but their very structure is such that, after all possible allowance has been made, he cannot be absolved from the charge of vulgarity.

Apart from this, the structure of "Brighton" and "Truth" is in a measure noteworthy. It shows a genuine talent for the invention of comic situations, with little or none for the construction of a logical or symmetrical plot. "Brighton" especially is a quite formless farce, consisting of a string of very amusing but almost entirely unconnected episodes. "Truth" has more compactness of construction, but is spoiled by the pitiable anti-climax of the third act.

Had Mr. Howard produced nothing but these two farces one would have concluded that his main strength lay in comic dialogue, in which he has a peculiar art of his own. His personages do not talk epigrams and puns with no relevance either to their character or to the action. His "points" and "good things" do not as a rule dwell in one's mind; yet the dialogue never fails in humour, for its fun grows naturally out of character and situation. This is comic dialogue as it should be—and as, on the English stage, it generally is not. The same merit characterizes "The Old Love and the New." The dialogue tells the story and exhibits the characters clearly, interestingly, and brightly. It is not without special points. Many of the lines assigned to George Washington Phipps, for instance, are extremely funny in themselves, and the humour is never marred by the ill-taste to which I have referred above. But the chief merit of the play is the intimate welding, the organic unity, of plot, character, and dialogue. Points should grow like the flowers on a laburnum, not be stuck on like candles on a Christmas tree; and this condition Mr. Bronson Howard's points almost always fulfil.

On the first night of "The Old Love and the New" it impressed me as one of the strongest and healthiest plays I had seen for long on the English stage, but I remember feeling doubtful as to its financial success, on account of its length and general seriousness of tone. My doubts have proved groundless. It had two long runs in London, and was altogether a genuine success. I can imagine few more hopeful signs for the future of the English stage.

"The Old Love and the New" deals with familiar materials, but is none the worse on that account. The playwright who in these days should go about to find an absolutely new motive, would have little more chance of success than an alchemist in the search for the philosopher's stone. A score of plays will occur to every one in which a daughter marries to save her father from ruin, and sacrifices the happiness of her life. Even the particular development of this theme, in which the wealthy husband is ignorant of the sacrifice, and imagines himself possessed of his wife's love, is by no means entirely unknown. It is in the working out of his material that Mr. Bronson Howard shows his art. He presents it in new lights, evolves from it new situations, and dresses the story in dialogue of unusual grace and finish. How much of this may be due to Mr. Albery, I cannot tell. In one or two of the touches that master of dialogue revealed himself unmistakably, and I believe that at least one character who appeared in the American version has been suppressed; to wit, the aged husband of the juvenile Mrs. Brown. This alteration, which seems a manifest advantage to the play, is probably due to Mr. Albery; and he may have introduced several similar modifications. But as the groundwork of the play is admittedly Mr. Howard's, I must treat it as his throughout, and let Mr. Albery take to himself what is his due.

The first act is the most dangerous, for here the material is most conventional. Perhaps, also, the conventional element is too much dwelt upon, particularly in the scene where Westbrook tells his daughter of his ruin. This passage, if it could not be treated in a more novel fashion, might with advantage have been shortened. But from the moment of Stratton's entrance, when we understand his attitude towards Lilian and appreciate the double deceit of the selfish old father, we find that out of the old dramatic germs a new problem has grown. Our curiosity is aroused to precisely the requisite extent. We cannot guess the probable solution, but we see opportunities and speculate upon them with more than usual interest.

The character of the Comte de Carojac brings the second act at one or two points into rather dangerous proximity to hackneyed French melodrama. His rhapsody before the picture should be curtailed. Even if the Comte had the bad taste to continue his pretended soliloquy beyond a few moments, Lilian should have the good taste to interrupt him. Another inartistic touch is the story of the portrait, which, well-imagined in itself, is spoiled by the artificial exactness with which it is made to coincide in every detail with the situation in progress. On the other hand, the scene between Lilian and her discarded lover Harold Kenyon is admirably conceived and written, and the concluding situation is original and striking.

It seems to me a pity that the second, third, and fourth acts were not run into one, or at most two. They are in effect one act in three scenes, so far as the development of the action is concerned. The duel in the third act is excellently managed, and the situation to which it leads is powerful. But this situation might have been retained had the duel been supposed to take place near Stratton's house, and Kenyon been carried dying into Lilian's drawing-room. This might have been done with scarcely more violation of dramatic probability than is involved in the appearance of Stratton and Lilian at the close of the duel. The change of scene would thus have been avoided, and the piece materially curtailed. But one cannot quarrel with an arrangement which produces such an effective scene as that of the duel. The last few words uttered by Stratton are almost its only fault. The curtain should fall upon him taking his wife in silence into his arms.

The dramatist's skill is perhaps seen at its best in the fourth act, or, as I should prefer to call it, the last scene of the second act. It consists almost entirely of the explanation between Stratton and Lilian, which is worked out with remarkable delicacy, subtlety, and insight. The news of Kenyon's death brings down the curtain on an excellent crisis. A more conventional dramatist than Mr. Howard would have kept Lilian on the stage until the arrival of the letter, and ended with a commonplace situation of despair and hysterics. Mr. Howard's art is more original and truer.

That the fifth act should be somewhat of an anti-climax is unavoidable under our present dramatic conditions. The premises, logically worked out, would lead in nature, and consequently in the highest art, to a tragic conclusion. The taste of audiences, on the other hand, demands a "happy ending," and Mr. Howard had simply no choice but to contrive, as gracefully and as dramatically as he could, a reconciliation between the husband and wife. He has done so very gracefully, and the only point to which practical objection can be made is the very close, where, as in the third act, he has overlaid his situation with unnecessary talk. Still the conclusion is inartistic. Kenyon is dead and cannot be brought to life again, and we are irresistibly certain that his ghost will form an unpleasant third in the conjugal *tête-à-tête* of Stratton and Lilian. An uncompromising pessimist would have killed off Lilian also at the end of the fourth act. A moralist would have done the same, but would have brought in the element of justice by giving her some part in her father's deceit at the beginning. Either ending would have been better art, but Mr. Howard, being neither a moralist nor a pessimist, but simply a dramatist, is quite right in preferring success with a good drama to failure with a better one. A curious instance of the way in which the mere theorist is apt to overlook practical advantages of stage effect is afforded by the circumstance that the duel scene which I regard as an excrescence on the play, is the very passage which formed the germ of the drama in the author's mind. It was Gérôme's picture "Un Duel de Pierrot" which suggested to Mr. Howard the motive of "The Banker's Daughter."

The serious dialogue of the play is even better than that of the lighter passages, to which I have alluded above. It is written in strong, nervous English, with scarcely a strained point, and scarcely a melodramatic turn of phrase. So few are the faults of the diction that even a slight blemish like Lilian's use of the phrase "Nor has that trust been betrayed"—a literary, and not a colloquial, form of speech—jars upon one's ear, which in a worse written drama would never notice such a trifle. The great fault in the mere technique of construction seems to me to be an abuse of the soliloquy. There are at least half a dozen long and needless soliloquies—sometimes comic, in which case they are not so objectionable; but sometimes serious, when they are of extremely bad effect. On the whole, the play is, both from a literary and a dramatic point of view, so unusually good that one cannot but regret that Mr. Howard has been so long in following up its success with another work of the same character.

MR. H. A. JONES.

THOUGH neither long nor eventful, the career of Mr. Jones as a dramatist has been promising. It began, so far as London is concerned at any rate, with a comedietta entitled "A Clerical Error," produced at the Court Theatre. Its idea is this:—Minnie Heritage, ward of the Rev. Richard Capel, loves her guardian's nephew, Dick Capel, a ne'er-do-well, of whom nothing has been heard for three years. Her guardian, not suspecting her attachment to his nephew, asks her to become his own wife. Out of a sense of duty, she consents. Scarcely has she done so when the nephew turns up, an entirely reformed young man. The vicar's eyes are opened to his mistake by Perry, the old butler, who does not wish his master to marry. On hearing of the old attachment between his ward and his nephew, he pretends that his proposal to Minnie was merely "one of his jokes"—for he is of the jocular school of clergymen—to test her constancy to Dick. He joins their hands as the curtain falls, and we are not given clearly to understand whether the happy pair see through his "joke," and appreciate his self-renunciation.

This motive is far from new, and in its working out there are a good many elements of the commonplace.

The jocose vicar is scarcely an original creation, and the bibulous butler is one of the stock-characters of farce. The idea of making the heroine scribble what she hopes will be her married name over a piece of paper, and then leave the tell-tale paper lying about for every one to read, is at least as old as Polly Eccles, if not older. The scene, too, where the vicar, in the first burst of his grief on learning his mistake, sits motionless for several minutes, with his head buried in his hands, is managed clumsily. Yet there were enough good points in the piece to make one expect better things from the author. The two chief characters—the vicar and the butler—were pleasantly drawn, and there were several touches of genuine humour in the dialogue. Moreover, there was a pleasant honesty of sentiment in the piece, and an evidence of serious effort which went far to redeem its defects. Unfortunately Mr. Jones's second production, a comedietta entitled "An Old Master," showed the same faults in an exaggerated form, with the addition of an extreme naïveté of construction. The very title indicated a lack of judgment, since it suggested, to all appearance intentionally, a much more interesting theme than the one actually dealt with. When we hear of "An Old Master" we naturally expect a play turning upon art; but the Old Master depicted by Mr. Jones has nothing whatever to do with art, being simply a country schoolmaster. Thus the equivoque in the title is both unmotived and unwise, since it leads us to form higher expectations than the author is prepared to fulfil.

The most important work Mr. Jones has done as yet

is his dramatization of "A Prodigal Daughter" by Mark Hope, entitled "His Wife." The novel, which is somewhat after the style of Mr. Charles Reade, deals with the abuses of prison life, with a side-glance at the old story of private lunatic asylums. Both these subjects Mr. Reade has treated, scarcely more powerfully than they are handled in "A Prodigal Daughter." The author shows an unlimited and even superabundant fertility of invention in the matter of incident. Mr. Jones's task, therefore, has been mainly one of selection, and he has compressed the original story into his narrow limits with no little skill. The modifications introduced are mainly these: Margaret Field does not take revenge on the man she claims as her husband, by blinding the woman he loves, but is merely arrested for trying to extort money from him; Frank Christy and Rose Graham are entirely suppressed, Colonel Forester's betrothed becoming Nelly Christy; and Forester, instead of meeting his death in a heroic fashion, shoots himself like the cur he is. The drama has thus one or two positive advantages over the novel. No attempt is made to whitewash the crimes of Forester, who, with his accomplice Frank Christy, is represented in the novel as committing perjury, seduction, and every species of cruelty short of murder, and yet as retaining his self-respect and believing himself a rather meritorious and ill-used member of society. Moreover, the suppression of Frank Christy makes Michael Christy's conduct in ruthlessly insisting upon clearing up the case of Margaret Field a little less improbable. In the novel one is always feeling that though Michael is acting as every honest and right-minded man should act, his situation with respect to his brother is altogether too painful for him to retain his equanimity as he does. On the other hand, the growth of Michael's love for Margaret Field is in the play left very much to the imagination of the audience, and is indeed little short of inconceivable.

So much for the main motives of the play. In the details of construction some faults and some peculiarities are to be noted. The situations upon which Mr. Jones brings down his curtain are, as a rule, rather unusually conceived. He has a contempt for tableaux which would delight the heart of M. Zola. The curtain generally falls upon a conversation at the point where Margaret Field is too much overcome by her feelings to continue it. This is particularly notable at the end of the second act. Michael Christy is starting for London to bring down Margaret's child, and she makes him a long speech of little domestic directions, at the end of which Michael shakes hands with her and the curtain falls—a situation which is certainly not vividly exciting. I do not blame Mr. Jones for this abstinence from the picture-poster style of concluding his acts. I merely note it as a peculiarity, which might, under some circumstances, be deserving of positive praise. Now and then there is a little clumsiness in the development of the story. Margaret's recital of the circumstances of her marriage in the presence of Michael and Riddell, who must both have been perfectly familiar with her story long before, is very inartistic, and there are other less obtrusive defects of a similar nature. Mr. Jones might, too, be a little less timid in the matter of sensation. Except in the mad scene, all physical sensation—the struggle for the marriage certificate, Forester's suicide, &c.—is relegated behind the scenes with a scrupulousness worthy of a classic tragedy. For myself, I can see no harm in a sensation drama being sensational. This respect for the decencies of the stage is in modern times generally a sign of the author's timidity and lack of confidence in his interpreters rather than of artistic scruples. There is a wide region of possibilities between the physical brutalities in which French dramatists so often indulge, and the classic quietism which relates the incidents instead of letting us see them.

The dialogue is, as a rule, quite unobjectionable, though one or two speeches jar from a lack of dramatic fitness. When Riddell propounds to Forester his scheme for procuring a false Captain Field, Forester remarks humorously, "And I thought I was a villain!"—a speech which no one under the circumstances would ever make. Still feebler is one of Forester's speeches in the last act. Just as he is on the point of being married to Nelly Christy, his wife, whom he believed to have been murdered by his own servants, appears before him, and tells him that she is not only alive, but determined to show him up. Hereupon Forester—who, by the way, has testified only the mildest surprise at the appearance of the woman he supposed to be murdered—remarks, "This is pleasant news for a man on his wedding morning." The situation is a difficult one, it is true, and Forester might naturally feel rather embarrassed for appropriate conversation; but he certainly would not say the words Mr. Jones puts in his mouth. The part of Barby Haggitt, too, is one in which Mr. Jones seems to have tried a touch of naturalism with an effect which in one or two speeches is rather startling. On the whole, however, the play treats a difficult subject with a good deal of tact, and is a great advance both in construction and dialogue upon its author's earlier works.

Mr. Jones, in fine, seems to possess a good deal of culture and a great deal of earnest aspiration, which may go far to supply the place of some more strictly dramatic qualities in which he is rather lacking. He has done too little as yet to permit one to predict with any certainty what may be expected of him; but he has done enough to establish for his future efforts a fair claim to respectful attention.

MR. PAUL MERITT.

THE old Eagle Theatre in the City Road, lately known for some inscrutable reason as the Grecian, and now a theatre no more, has formed the nursery of a whole school of playwrights. It has been a very active and productive school, and has lately been extending its activity into the West End, so that one cannot disregard it as purely transpontine. I place the name of Mr. Paul Meritt at the head of this paper, but what I have to say refers almost equally to Messrs. Pettitt and George Conquest, while of late Mr. Augustus Harris has become an active member of the partnership.

The following list of the works this school has produced, though by no means complete, will serve to prove its productiveness. Mr. Paul Meritt alone has written "Sid, or the Family Legend;" "Chopsticks and Spikins;" "Pickles;" "Glin Gath;" "Word of Honor;" "Rough and Ready;" "The Olive Branch;" "The Golden Plough;" "Stolen Kisses;" and "New Babylon." In collaboration with Mr. Pettitt he has written "British Born;" "The Bread Winner;" "Brought to Justice;" "The Lost Witness;" "The White Cliffs of Albion;" "The Worship of Bacchus." In collaboration with Mr. Harris,

"Youth." In collaboration with Messrs. Pettitt and Harris, "The World." In collaboration with Mr. Tom Taylor, "Such is the Law," and in collaboration with Mr. George Conquest, "Seven Sins;" "Hand and Glove;" "Velvet and Rags," and "Mankind." Mr. Pettitt alone has written "The Black Flag" and "Taken from Life;" and Messrs Pettitt and Conquest have collaborated in "Dead to the World;" "Bound to Succeed;" "The One Eye'd Pilot;" "Neck or Nothing;" "The Sole Survivor;" "Sentenced to Death;" "During Her Majesty's Pleasure;" "Notice to Quit;" "The Green Lanes of England;" "The Royal Pardon;" "The Queen's Colours." Finally, Mr. George Conquest has written "The Elixir of Life;" "The Hanged Man;" "The Realities of Life;" "A Moment of Terror;" "Lion's Love;" "The Rescue on the Raft;" "The Lost Wife;" "The Streets to the Hulks." This formidable list is largely composed of works strung together almost at haphazard to please an east-end audience, in point of art not much above the old Italian "Commedie a soggetto" in which a plot was given to the actors and they were left to work out the dialogue for themselves. A sufficient number of accidents and offences, crimes and catastrophes, were strung together, often with a good deal of melodramatic invention; a hero and heroine, one or two villains, and a male and female comic character were provided; and then the dialogue was written in consultation with the stage carpenter, to suit the prisons and precipices, shipwrecks and waterfalls which happened to come in handy. But on dramas intended for the west-end a little more care and elaboration has been expended; until finally a new dramatic product has been evolved, or rather a new development of the old sensation drama.

In a clever skit published some time ago, Mr. W. S. Gilbert puts in the mouth of "a dramatist" the following opinions: "It is easy to write an original play that shall succeed. Every play which contains a house on fire, a sinking steamer, a railway accident, and a dance in a casino, will (if it is liberally placed on the stage) succeed in spite of itself. In point of fact, nothing could wreck such a piece but carefully written dialogue and strict attention to probability. Avoid those two stumbling-blocks (and nothing is easier than to avoid them), and your piece will succeed triumphantly." It is not difficult to guess of whom Mr. Gilbert is thinking in writing these words. He has in his mind, partly no doubt Mr. Boucicault and Mr. Charles Reade, but mainly Mr. Paul Meritt and Mr. Henry Pettitt. In this case, as in many others, Mr. Gilbert's satire is more clever than just. The style of drama which these gentlemen produce may not be very exalted, but it supplies a legitimate demand, and a demand which will continue to exist until the human mind ceases to be stirred by hairbreadth 'scapes and moving accidents by flood and field. In his reference to "carefully written dialogue," Mr. Gilbert is quite unjust. The dialogue of a successful "realistic drama," such as Mr. Paul Meritt produces, is after its kind, very carefully written. It is not good from a literary point of view, but it has often a certain quality of wit, and a great deal of feeling and nervous force. It is not characterized by the elegant cynicism of Mr. Gilbert nor by the quibbling ingenuity of Mr. Byron. It is not always highly polished or strictly natural; but it is what it professes to be—good, forcible, melodramatic dialogue. In the matter of probability, again, Mr. Gilbert exaggerates wildly. The art of the melodramatist lies, not in throwing probability overboard altogether, but in having the taste to know exactly what liberties he can take with probability, without incurring the ridicule or losing the interest of his audience. Or, putting the matter in a different light, we may say that his art is to render probable the improbable—to carry away the imagination of his audience so that it does not apply prosaic criticism to what moves and excites it. The dramatist may give his hero as many lives as a cat; he may override gravitation, re-arrange astronomy, and construct a geography of his own; he may snap his fingers at laws, physical, chemical, or psychological; he may do all this, so long as he does it in such a manner that his audiences shall for the moment overlook or excuse his revision of the universe. Mr. Gilbert's sneer, then, is to be taken with very large reservations.

It is not my purpose to write an apology for the sensational drama. Personally, I have no great taste for it, and I regret that it absorbs so much of the attention and money of the public, which might otherwise go to the support of higher and worthier forms of art. But it is a form which has its justification in an irrepressible demand on the part of British human nature in its present stage of progress. It is largely an outcome of the modern newspaper. It is a collection of exciting "crimes and disasters" welded into dramatic shape. It forms an exact counterpart to the idea of modern life gathered by an habitual student of the police paragraphs, law reports, and "special" columns of the *Daily Telegraph* and the lower-class Sunday newspapers. It is mainly supported by that immense section of the lower-middle classes which gets its whole culture from newspaper reading and the study of cheap fiction. In short it is a necessary outgrowth of modern English life, and not in its way an unhealthy one.

Even for audiences which may claim a little higher culture the sensation drama is not without a quite comprehensible charm. Gaboriau's novels, as an enterprising publisher has recently informed us, are the favourite reading of Prince Bismarck, and Macaulay in his moments of relaxation used to weep over the silliest feminine romances of the day. In the same way it is occasionally refreshing to let one's critical faculties lie dormant and allow oneself to be carried lazily along on the stream of a sensational story. If the writing is good it interests, if bad it amuses. The comic acting is sometimes funny, the heroic and melodramatic almost always. To any one with a sense of humour the scenic effects afford an inexhaustible store of amusement—pasteboard race-horses careering in wild jerks along the farthest groove, boats sailing gallantly away with their sails flapping against the mast, steamboats exploding with the measured deliberation of well-regulated clockwork. As for the "barons and squires and knights of the shires" who wander through these remarkable productions, they are irresistibly comic. In short, "New Babylon," "The World," "Youth," and "Mankind," have for me all the attraction of Mr. Gilbert's burlesque, with the additional advantage that their naïveté is genuine. Their morality is, as a rule, quite unexceptionable, except when they set themselves to be moral, as in the case of "Youth." The ethics of that stirring drama are of the most startling description, but are so plainly and ludicrously fallacious that they cannot possibly do any harm.

Thus I confess to a certain tenderness towards this style of work, because it is frankly bad and unpretentiously amusing. Yet I never see one of Mr. Paul Meritt's plays without feeling that there is in them a talent fit for better things. He has a power of invention and a dramatic force which might almost have furnished forth a Dumas père or D'Ennery. Such plays as "Glin Gath" and "The Golden Plough" show that only culture and taste are lacking to make of him a melodramatist after the French rather than the English model. They are vigorous and excellent rough sketches of dramas. If Mr. Meritt had carefully rewritten them, developed his situations instead of merely elaborating his tableaux, smoothed down impossibilities, polished his language, and made his baronets a little less like greengrocers in disguise, the plays would have been admirable in their kind. Unfortunately Mr. Meritt has no culture, and nourishes a hearty contempt for those who have. Some of my readers may remember a manifesto which heralded "The Worship of Bacchus," in which he openly sneered at "literary merit." It conveyed the impression that Mr. Meritt, in Mr. Labouchere's phrase, considers an English dramatist to be the noblest work of God, and holds that he and Mr. Pettitt are English dramatists *par excellence*. So they are—but the phrase is double-edged. The fact is that Mr. Meritt began his career by writing for audiences who would accept anything he gave them so long as it was stirring enough, to whom style was a dead letter, and on whom even grammar would have been thrown away. As he worked westwards he found audiences more difficult to please, but he chose to attract them, not by more careful style, but by more elaborate and novel sensations. This was no doubt the tendency of his organization, fostered by early circumstances and training. The material results have probably been greater than any he could have attained by following the better course. He might have been a dramatist and he has elected to be a play-carpenter. He has proved himself wise—or fortunate—in his generation.

MR. HERMAN CHARLES MERIVALE.

THOUGH Mr. Merivale has scored several successes, he can scarcely be called one of the popular dramatists of the day. He writes too well and too carefully for that bad eminence. In farce, in so-called tragedy, in romantic drama, and in modern drama, he has given the stage some of the best work it can boast. But he is not one of the authors whom managers, actors, and actor-managers besiege for plays, and whose weakest efforts are certain of acceptance on the mere strength of their signature. Unless the conditions of the stage improve more rapidly than can fairly be hoped at present, Mr. Merivale is not likely ever to become one of those autocrats of the boards, and for the sake of his artistic development it is to be hoped that he may not. When an author finds his name on the bill sufficient to secure at least a certain amount of success, he is apt to neglect to put his thought and his wit into the play. Yet it is to be hoped and expected that Mr. Merivale may give us much good and successful work in the coming years, and that his popularity may rise, if not to fever-point, at least to a fair and steady average temperature. I may confess at once that he is one of those among our younger dramatists to whom I look with most confidence for work which shall contribute to the regeneration of the stage.

In one respect Mr. Merivale occupies an exceptional position among dramatists of the day. He is the only one who has consistently and systematically recognized the value of collaboration. All his most important work has been done in collaboration. "Time and the Hour," "Alone," and "All for Her," were written in collaboration with Mr. Palgrave Simpson; in "Forget-me-Not" Mr. F. C. Grove had a share, and on the title-page of "The White Pilgrim" we read "The legend by Gilbert à Beckett." This may mean that Mr. à Beckett suggested the subject, or that he wrote the portion dealing with the legend of Earl Olaf's Vow. It is generally understood that in these plays Mr. Merivale is responsible for almost all the dialogue, while it is of course impossible even for the authors themselves to estimate exactly the part played by each in the construction. In dealing with these plays, then, I cannot be always introducing conjectural saving clauses as to the amount of credit or discredit due to the respective authors. I shall treat them as entirely Mr. Merivale's.

Before I leave the subject, one word as to the principle of collaboration. The rarity of this form of work seems to me one of the causes of the weakness of the English drama. In France, since the days of Scribe, collaboration is as much the rule as in England it is the exception. To attribute the inferiority of English work solely or even very largely to the absence of collaboration would of course be a wild instance of *post hoc, ergo propter hoc* reasoning. But neither is it without its effect. In every dramatic work there are two elements—construction and dialogue. Perhaps we are too much inclined to draw a hard and fast line between these, for it is almost impossible for a badly-constructed work to have really good dialogue. If the construction is bad, the dialogue may be clever, witty, poetical, but it can scarcely be natural and good. Nevertheless, it is clear that different mental faculties are appropriate to the production of these two elements. They have no doubt a tendency to appear in conjunction, but the tendency is far from invariable. Their conjunction is presupposed in every really great dramatist, but if none but really great dramatists were to write dramas the supply would be limited. Consequently it seems to stand to reason that an association of two men, each possessing one of these faculties in a larger proportion than the other, might produce, in place of two mediocre playwrights, one good dramatist. But, that a collaboration may be advantageous, it is not necessary that one of its members be exclusively a constructor, and the other exclusively a writer of dialogue. Such a combination seldom occurs. In the drama it is very frequently the case that two heads, even with equal and equally divided faculties, are better than one. The mere verbal discussion of a theme often suggests possibilities and developments which would never have occurred to a single thinker. Each member of the dramatic firm acts as a corrective to the other. Every one has his little idiosyncrasies, blinding him to faults of style or errors of taste in his own work. When two people are at work on a play, it is subjected to a continuous, careful, and often tolerably unbiassed criticism, in the very course of its growth. The mere reading of a completed play to friends or to the actors is far from having this effect. Friends are careless, inattentive, insincere and often incompetent critics, while each actor, it is notorious, thinks only of his own part. If sincerity and competence could be insured in the friend to whom the play is read, he would be in the best sense of the word a collaborator. Thus Molière, it is said, had at least one valuable collaborator—his cook. But Molière, aye and Shakespeare, had other collaborators—the earlier dramatists, whether Spanish, French, or English, whose plays they rewrote. For myself, I have not the smallest doubt that even this form of collaboration, though not the most valuable, was of advantage in many cases, even to the two supreme dramatists. It may be said, with a certain bitterness, that this form of collaboration is prevalent in England to this day, when English authors "collaborate" with their French contemporaries. Unfortunately, for obvious reasons of morality and sometimes of prudery, adaptations from the French too often result in the ruin of the original as a work of art; but on the other hand I could name several instances in which the English adapter has positively improved on the French work, thus showing that two heads are better than one, or three than two. And again, the absence of any habitual system of collaboration in England leads to the total loss of many a work which contains valuable material.

How often do we hear of a work being sent by a young writer to a French manager, who, recognizing in it the "stuff," though without the proper handling, sends it to a more experienced playwright for re-arrangement, the names of both appearing ultimately on the title-page of the play in its definitive form. It stands to reason that English managers must frequently receive plays to which this system might with advantage be applied; but who has ever attempted it? I do not remember a single instance, and even if one or two can be adduced, the *system* certainly does not exist. The result is that plays which might otherwise be of great value are condemned to obscurity—and not only plays, but their authors along with them.[1]

[1] Mr. Merivale writes:—"Believe me that I do not write as a 'disappointed greengrocer,' for I have written very few plays, which have all been acted (with one or two just finished exceptions which have been paid for). But many are sent me, and I read many. And on the strength of them I will undertake to say that if there were any 'system' in English theatrical management whatsoever by which the work of unfledged but promising dramatists were placed for 'collaboration' in older and abler hands by the managers to whom it was submitted, with the necessary security of production, we should have English playwrights by the score, as French ones grew up in France under the shadow and help of Scribe. But it is of no use. I read somewhere the other day of the despair of Mr. and Mrs. Bancroft over the MSS. submitted to them. The other day, a dramatist—not untried either—sent me the sketch of what struck me as a most admirable play. I advised him to send it at once to the Haymarket, where they said they wanted one. He answered that between ourselves he had done so, and they saw nothing in it they could use. It was pure modern comedy. Desirous of confirmation in my opinion, I got the sketch shown to Mr. Boucicault, and he said it was a most admirable plot. And so everywhere."

And now to return to Mr. Merivale, to whom the latter part of this digression has no particular relevance.

After opening his career with one or two unimportant adaptations, Mr. Merivale made his first considerable effort in "Time and the Hour," produced at the New Queen's Theatre in 1868. It is a rather crude melodrama, in which the confession of a crime by the criminal in a state of somnambulism, which afterwards produced such great effect in the "The Bells," forms the catastrophe. There are some happy touches of dialogue, and the cockneyism of one of the characters is made to afford amusement much more dexterously, one might almost say legitimately, than is usually the case. But the plot is commonplace and full of impossibilities, and altogether the play can scarcely pretend to rank as a literary production. Its cast, by the way, was remarkably strong, including Mr. John Clayton, Mr. J. L. Toole, Mr. Lionel Brough, Mr. Alfred Wigan, Mr. H. Standing, Mr. W. H. Stephens, Mr. Gaston Murray, Miss Henrietta Hodson, and Miss Nelly Moore.

An adaptation of Ponsard's "Le Lion Amoureux," under the title of "A Son of the Soil," was Mr. Merivale's next work, produced at the Court Theatre, in 1872. Unfortunately the adapter fell into the trap laid for him by the author, and wrote a considerable part of the play in blank-verse, which detracts from its reality and ruins its movement. Ponsard may have been right in choosing verse as his medium. I have not sufficient appreciation of the advantages and disadvantages of French Alexandrines to form an opinion on the subject. But in English there can be little doubt that the application of verse to a theme so prosaic as that of "Le Lion Amoureux" is a great error. Neither Martel nor Beatrice has a single thought to express which could not equally well have been couched in plain prose, while the use of the verse tempts the adapter into exaggerated tirades, which have their counterpart in the French, no doubt, but become doubly questionable in English. Mr. Merivale has since shown us that he can write excellent and genuinely impassioned prose; and surely a passage like the following would have been much more effective in that natural vehicle of expression:—

Martel. That a man,
Other than I, should live to be your lord,
Makes my blood boil within me! I am jealous
Of who comes near you—could have struck down dead,
Here where he stood, that fool who kissed your hand!
Why do you wear that dress—why fall so low?
Leave such things to the shameless, you whose crown
Of glory is your spotless purity!
That you should let a man see you like that!
(BEATRICE *moves.*)
Oh, pardon me, I knew not what I said!
But I no longer know myself, my brain
Is turning. Hardened soldier as I am,
I tell you I could find it in my heart
To throw myself down at your feet, and *cry!*
Beat. Don't speak like that. Louis, you frighten me,
It is no fault of mine, indeed, *indeed,*
If I was pledged before I met with you.

Cannot you like a woman—as a friend,
Without this passionate and violent love?
Listen, my friend, my dear friend. You will let me
Give you that name? Some one is coming. Hush!

The school-boy exercise of paraphrasing blank-verse in prose, if applied to this passage, would improve it, besides giving it a much better chance of being properly spoken on the stage. Whatever may be the case in France, in England it is much better to have poetry without verse than verse without poetry. That should be the motto of the English "school of good sense." Moreover, a modern play, composed partly of verse and partly of prose is a hybrid monstrosity which not even the authority of Shakespeare can excuse. As regards construction, Mr. Merivale follows Ponsard pretty faithfully, with the exception of a modification of the conclusion which is perhaps more ingenious than judicious.

Next on Mr. Merivale's roll we find "Alone," produced at the Court in 1873. This play has a pathetic and well-imagined subject. A father has been estranged from his only daughter under a false belief in her misconduct, and has afterwards become blind. The daughter introduces herself under an assumed name into his house, as reader and housekeeper, and ultimately succeeds in overcoming the bitterness with which he regards her, and in convincing him of her innocence. The theme strikes one as admirably adapted for a short idyllic play in two acts, something in the tone of the first scene of the second act of "Alone," as it actually stands, in which the daughter is represented reading aloud from

"King Lear" to her blind father. Unfortunately, as it seems to me, the authors have extended it to three acts and tried to make it strong and lively as well as pathetic. The result is a strain of probabilities, a repetition of similar situations, a style of dialogue which is constantly verging upon the "comedy of no-manners," and a sacrifice of consistency and truth of character. This is especially felt in the case of the blind father, Colonel Challice. The character is evidently intended to be sympathetic—at any rate it is not satirical. But our sympathy is destroyed, firstly by the unreasoning and cruel bitterness of his feeling towards his daughter, whose supposed fault, at the very worst, bore no resemblance to the enormities of Regan and Goneril; secondly, by his treatment of the parasite, Stratton Strawless, whom he permits to remain about him as a sort of butt for the arrows of his misanthropy. His toleration of the coarse vulgarity of Strawless greatly lessens our esteem for him, and the outspoken rudeness with which he meets it rather heightens than softens the unpleasant effect. There is some clever dialogue in the play, however, and several of the scenes are effective on the stage. It has been more than once revived since its original production.

We now come to "The White Pilgrim," the first of the three plays upon which, as yet, Mr. Merivale's reputation is mainly founded. It was produced at the Court Theatre in the spring of 1874.

Among those amateurs of the drama who have seen and remember everything, "The White Pilgrim," now almost forgotten by the general public, is a sort of superstition, believed in much more devoutly in England than it ever was in Mr. Merivale's Finland. Time after time at the mention of Mr. Merivale's name, I have been met by the inquiry, "Have you seen 'The White Pilgrim?'" followed by its eulogy as the finest of modern poetical dramas. Unfortunately I have *not* seen "The White Pilgrim," and this fact must be taken into account in connexion with the remarks I have to make upon it. The play may be, and no doubt is, very picturesque and effective on the stage, aided by proper accessories of scenery, costume, music, and what may be called theatrical chiar'oscuro. But a literary work—and a "tragedy," for so the author does not hesitate to call it, must surely be a literary work—should remain erect without theset rappings. The silk gowns of our great-grandmothers could stand alone, it is said, but so could the women inside them. A good figure does not depend for support upon its stays.

Let me not be understood to say that it does not merit its reputation. It is certainly one of the best, perhaps the very best, poetical play of the past ten years. It contains numerous and striking beauties, and it proves in Mr. Merivale the existence of the real poet, which most poetical plays disprove in their authors. It is only when tried by a really lofty standard that it falls short, and the fact that it suggests and even demands that lofty standard is in itself sufficient proof of its merits as compared with most contemporary productions.

It has two great faults, the first of motive, the second

of detail, but at the same time in a measure connected with each other. The first is a vagueness, a lack of definition, in the supernatural machinery, which gives to the events of the play a fortuitous character, depriving them, as it were of background, or more properly of foundation. My meaning is difficult to express, but will perhaps become clearer if I give a short account of the action. Harold, a young lord of Finland, is represented as of weak character, vacillating between good, embodied in a Christian lady, Thordisa, whom he loves, and evil in the person of a deformed Pagan knight, Sigurd, who has been his guardian and monitor from childhood. At the opening of the play Thordisa resumes her beneficent sway over him, after a lover's quarrel, but unfortunately she is forced to leave upon a distant pilgrimage, which will occupy a month. Sigurd, after trying in vain to get Harold to return to a drinking-bout with their boon-companions, taunts him with Thordisa's empire over him, and declares that it has made him degenerate from the manly virtues, or vices, of his fathers. To clinch his taunts he dares him to repeat the oath once taken by his ancestor, Earl Olaf. This terrible oath was uttered at a time when there was war between Finland and Normandy. After invoking various heathen deities and sanctities, it winds up as follows :—

Ere the world's unmeasured bound
Once the sun hath travelled round,
Should but foot of Norman fall
In the shadow of my wall,

Yonder moon of silver stain
Shall not wane and wax again,
Ere with sure and secret blow
I will lay that Norman low!
By mine own hand he shall die,
Meed of Norman perjury!
If he fall not so, then Death
Call for me that break my faith!
Hear mine oath, and mark it well,
Be my witness, Death and Hell!

Scarcely has he uttered the oath, when the White Pilgrim, emblem of death, crosses the stage unseen, and a trumpet blast is heard outside the castle. On the gates being opened, there enter the Lord Hugo and his wife Lady Isabelle, just shipwrecked on the coast in a vessel from Normandy.

The three remaining acts occur a month later, just as the time is running out within which Harold has sworn to slay his guest. Harold, in a state of despair, feeling himself delivered over to the powers of evil, and for ever shut out from Thordisa and goodness, has fallen in love with Lady Isabelle. Sigurd and his own guilty passion prompt him to fulfil his vow and murder Hugo, while the remnants of good in his nature, and his memory of Thordisa, force him to forbear. At this juncture Thordisa returns, and despite Harold's faithlessness, devotes herself to saving him from committing the crime, even at the cost of the penalty he has invoked upon himself. In this she of course ultimately succeeds. His love for her returns in all its force, and Hugo and Isabelle are suffered to depart scatheless. Scarcely have they done so when—

The bell strikes one, and the WHITE PILGRIM *appears. Both pause, chilled and horror-stricken. The* PILGRIM *advances.*

Har. (*dazed*). I do not know that form.

Tho. Ah, God, I do!

Har. (*facing the* PILGRIM, *who has come down between them.* THORDISA *has fallen back*).

Yes, it is coming. I am not afraid.
Why, this is sleep—no worse: who art thou, then?
What is thy message?

Pil. To the restless—rest!

(*Unveils to* HAROLD, *who sinks at her feet.* THORDISA *springs forward, as the veil closes again.*)

Tho. Harold!

Har. Why, Death is not so hard as Life.
'Tis better so, belovèd, better so! (*Dies.*)

Tho. Oh, not alone! Dear Spirit, look on me!
I know my heart is breaking, is it not?
For if it were not, it were worse than stone.
I must go hence: I will not stay behind!
Sweet Spirit, let me not! unite us now
In the one union we may ever know—
We that so loved each other! Oh, draw back
The envious curtain that enfolds you both,
And let me see the face behind the veil!
(*Triumphantly.*) My heart is broken!

Pil. (*unveiling to* THORDISA). Like a tired child!

(THORDISA *sinks down by* HAROLD'S *side.*)

Tho. Darling, you will not be a stranger there! (*Dies.*)

Perhaps the something which is lacking in this theme

may be most shortly described as *tragische Schuld*, though that does not precisely express my meaning. The whole play turns upon a coincidence—Sigurd's whim of egging Harold on to repeat Earl Olaf's rather unmeaning oath, followed by the chance arrival of the Norman guests. True, the tragedy of real life turns upon such coincidences, and it is an open question whether the artist is or is not permitted to make free use of them. But it is not real life which Mr. Merivale is representing. It is a fantastic world which we can only grant the artist on condition that he takes full advantage of the licence allowed him. We suspect the hand of the gods behind these coincidences, but we should be allowed to see it. In a drama of real life to show us the finger of fate is to falsify the picture, since we know that fate, if it exists at all, is invisible on the small scale of individual human life. But in a world arranged by fantasy, we demand to see the workings of the mills of God. Since we accept the supernatural in the appearances of the "White Pilgrim," we could with no more effort, indeed with less, accept a complete and adequate supernatural machinery—I do not mean in bodily form, of course, but clearly and logically visible in its effects. Even the inherited Fate of the wildest German *Schicksals-Tragödie* would give the drama a basis which it at present lacks. It hangs like Mahomet's coffin, apart from the natural and yet not entirely in the supernatural. It should not have been difficult for Mr. Merivale to have taken a bolder flight while he was about it. He has suggested vaguely in the fact of Thordisa's Christianity and Sigurd's heathenism what might perhaps have served as the germ of an adequate motive for the tragedy. Harold, wavering between the two faiths, migh have fallen a victim to the wrath of the departing gods of his house, driven out by the fated encroachments of the new faith. I offer the suggestion, not as in itself good, or even feasible, but as illustrating my conception of the species of groundwork which is lacking to the play.

The error of detail to which I have referred, springs from the same source. Mr. Merivale places his drama in Finland, a perfectly definite locality, refers to Normandy, an equally definite and better known region, and gives his characters Scandinavian or at any rate Teutonic names. It would have been much wiser to have invented a land "east of the sun and west of the moon" for his fantasy, or at any rate to have placed it in one of the realms of romance which the poets have invented for him so plentifully. True, most of us do not know very much more about Finland than about Fairyland—but we all have this negative knowledge, that at the time of the introduction of Christianity into Finland the state of society had not the remotest resemblance to that represented by Mr. Merivale, which is Arthurian and not in the least Scandinavian; while Finland itself, be it noted, was more Slavonic than Scandinavian, probably with a strong intermixture of Turanian race. But even if we take "Finland" to denote vaguely some part of Scandinavia, as Mr. Merivale, from his names and his mythological allusions, apparently means that we should, his representation of society only becomes more glaringly false, since most of us have more or less definite ideas of the beginnings of Scandinavian civilization. This contrast between the nomenclature of the play and its matter obtrudes itself upon us in the lighter passages, between Rolf and Gerda, the faithful followers of Harold and Thordisa respectively. In the very first scene we have the following touches :—

Rolf. I took you for an angel.
Gerda. So I am,
Or so you used to say.
Rolf. Yes, so I did,
And so I do, and so I always will,
Till better knowledge kill the simile.

And again :—

Rolf. Mock me as you will,
I yet will draw you to my lure some day,
Or else may the White Pilgrim call for me.
Gerda. What's that?
Rolf. A legend in my family.
Gerda. You have a family and make love to me?
Rolf. My master's family is to me as mine.
I spoke in metaphor.
Gerda. Let that alone;
Plain speaking suits you better.

These two scraps of dialogue may stand as specimens of a great deal of commonplace—I had almost said vulgar—banter between these two characters, occasionally assisted by Sigurd, which would deface the play were it located in the Mountains of the Moon. Strange that Mr. Merivale should not see that a tasteless play upon the word "family" is out of keeping with the whole tone of his poem—for a poem it should be. But the fact that these personages are supposed to be pagan or half-Christianized Scandinavians, makes doubly ludicrous this discussion of "similes" and "metaphors." The Northmen spoke in metaphors, but they did not know what they were.

Otherwise the style of the play is excellent, and the blank-verse is of an order much superior to the ordinary blank-verse of the modern English stage. Take as a specimen the following extract from the White Pilgrim's address to Thordisa:—

> Miscall me not! ye know not what I am,
> But ye shall see me face to face, and know!
> I take all sorrows from the sorrowful,
> And teach the joyful what it is to joy.
> I gather in my land-locked harbour's clasp
> The shattered vessels of a vexèd world,
> And even the tiniest ripple upon life
> Is, to that calm sublime, as tropic storm.
> When other leech-craft fails the breaking brain,
> I, only, own the anodyne to still
> Its eddies into visionless repose.
> The face, distorted with life's latest pang,
> I smooth, in passing, with an angel wing;
> And from beneath the quiet eyelids steal
> The hidden glory of the eyes, to give
> A new and nobler beauty to the rest.
> Belie me not; the plagues that walk the Earth,
> The wasting pain, the sudden agony,
> Famine, and War, and Pestilence, and all
> The terrors that have darkened round my name,
> These are the works of Life, they are not mine,

Vex when I tarry, vanish when I come,
Instantly melting into perfect peace,
As at His word, whose master-spirit I am,
The troubled waters slept on Galilee.
Tender I am, not cruel : when I take
The shape most hard to human eyes, and pluck
The little baby-blossom yet unblown,
'Tis but to graft it on a kindlier stem,
And, leaping o'er the perilous years of growth,
Unswept of sorrow, and unscathed of wrong,
Clothe it at once with rich maturity.
'Tis I that give a soul to memory;
For round the follies of the bad I throw
The mantle of a kind forgetfulness ;
But, canonized in dear Love's calendar,
I sanctify the good for evermore.
Miscall me not ! my generous fulness lends
Home to the homeless, to the friendless friends;
To the starved babe, the mother's tender breast,
Wealth to the poor, and to the restless—rest !

The opening scene, with its psalm from the chapel alternating with a convivial strain from the banquet-hall, recalls a saying of the elder Dumas—I quote from memory—that Victor Hugo always needed tombs, dirges, and drinking-songs for his dramatic effects, while all that he, Dumas *père*, required, was a stage, four walls, and a human passion. Mr. Merivale may plead that it is better to err with Hugo than shine with Dumas ; but, authority apart, there is something melodramatic, or worse, operatic, in such an opening, which may be effective but is meretricious. The drinking-song itself, however, has a

Horatian echo which proves Mr. Merivale to be a facile, if not very original lyrist:—

Ha, ha, ha! the rich wine flashes
Ruby red:
There's no heat in dead men's ashes;
They are dead:
Just a while, for love and laughter
Lasts the light;
Seize the day! what follows after
Is the night!

Ha, ha, ha! the grass grows greenly
From the tomb;
And the night winds whistle keenly
Through the gloom:
Deep our draught, our slumber deep is;
Let us fill
To the dead, whose sober sleep is
Deeper still!

"A Tale of Two Cities," one of the most mannered and least spontaneous of Charles Dickens' works, contains towards the close some passages which deserve to rank with his very best. The book belongs, as every one knows, to the later period of his life when "the good genie of modern fiction," under the influence of Mr. Wilkie Collins, paid much greater attention to the dramatic construction of his work than in his earlier and more naïve stage. It is not wonderful, then, that the material for a good drama should have been found in "A Tale of Two Cities," and especially in its concluding chapters. At the same time Mr. Merivale did wisely in merely using the motive and not attempting to dramatize the book. The drama of the French Revolution yet remains to be written. Mere individual episodes thrown against that vast and lurid background are apt to be dwarfed by it. In "All for Her" Mr. Merivale has chosen a smaller and simpler stage on which to make his figures move. A domestic drama is more in proportion with the Rebellion of '45 than with the Reign of Terror.

And an excellent play it is, the least faulty if not the best of all Mr. Merivale's works. It is romantic without bombast, and a little romance now and then is very refreshing. The character of Hugh Trevor, the Sidney Carton of the drama, is of a type for which Mr. Merivale seems to have a certain predilection, since he has in another instance been very successful with a somewhat similar personage—Sir Horace Welby in "Forget-me-Not." A fine nature shining through a mask of cynicism and even of misanthropy has again and again been made effective on the stage, but seldom more so than in Hugh Trevor. He is a much more living and solid figure than the Robertsonian cynics, all cast in one mould, who were so popular a few years ago. Mr. Gilbert, in "The Ne'er do Well," made a similar attempt, but with very indifferent success. Indeed, we must go to the novelists or to the French drama to find an equally successful character of the type. Moreover, the intrigue of "All for Her" is strengthened by an ingenious sub-plot, intimately welded into the main action, which, in the second act especially, leads to some very effective scenes.

I am not so sure of the judiciousness of the part played by Mary Rivers in the drama. It is perhaps carrying the romantic a little too far, not to mention that, in point of taste, a woman masquerading in male attire is always questionable. One of the motives for her introduction is no doubt to let her replace to a certain extent the seamstress of Dickens' story, by whom the pathos of the catastrophe is so skilfully heightened.

"Citizen Evrémonde," she said, touching him with her cold hand, "I am a poor little seamstress who was with you in La Force."

He murmured for answer, "True. I forget what you were accused of?"

"Plots. Though the just Heaven knows I am innocent of any. Is it likely? Who would think of plotting with a poor weak little creature like me?"

The forlorn smile with which she said it so touched him that the tears started from his eyes.

"I am not afraid to die, Citizen Evrémonde, but I have done nothing. I am not unwilling to die if the Republic, which is to do so much good for us poor, will profit by my death; but I do not know how that can be, Citizen Evrémonde. Such a poor, weak little creature!"

As the last thing on earth that his heart was to warm and soften to, it warmed and softened to this pitiable girl.

"I heard you were released, Citizen Evrémonde. I hoped it was true?"

"It was. But, I was again taken and condemned."

"If I may ride with you, Citizen Evrémonde, will you let me hold your hand? I am not afraid, but I am little and weak, and it will give me more courage."

As the patient eyes were lifted to his face, he saw a sudden doubt in them, and then astonishment. He pressed the work-worn, hunger-worn young fingers, and touched his lips.

"Are you dying for him?" she whispered.

"And his wife and child. Hush! Yes."

"O you will let me hold your brave hand, stranger?"

"Hush! Yes, my poor sister; to the last."

The exquisite pathos of the little phrase "You will let me hold your brave hand, stranger," could only be reproduced in a precisely similar situation, which was clearly impossible in "All for Her." In comparison with the above passage Mr. Merivale's scene is very conventional and tame.

Mary. Lord Edendale!

Hugh. The boy Rivers! All is not safe yet! How came you here?

Mary. My lord, I am sent by Colonel Damer.—Ah! Hugh!

Hugh. Hush, for your life! I am Lord Edendale!

Mary. Ah! you are going to die for him! You shall not do it.

Hugh. Peace!

Mary. I cannot hold my peace. Here!

Hugh. Silence, I say. What right have you to question what I think fit to do?

Mary. What right! What right! The right of a woman who has loved you from a child. I am that Mary Rivers, whose life and honour you saved—and I will not let you die! Help!

Hugh. Listen to me for a moment, Mary Rivers. You have loved me, you say.

Mary. All my life!

Hugh. I charge you by that love, Mary, to be silent now! We shall meet, I pray, where I am going. There is mercy in that great hereafter, which I am soon to understand.

Mary. Oh! let me die with you!

It was of course necessary that Hugh Trevor should be recognized, else half the pathos of the catastrophe would have remained undeveloped; but I cannot help thinking that the recognition might have been brought about more neatly and effectively. There is this tantalizing circumstance in both the book and the play that the dramatic possibilities remain unexhausted, since the woman for whose sake the sacrifice is made never recognizes it, or rather can only recognize it after both book and play are ended. We feel that the drama *should* culminate in one flash of comprehension and recognition on Lady Marsden's part, of the crowning act of devotion that is being rendered her. It should be so arranged that for her to refuse the sacrifice would be useless, so that she can only convey her mute thanks to her adorer. This, I repeat, would be the culminating moment of the play—were it only possible, Unfortunately it is not, at any rate without a gigantic strain of probability. Even as it is probability is, sufficiently strained in the last act, which is, from the necessity of the case, structurally the weakest. We feel that Carlisle Gaol is conducted on very extraordinary principles, and under very lax regulations. Furthermore, the necessity for ending the play with a tableau instead of a situation is unfortunate, and Hugh Trevor's "last dying speech" is inartistic. It is taken from Dickens, who, however, only makes Sidney Carton think it. This of itself is improbable enough, for the emotions of a man in such a situation, could we only get at them, would, I think, be found to be of a kind untranslateable into any form of thought that can even mentally embody itself in words. His verbal thoughts, if I may use the expression, are probably occupied with the veriest trifles—the number of steps to the scaffold, the colour of the executioner's beard, or the ticking of the sheriff's watch.

The history of "Forget-me-not" is both interesting and instructive. It was originally written for Mr John Clayton, or at any rate the part of Sir Horace Welby was originally destined for him. For many years his influence and that of the authors—not to mention the merits of the play—were exerted in vain in the attempt to secure for it a hearing. At last Miss Geneviève Ward an American actress, happened to take the Lyceum for the autumn season with the view of securing a footing in London. Her first attempt proved disastrous, her second secured at best a success of esteem, and as a last resource at the end of her season, she determined to give "Forget-me-Not" a trial. The play was at once recognized by the critics as a very remarkable piece of work, but the fortunes of the theatre were beyond retrieval. Another lapse of several months occurred, and then a fortunate opening was found at the Prince of Wales's Theatre. The piece was adequately mounted, Mr. Clayton assumed the part originally intended for him, Miss Ward repeated her remarkable performance of the heroine, and adventitious circumstances, including an unwonted exertion of Royal patronage, secured for it a genuine success, financial and artistic. Thus it is merely the result of a series of happy chances, that "Forget-me-Not" is not at the present moment reposing in Mr. Merivale's desk, or at best remembered by a few theatrical enthusiasts as a clever piece thrown away upon the barren soil of an autumn season.

Such is the external history of the play. Let us now attempt to trace its probable genesis and development, always an interesting task in the case of any serious play. Mr. Merivale has had for collaborator a Mr. F. C. Grove, otherwise unknown, I believe, in the theatrical world. This gentleman, one may guess without too much rashness, probably suggested the theme, whose germ evidently lies in Article 148 of the Code Napoleon, which provides that a son under twenty-five cannot legally contract marriage without the consent of his parents, while it is also provided that the parents must formally impugn the marriage within a year of its coming to their knowledge—otherwise it is valid for all time. In the difficulties and anomalies which might clearly arise from such provisions there lay the evident material for a drama. The question was what form the drama should take. And now the authors imagined a striking dramatic contrast and a novel catastrophe. The contrast was that between a type of pure and graceful English maidenhood, and a Ninon de l'Enclos, the ever-youthful and ever dangerous Circe of a French aristocratic gambling-hell. The catastrophe was brought about by the use of abject physical fear as a dramatic motive. Stephanie de Mohrivart, *alias* Forget-me-Not, holds Alice Verney under her thumb, through her power to impugn the marriage of Alice's sister Rose with her son, the Vicomte de Brissac, who had died a few months after the marriage. This power she holds *in terrorem* over Alice to force her to ruin her own character and position by introducing the notorious Forget-me-Not into Roman society under the sanction of the Verney name. And now comes a very cleverly imagined complication. There arrives in Rome a certain Sir Horace Welby, a rolling-stone who has gathered a good deal of moss, and an old friend and warm admirer of Alice Verney. He sees that something is weighing upon Miss Verney's mind, and is all anxiety to aid and protect her—when the skeleton in the cupboard suddenly confronts him in the person of Forget-me-Not, whom he has known only too well in her old Parisian days. Without precisely knowing the circumstances of the case, he undertakes to rid Alice of her tyranny, and in the battle that ensues between him and Forget-me-Not lies the main action of the play. At first he is routed at all points—materially by the revelation of Stephanie's power, as the mother of the husband, to annul the marriage of Alice's sister; morally by Stephanie's only too plausible demand to know by what right he, Sir Horace Welby, assumes the position of a protector of virtue and innocence.

Sir H. What do you mean to do?

Ste. To stay in this house, and go into the world with Alice, as her dearest friend, for six weeks.

Sir H. At the end of that time the marriage will be valid and by your own showing you can do no harm. What can a woman with your antecedents do to gain a position in six weeks?

Ste. With the countenance of the Verneys, everything. The world will believe them, when they declare, as they will, how misrepresented I have been. . . . After all, is what I ask so very terrible? I promise to be as good as gold, as pure as ice, as intensely respectable as poor old Foley. I shall do your Alice no harm.

Sir H. No harm! Why your very presence is an insult to her! Your incarnate wickedness poisons the air she breathes, as your schemes darken her beautiful and upright life. If you stay in the house with her for six weeks, she will droop and wither like a blighted tree. Oh, Alice! my Alice! I would die to save you a passing pain, and I cannot sweep this contamination from your path!

Ste. No, you cannot; and you shall not. You shall have cause to remember these words that you have said to me. I will sit at you darling's table, and sleep in your darling's arms. She shall be kind to me, and fond and loving, and shall learn to look to me for guidance and example. I will distil into her, drop by drop, the lessons that men have taught me. I will disclose to her, little by little, the sort of life that is led by sensitive lovers like you—you, who talk about blight and contamination to the partners of your luxuries, the victims of your selfishness, the playthings of your pleasure! Is there no blight, no contamination, that a past like yours would throw upon the baby-innocence that you would link with it? Why may a man live two lives, while a woman must stand or fall by one? What was the difference between us two, Sir Horace Welby, in those bygone years, that should make me now a leper, and you a priest? that should give you the right to say to me, "You are Vice, and I am Virtue! sin on, or I damn you?" Who and what are you, that you should dare to talk like this? There would be no place in creation for such women as I, if it were not for such men as you! . . . . I have listened once to you, I shall do so no more. Alice, I say, shall be my dearest friend, and you my very humble slave and servant to command. Talk to me again as you have done to-day—try to thwart me in this matter—yield me before the world one jot less deference than you would pay to the proudest gentlewoman you know, and I swear to you by the dome of St. Peter's there, that I'll drive that pale beauty of yours into a convent, or into the Tiber. Have you anything to answer now, most crafty baronet? No! as I expected, dumb.

This is what specially pleases me in the play. The authors have not been contented with working up their dramatic material, but have ingeniously, yet naturally, made it relevant to a great moral problem of the day, or rather of all civilized time. In this respect it stands almost alone in the modern English drama, though it has counterparts in every serious work of the great French dramatists. I am not concerned with the justice or injustice of the sarcasms which Stephanie flings in Sir Horace's teeth, or of the answer to them which is shortly afterwards placed in the mouth of Alice Verney. I regard the latter especially as pretty sophistries, all the more natural from their logical feebleness.[1] But that is not the question. The stage should not attempt dog-

[1] A considerable portion of them is suppressed in representation, probably as being too advanced for audiences who insist on judging dramatic utterance in itself, apart from its fitness in the situation.

matically to solve moral problems, but should be content to suggest, pose, and lightly discuss them, as they are suggested, posed, and lightly discussed in every-day real life. We may draw our own most serious conclusions from what we see on the stage, but it is not the business of the dramatist to draw them for us through the mouths of his characters. In "Forget-me-Not" this distinction is kept clearly in view. The dramatic interest is intimately welded with an ethical interest, which, however, is never suffered unduly to preponderate. The symmetry of the play is excellent.

Thus, up to the last scene of the second act, Stephanie is triumphant, when chance places under Sir Horace's hand the one piece in the whole human chess-board by which he can checkmate her. Only a short time previously the name of Mohrivart had been rendered doubly notorious throughout Europe by the tragic death of Stephanie's husband, the old Marquis. Among the victims of their gambling-hell was a Corsican named Benedetto Francini, who had been entrapped by a skilfully encouraged passion for the wife to lose all his money to the husband. As soon as he was reduced to beggary he was ignominiously driven from the house, and saw how cruelly he had been duped. One night he returned and murdered the Marquis, but failed to carry out the principal aim of his revenge, namely the murder of Stephanie, who escaped with a slight wound. He was condemned to the galleys for life, and Stephanie was thus relieved from all fear of his vengeance. But at the end of the second act, Sir Horace Welby recognizes in

Barrato, a Roman police spy whom he has had occasion to employ, the veritable Benedetto Francini, who has been permitted to escape from Toulon owing to his conduct in assisting the authorities to suppress a rising of the convicts. His desire for vengeance upon Stephanie would be as strong as ever, but that he believes her to be dead. This information causes Stephanie, in the last act, to fall, by one blow, from the summit of arrogant confidence to the depth of abject terror. Sir Horace points out that if she insists on remaining in Rome, Francini cannot fail to learn that she is still alive, even without any action on his (Sir Horace's) part, Stephanie accedes to all the terms proposed, formally recognizes the marriage, and makes a precipitate escape, the effect of the conclusion being worked up by means which, if a trifle theatrical, are so telling as to form their own sufficient excuse.

So ends a play which is not only good in comparison with the general run of original English dramas, but is absolutely and in itself an interesting and powerful work. Yet it is very far from being faultless. Its construction opens some very interesting questions. The secret of Stephanie's power over Alice is carefully kept from the audience until towards the end of the second act, that is, for more than half the play. Such a proceeding is against all established rules of dramatic construction, but in the present instance I am not prepared to condemn it, or even to assert that it is not absolutely one of the merits of the play. A still more difficult question lies in the occasional violations of probability necessitated by the author's determination to bring the whole action into one scene. This is a course for which, personally, I confess to an extreme weakness. The commercial value of a play, I believe, is undoubtedly injured by its confinement to one scene, since the ignoble vulgar demand "for their money" at least three elaborate sets, as gorgeous as Tottenham Court Road can make them—and the ignoble vulgar in this respect are to be found in the stalls as well as in the pit. But surely even the most ardent devotee of stage furniture should have been satisfied for one evening with the solidly and tastefully mounted Roman salon with its view over the Ludovisi Gardens, in which the play was put on at the Prince of Wales's. Of the gain in closeness, crispness, and symmetry of action which usually goes along with concentration upon one scene, I have not thc smallest doubt. But it is a question whether these advantages are not dearly bought at the price of such anomalies as, for instance, the appearance of Barrato in the Verney's drawing-room, in Act I. It is a question on which my own mind is divided, so I content myself with stating it without further discussion.

On the other hand there cannot, I think, be any doubt that the so-called lighter passages of the play are very much beneath the level of the rest. "Comic relief"—a term which suggests though it does not cover a multitude of sins in the English drama—is afforded by a companion of Miss Verney, Mrs. Foley, and a certain Prince

Malleotti, who is conceived in a spirit of outrageous and grotesque caricature. He talks a dialect such as no foreigner ever dreamt of, but much more closely related to French than to Italian. His strained vulgarisms, whether of compliment or of impertinence, are wearisome as well as inartistic. In the last act the authors absolutely make him drunk in Miss Verney's drawing-room—surely a gratuitous insult to the Roman aristocracy. It is true that the offensiveness of the character was almost always exaggerated in performance, English comedians having apparently a rooted conviction that all foreign noblemen have something defective about their shoulders and elbow-joints. But the authors had laid down only too clearly the lines upon which the actors' farcical conceptions were built. A blot of such dimensions upon a play otherwise so excellent is very much to be regretted.

Two other serious plays by Mr. Merivale remain to be considered, both founded on material supplied by Goethe.

One of Uhland's ballads describes how a serving-man has murdered his noble lord, for "the serving-man himself would fain be a knight." He sinks the body in the Rhine, puts on his master's armour, and mounts his gallant charger. But, as he is riding across the bridge, the horse shies, rears, and flings him off into the swift river. He struggles and swims with all his might, but the heavy armour drags him to the bottom. One is reminded of this legend by the relations of some of our dramatists to Goethe. A busy fiend seems to be perpetually whispering in their ears how easy it would be to "convert" his intellectual trappings to their own use. They yield to the temptation and, I will not say murder, but at least maim the Master, and appropriate his stories and characters. But his steed is too fiery for them, his panoply too heavy. Their presumption invariably ends in half-tragic, half-ludicrous discomfiture.

Mr. Gilbert attempted to "dramatize" Faust in "Gretchen," Mr. Merivale tried to modernize it in "The Cynic." The latter was not quite such a deadly failure as the former, because it appealed more strongly to the modern public, and, though at least equally faulty in conception, was greatly superior in execution. Yet it was distinctly a failure; and this, in spite of the great ingenuity and pains which had evidently been expended on the characters and dialogue, was natural and inevitable. Is it possible to conceive a satisfactory adaptation to modern life of the story of Faust? Miss Thackeray has fancifully paraphrased our nursery tales in the form of modern novelettes; but, on the one hand, much is possible in narrative which is impossible on the stage; and, on the other hand, the characters with which she had to deal were mere abstractions, lay-figures, dreams or allegories, not beings into whom one of the poets of all time has once for all infused the very breath of life. We have no very definite preconception as to the character of the last Mrs. Bluebeard, and are not likely to be shocked at any rational filling-in of the vague outlines provided in the original tale. But Margarete we know intimately and warmly love, so that a pseudo-Margarete strikes us at once as an impostor. She is at best a caricature, at worst a profanation. If Mr. Gilbert's disappointed monk and moralizing maiden were inferior to Goethe's creations, how much more do Mr. Merivale's lackadaisical and utterly unprincipled lover and flirting grass-widow seem insignificant, not to say contemptible, beside them! For, of course, all excuse for Faucit's wickedness, and therefore all sympathy with his character, has disappeared with the supernatural agency which leads his prototype on, so that we merely despise instead of pitying him; while Daisy Brent's narrow escape from falling from a state of anything but innocence, is profoundly uninteresting to us. On the other hand, Satan Lestrange, the counterpart of Mephistopheles, is an effective enough though somewhat conventional figure; but even his part is spoiled by the semi-supernaturalism, the pseudo-omniscience with which he is invested. Such timid attempts at compromise are at once far less effective and far more incredible than a bold and frank use of the supernatural.

From Goethe, too, was borrowed "The Lord of the Manor," produced with scant success at the Imperial Theatre early in 1880. It was avowedly suggested by "Wilhelm Meister's Apprenticeship," but the scene was removed to England, and various other modifications were necessarily introduced. There is a dramatic element in Goethe's great novel which must often have attracted dramatists, but there are difficulties in dealing with it which must almost as often have frightened them away from it. I do not know whether it has ever been popular on the German stage, and its operatic popularity is no criterion of its value for the non-musical stage. However, the characters of Philina, Laertes, Wilhelm, and above all, Mignon, together with the dramatic motive of the struggle between Philina and Mignon for Wilhelm's love, seemed to Mr. Merivale too tempting to be neglected. Unfortunately Mignon, though one of the most beautiful, is one of the wildest of poetic creations. The motive and meaning of her character lie in the horrible circumstances of her birth, which for obvious reasons cannot be made use of on the stage. Mr. Merivale's Sybil was consequently devoid of the element of unearthliness which, in the novel, raises her history into the region of the highest poetry. She was merely an earthly child stolen by mountebanks, and consequently came dangerously near the limits of melodrama. The same remark applies to "Crazy Dick," the terribly disenchanted form in which Mr. Merivale presented Goethe's Harper. As for the romantic Wilhelm Meister, whether by the author's intention or by the fault of the actor entrusted with the part, he became a middle-aged and staid country squire. On the whole, it was evident that Mr. Merivale had undertaken a hopeless task, and the excellent touches of dialogue which the play contained did not avail to retrieve its fate.

Three other lighter productions remain to be noticed. "Peacock's Holiday" is an adaptation of Labiche's "Voyage de M. Perrichon," and retains a good deal of the profound knowledge of human nature whose cynicism the great French humourist veils under a cloak of irresistible fun. But Labiche, perhaps unavoidably, loses enormously in adaptation to the English stage. It is difficult to recognize in "A Phenomenon in a Smock Frock" the subtle humour of "Le Misanthrope et l'Auvergnat;" and "Peacock's Holiday," if it has not suffered quite so much in transplantation, gives but a feeble idea of "Le Voyage de M. Perrichon." Mr. Merivale's dialogue, however, is very bright; and the same may be said in an even greater degree of his brilliant little farce "A Husband in Clover." Throughout this rapid duologue the wit is unflagging, and just sufficiently strained to suit the pleasant extravagance of the action. Lastly, a word with reference to Mr. Merivale's one excursion into burlesque, "The Lady of Lyons Married and Settled," produced at the Gaiety in 1878. The idea is an excellent one. No play that ever was written lends itself so readily to burlesque, and there is none that one need have less compunction in burlesquing. The execution of the idea, though occasionally marred by the exigencies of the theatre and company for which it was destined, is full of genuine humour, and seldom degenerates into childishness. Still I, for one, do not regret that this is the only burlesque—he himself entitles it a "vaudeville"—included in Mr. Merivale's list.

As I write, there are rumours of several new plays shortly to be expected from Mr. Merivale's pen, one of them being a dramatization of "The Bride of Lammermoor," officially promised at the Lyceum. It is understood, moreover, that Mr. Merivale, after a long illness which he has recently suffered, has given up his practice at the bar, and intends to devote himself entirely to literature. If his coming works answer to the promise of those I have here imperfectly reviewed, this resolution should be one of good omen for the English drama.

MR. ARTHUR W. PINERO.

THERE have been people who have held that no one but an actor can write a good acting play. Such a position is clearly absurd, but it is nevertheless true that an actor's practical experience of the stage often assists him in producing pieces which are effective behind the footlights. Mr. Pinero, according to his own account, was a dramatic author before he was an actor, having written a three-act comedy at some fabulously early age; but he was an actor long before he was a successful author. After serving his apprenticeship in the provinces, mainly at Edinburgh, he joined Mr. Irving's company at the Lyceum. Here he had an opportunity of producing one or two short and bright opening-pieces, of which "Daisy's Escape" and "Bygones" dwell in my memory as happy blendings of humour and pathos. Another one-act piece, produced at the Folly under the title of "Hester's Mystery," dealt with a rather dangerous theme, but dealt with it cleverly. It is, however, on his three-act plays that Mr. Pinero's reputation rests. Each of these shows sufficient promise to warrant a hope that we have in their author a playwright of genuine talent, whose more mature work will take a prominent and honourable place upon the stage in coming years. Consequently I need not apologize for the following study, though it may seem more detailed than the importance of the plays justifies. A searching criticism is often the highest compliment which can be paid to a piece. To break a butterfly on the wheel is not only absurd but impossible. A play must have bone and muscle in it before it can afford any material for the dissecting-knife.

I have spoken of Mr. Pinero's "three-act plays," for "The Money-Spinner," though produced in London in two acts, was originally a three-act play, and should, I think, have retained that form. The first act, in Baron Croodle's gambling saloon, would have sufficed to render clearer and more conceivable the relation between Millicent and Lord Kengussie, and might even have placed in a more consistent light the character of Harold Boycott. I use the conditional mood in speaking of this first act, for I have not seen that which Mr. Pinero actually wrote, as it has only been played in the provinces. It may not have fulfilled the ends indicated, but there is no reason why it should not. Leaving this apart, however, let us look at the play as it was placed on the stage at the St. James's Theatre, with the original first act suppressed.

In the first place, then, the wonder is that with such an unsympathetic theme, Mr. Pinero has succeeded in producing such a sympathetic play. Its matter is open to criticism at almost every point. The expedient of making Harold Boycott embezzle the money to save his bankrupt father is thin and ineffective. It substitutes weak-minded folly for selfish criminality, and the substitution is scarcely an improvement. In Mr. Pinero's place I should have been inclined to remodel the character of Harold, and with it the relation between him and Millicent, making him more thoroughly unworthy of her devotion, and consequently heightening the effect of that devotion, and purposely concentrating all the sympathy upon her. This would have made the play more sombre, but also more logical. Then the point upon which the great situation of the play turns, namely Harold's refusal to allow his wife openly to ask for Lord Kengussie's aid, is insufficiently motived. It is a piece of Quixotism, grossly inconsistent with the rest of his character. True, such inconsistencies do often manifest themselves, but no dramatist should make his play hinge upon an improbable eccentricity of character. His undoubting acceptance of Millicent's implicitly-propounded theory, that it is better to win a man's money at cards than simply to borrow it, is also a little startling. It is explained in her case by the facts of her bringing up, but Boycott is not supposed to have any of the gambling taint in his nature. Thus the whole play is founded on a series of inconsistencies in Boycott's character, which tax our powers of belief to the uttermost. Yet with all this the author—assisted no doubt by the actress—has managed to impart such sympathetic quality to the character of Millicent, that we keep both our moral and our artistic sense in abeyance for her sake. Not that she, in herself, offends our moral sense. She is not put forward as an ideal. Her nature is a fine and pure one obscured by early training and surroundings. She is tempted, and for the moment succumbs to the temptation. There is nothing immoral in this, for our sympathy is demanded, not for her error, but for the devotion which caused, and the humiliation which expiated it. What moral offence there is in the play lies in the character of Boycott, for whom our sympathy is sometimes expected at very questionable junctures.

We now come to defects not inseparable from the motive, and thus more directly blamable on Mr. Pinero himself. His dramatic technique, his method of telling and developing his story, stands greatly in need of improvement. The first thing that strikes one is his inordinate abuse of the expedient of soliloquy, or at least monologue addressed to the audience and inaudible to the rest of the characters on the stage. Even a short "aside" is always awkward, and Mr. Pinero's asides are anything but short. This struck me so early in the play that I took the trouble of counting the soliloquies and other monologues as they occurred, and found that there were exactly seven in each act. The play opens with a soliloquy by Faubert, and in his case and that of Margot the expedient is peculiarly clumsy, as French detectives and *concierges* are not in the habit of conversing with themselves in broken English. Then Boycott has a monologue on embezzlement and suicide over his morning newspaper. Next Margot gives the audience her opinion of Faubert, and Faubert soliloquizes over Croodle's luggage. The matter of the fifth soliloquy I do not remember, but the sixth and seventh are allotted to Millicent, the one immediately after the revelation of Boycott's guilt, and the other at the end of the act. I need not detail the monologues of the second act, which are quite as long and out of place, the most objectionable being that in which Faubert kindly initiates the audience into the secret springs of his policy, while the game of écarté is in progress. This is a trick of which Mr. Pinero should be able easily to cure himself. He has fallen into it, sometimes from the mere wish to get in a "point" at all hazards, but generally from the more laudable desire to avoid long explanations in dialogue. He wishes to make his story tell itself, without any set exposition, and he has in a sense succeeded, but at a too great sacrifice. Soliloquy should be almost entirely tabooed in serious modern plays. It is all very well in farce and in the poetical drama, but it destroys the commonplace realism which is the very foundation of art in such plays as "The Money-Spinner." A few broken exclamations under high emotion is all the soliloquy that strict art should permit, for high emotion does in many cases manifest itself in speech. A spoken chain of reasoning like that of Faubert in the second act is an enormity only permissible in Shakespeare. It is a method much in vogue in the Chinese drama, but this form of "Chinese cheap labour" should be strictly excluded from the West.

A yet more radical weakness in "The Money-Spinner" is the way in which the concluding situation is frittered into a series of small effects, instead of being concentrated in one great climax. From the moment of Lord Kengussie's discovery of Millicent's error, there should be no break in the emotional chain, and the conclusion should be worked out in about half the time it actually occupies. As it is, we are perpetually on the brink of a situation which we never reach. First this character, then that, has to be disposed of. There is a long break in the emotional chain while Kengussie is dealing with Faubert, leaving Millicent, Boycott, and Dorinda with nothing to do but to turn their backs to the audience and look aimlessly out of the windows. Then Mr. Pinero insists on having a clear stage for Millicent's confession to Kengussie, and Boycott and Croodle have consequently to be got rid of, while Dorinda very unnecessarily plays the eavesdropper. I do not see the necessity for a single exit or entrance after the discovery of Millicent's cheating. The action might have been developed through a series of minor situations to a very strong final tableau. The interest should burst into a great blaze at the end, whereas it merely flickers on uncertainly and tremblingly. The conclusion is saved by some good dialogue, and by admirable acting, but the author has somehow lost the dramatic grip of the situation.

The character-drawing, though rather of the Robertsonian school, is clear and good, and in the case of Croodle, genuinely humorous. All the "business" with the flask, however, should have been ruthlessly suppressed. Its sole merit is its antiquity. It is vulgar and commonplace, and merely serves unnecessarily to heighten the resemblance between Croodle and Eccles in "Caste." The character of the old adventurer is strongly enough marked to do without any mechanical trickery of this sort. The idea of raising a laugh at the end of the first act by means of this irrepressible flask is simply pitiable.

The dialogue is in some respects the strongest point in the play. It is not very brilliant, but nervous, and altogether good. There are one or two touches of conventional stage phraseology which might be eliminated, and now and then Mr. Pinero shows a tendency to introduce irrelevant and incongruous comedy into serious situations. The worst instance of this is at the very end, where the exit of Kengussie is spoiled by a piece of pointless flippancy on Dorinda's part, very unnatural immediately after the emotional crisis through which she had just passed, and very much out of tune with the situation as a whole.

The technical part of the construction of "The Money-Spinner" would probably have been much better had not Mr. Pinero's evil genius led him to imagine for his scene a room with a balcony. This balcony was altogether too convenient. Whenever a character was in the way he or she was seized with an irrelevant longing for fresh air and a view of Rouen, and wandered out upon the balcony. The expedient was as simple as a harlequin's mask, and about as artistic. The moment a personage was felt to be in the way, hey! presto! he sidled to the balcony and was as invisible—as harlequin with his mask down. In "Imprudence" there is no balcony, and in technique of construction, in the arrangement of exits, entrances, &c., it is a great advance on its predecessor. I am surprised to see it stated that it is one of Mr. Pinero's "early works," and, in date of composition, considerably anterior to "The Money-Spinner." If it was really written before that unsophisticated drama, it has surely been very thoroughly revised, in the light of the author's more recent experience.

Thin as it is, "Imprudence" seems to me to show more genuine promise than any of Mr. Pinero's former plays. It is easy to point out its faults and not so easy to point out its merits; but this is the case with all plays. Perhaps its merits may be best defined as freshness of comic invention in details, and neatness of dialogue, with very slight recourse to pun or "epigram." But it is unnecessary to attempt a definition at all. It is sufficient if I say that to my mind the play seems to reveal a fresh individuality, and to promise an infusion of new and not unhealthy blood into our theatrical life. Mr. Pinero's manner is not that of Mr. T. W. Robertson, nor of Mr. Gilbert, nor of Mr. Byron, nor of Mr. Burnand. His style is his own, and his effects, if not in themselves novel, are procured in a more or less original fashion. Even his construction, though it is his weakest point, shows an effort at something better than the ordinary invertebrate pulpiness of "original comedies." Mr. Pinero has tried to give his farce a backbone. It is not one of the ordinary molluscs which, with a wry face and a good deal of pepper and vinegar, one can swallow at a gulp, but which defy dissection and even elude the merest mastication. It is much more solid than this, and much higher in the scale of dramatic organisms. Mr. Pinero has gone about the work of articulation rather unskilfully, and the result is a marked spinal curvature; but even deformity is better than absolute formlessness.

A boarding-house has more than once furnished materials of comedy to novelists and dramatists. Charles Dickens and Mr. Henry James have both made large use of it, and a comedy called "Our Boarding-House," by Mr. Leonard Grover, has recently been popular on the American stage. In a three-act piece, called "Campaigning," produced at a Criterion matinée some years ago, the same material was used, and other instances could no doubt be cited. So far as I know, however, Mr. Pinero is entirely justified in claiming originality for his characters and plot. The character of Baines Durant, mischief-maker-in-general to the "Pension Lazenby," is certainly original, and is at the same time a somewhat extraordinary conception. He is represented as a sort of mischievous boy who boasts of having squandered a fortune, and to whom therefore all the other characters at once fly for advice and assistance. George Castleton, a young gentleman who is in that happy position, so common on the stage, of having a fortune left him on condition that he marries within a certain time, applies to Durant to get him a wife. Mr. Coxe Dalrymple, a broken-down Indian who finds his daughter Zaida an impediment in certain matrimonial projects of his own, applies to Durant to get her a husband. Castleton gives him fifty pounds, and Dalrymple ten pounds, as retaining fees, on his mere promise to interest himself in the matter—a circumstance which leads one to wonder longingly whether every boarding-house is such a Tom Tiddler's ground for young men who are gifted with cynicism and empty pockets. His profound strategic genius causes Durant to put these two commissions together, and conceive the possibility of marrying Castleton to Zaida Dalrymple. But now comes a third applicant for the counsel of this eccentric guide, philosopher, and friend. A certain Mr. Parminter Blake is alarmed at the way in which all the male members of the establishment are paying court to his wife, who seems in no wise to object to their homage. Him Durant advises to give forth that a flaw has been discovered in his marriage licence, and that consequently his marriage is null and void. The attentions of the gentlemen will at once fall off, he says, when they discover that Mrs. Blake is not a married woman. The boarding-house Iago has apparently forgotten that Castleton has just asked him, in procuring him a wife, to look out for one as like Mrs. Blake as possible, so that in his suggestion to Mr. Blake, he is cutting the throat of his own project with regard to Castleton and Zaida Dalrymple. Sure enough, Blake has no sooner whispered into Castleton's ear that there is a flaw in his marriage licence, than Castleton demands of Mrs. Blake a rendezvous in the dining-room after supper. Durant has meanwhile made an exactly similar arrangement with Zaida Dalrymple, and an elegant imbroglio is clearly imminent.

Mr. Pinero as a dramatic constructor has this in common with M. Victorien Sardou, that he concentrates his energies upon one great scene, to which everything else works up. M. Sardou, however, though not always scrupulous about his means, would scarcely have invented such an extremely attenuated ficelle as that of the supposed-lawyer's letter announcing that "a flaw had been discovered in Mr. Blake's marriage licence." That this childishly palpable ruse should deceive three sane men—Dalrymple, Rattlefish, and Castleton to wit—is a gross absurdity. It is fortunately not my business to reconstruct Mr. Pinero's play for him, but it would not be difficult to suggest several expedients which would at least have a little more appearance of rationality than this. Then the means taken to get Mrs. Blake and Zaida Dalrymple to the dining-room are unsophisticated in the extreme, and might very easily be improved. When once they are got to the dining-room, the scene which follows is amusing enough. The idea of the cupboard-bedstead is really funny, though it might perhaps have been better worked-up. Mr. Blake's hiding-place, too, might have been made more "probal to thinking," as Iago would say, though in this the upholsterer rather than Mr. Pinero was mainly at fault. A much more serious blemish is the behaviour of Miss Zaida Dalrymple. Mr. Pinero seems to have a Zola-like horror of the "personnage sympathique." He is determined that none of his characters shall deserve our respect for a moment, and he consequently makes Miss Zaida perfectly willing to marry Castleton through the delicate intermediation of Durant. The consequence is that she undergoes unnecessary humiliation when Castleton, enamoured of Mrs. Blake, will have nothing to do with her, and that she entirely loses our sympathy when in the third act she agrees to marry Durant. Mr. Pinero might surely leave to Mr. Gilbert such objectless cynicism.

The third act is not precisely an anti-climax, for it contains several amusing scenes. The idea of all the boarders insisting upon seeing Mrs. Lazenby, who is locked into her cupboard-bed, is really funny, and the audience seemed very much to relish the reconciliation between Mr. and Mrs. Blake, though to me it seemed a great deal more vulgar than comic. Mr. Pinero makes one or two slips in taste, of which this is the most prominent. Another is Durant's speech to Zaida, "If you were a fellow, I should slap you on the back and say you were a lucky dog," the use of the word "fellow" in this sense being confined to shop-girls and their swains. A further instance in which Mr. Durant's manners break down occurs in the second act, when, having demanded a serious interview with a lady, he calmly asks, "May I smoke?" and proceeds to do so without even waiting for the permission requested. There are several other cases in which Mr. Pinero's speeches or business sin against the canons of taste, which should hold even in the wildest farce, but they are excrescences —the vulgarity does not appear to be in the grain. Nevertheless, the piece would be greatly improved by their excision, and that of a few particularly puerile touches of dialogue, like the point in the third act where Durant says to Zaida, "May I call you a cab?" and she brilliantly retorts, "You're mean enough to call me anything."

It may be understood from this sketch that Mr. Pinero's work is far from faultless, and yet the impression it produces is altogether favourable. Its chief merits are, perhaps, negative. It is not a French farce painfully hewn into shape for the Procrustes-bed of English taste; its humour is not merely verbal; its action is not absolutely a negative quantity, and is not always being interrupted while the characters exchange broadsides of irrelevant puns. The existing works which it most resembles in style, both of construction and dialogue, are Mr. Bronson Howard's clever farces. What is mainly lacking both in it and in "The Money-Spinner," is firmness and consistency of construction, and in this respect Mr. Pinero's third play "The Squire" shows a great advance.

In the course of the very curious and interesting controversy which raged for some time after the production of "The Squire," Mr. Pinero published the memorandum in his note-book which formed the germ of the drama. It ran as follows: "The notion of a young couple secretly married—the girl about to become a mother—finding that a former wife is still in existence.

The heroine amongst those who respect and love her. The fury of a rejected lover who believes her to be a guilty woman. Two men face to face at night-time. Qy.—Kill the first wife?" This memorandum gives a tolerably complete idea of the motive of the play as performed. Nothing essential has been added to it, and nothing changed. The scene is laid in an English country district; the heroine is Kate Verity, a young lady who farms her own land, and is accordingly known all over the country-side as "The Squire," the husband is a certain Lieutenant Thorndyke, who marries Kate Verity under the belief that his first wife, an opera-singer known as La Sirène, is dead. From motives of revenge this woman has fostered the rumour of her death, but, being overtaken by illness and remorse, "drags herself to the spot where Lieutenant Thorndyke is," and there writes a confession, which she entrusts to Parson Dormer, commonly known as "the mad parson," to be conveyed to "the woman who loves Eric Thorndyke." This confession, the parson, who knows nothing of the secret marriage, reads as a warning to Miss Verity; and the great scenes of the play follow between Kate and Thorndyke, and between Kate, Thorndyke, and Gilbert Hythe, the rejected lover. Gilbert, finding Thorndyke in Miss Verity's room at dead of night, demands to know if he has the right of a husband there. To the question, "Lieutenant Thorndyke, is that lady your wife?" Thorndyke rather weakly replies, "In the sight of heaven, sir, yes." To the natural rejoinder, "But in the eyes of the law?" he answers,

"No!" and Gilbert is proceeding to shoot him, when Kate throws herself between them with the wild cry, "Gilbert! the father of my child." In the third act the interest is kept up by the danger of exposure of what seems like Kate Verity's disgrace. Parson Dormer has been informed by a treacherous servant of Lieutenant Thorndyke's midnight visits. On Kate refusing to exclude Thorndyke from her house—a rather unnecessary piece of defiance, since he is on the point of starting for India—Dormer summons the villagers in order to expose what he thinks her infamy. Under pressure of this fear she tells him the whole story. While he is announcing to the villagers the approaching departure of their mistress, Gilbert Hythe, who has been told the secret the night before, and is now the devoted friend of the lovers, rushes in and whispers something in his ear. His tone immediately changes. He will tell them, he says, why their lady is going away. She is going to marry Lieutenant Thorndyke, but the Lieutenant is going to India for some years, and of course his wife goes with him. Then, as Thorndyke and Kate look at him with faces of amazed hope, he says in a low voice, "You are a free man, Lieutenant Thorndyke, your wife is dead."

Into the question of Mr. Pinero's indebtedness to Mr. Hardy's "Far from the Madding Crowd," it is not necessary to enter at length. It seems to me that the resemblance of the play to the novel, or rather the importance of the resemblance, has been exaggerated. Kate Verity, like Bathsheba Everdene, farms her own land;

they both have a bailiff; they are both married to a soldier; in the novel this soldier is murdered by a lover of the heroine, and in the play Gilbert Hythe threatens to shoot him; in both works there is a servant-girl also in love with a soldier, and in both an old man who seems to consider his age a virtue. But the relations of the characters and their motives are entirely different. For instance, in the novel Boldwood shoots Troy because he is Bathsheba's husband, and has returned to torture and drag her down; in the play Gilbert Hythe tries to shoot Thorndyke because he is *not* Kate Verity's husband. Again, in the novel the servant-girl is in love with Troy, and is her mistress's favoured rival; in the play she is in love with another soldier, and some of the prettiest effects in the piece are got out of the mistress's sympathy for the girl's little griefs in the midst of her own great ones. It seems probable that the whole action of the piece is original, while the background, so to speak, is borrowed from Mr. Hardy—a liberty which Mr. Pinero would have done well to acknowledge, but which scarcely deserves the unsparing denunciation it has met with in certain quarters. Mr. Pinero was mainly indebted to Mr. Hardy for "the scent of the hay," which, to use his own expression, he wafted "over the footlights."

In point of construction, as I have said, "The Squire" is a great advance upon Mr. Pinero's former efforts. Up to the end of the second act the story moves forward, on the whole, easily and freely, through a succession of scenes in themselves amusing and at times truly pathetic. But in the third act Mr. Pinero loses to a great extent his grasp of the subject. And this is due not to any lack of dramatic power, but rather to deficient moral insight or moral courage. As an exposition of how a perfectly innocent woman may be driven almost to madness by fear of a diseased public opinion, added to the natural and instinctive shame of her sex, the story is really tragic. But the tragedy seems to me to lie in the very injustice and cruelty of this public opinion. Mr. Pinero and his audience, on the other hand, bow as low to the fetish as does Kate Verity. They accept the idol's decisions as the decrees of fate. They can pity the victims of its stony cruelty, but they cannot even conceive the possibility of dethroning it. Thus the Athenians who saw "Iphigenia in Aulis" pitied the victim, but did not think of rebelling against the bloodthirsty power which demanded her innocent life. Mr. Pinero may claim the precedent of Euripides, but unless two thousand years have passed in vain an English author and audience should surely have a freer and truer moral stand-point. Both dramatically and morally the play should have concluded with a protest against the fetish, instead of with the intervention of a *deus ex machina* which enables the heroine to elude its grasp, but leaves it standing in undiminished authority ready to devour the next innocent victim who may come in its way. "The Squire" is one of the many plays which prove that the English stage is hopelessly non-moral. Mr. Pinero might—by the grace of the Lord Chamberlain—have made his play moral; he has only made it conventional.

I do not object to the details of the *dénouement.* The device on which the curtain is brought down is really ingenious, and gives an air of freshness to an end plainly foreseen. But what I do object to is the sentimentalizing scene between Kate Verity and Thorndyke, which Mr. Pinero has seen fit to introduce. This scene is not only in itself unutterably feeble, but is doubly so from its position in the play. It is scarcely conceivable that a dramatist of Mr. Pinero's calibre could imagine, or induce intelligent actors to play a scene in which a woman on the brink of what she considers shame and ruin unutterable, devotes herself to the task of warning the man who has brought her to this pass against gambling, sitting up late, and taking too much wine. Shall Antigone at the moment of eternal parting tenderly caution her Hœmon against the night air, or Ophelia stoop to tie the garter left unbraced in Hamlet's frenzy?

This unhappy tendency to sentimentalizing has throughout injured dialogue otherwise strong, nervous, and commendably free from "brilliancy." In the powerful scene where Kate upbraids Thorndyke with the concealment of his first marriage, he consoles her by the information that he "heard his wife was dead, and sent red roses to strew upon her grave," which explanation Kate apparently accepts as quite satisfactory. Of minor faults the play has its full share. Agriculture and discipline on Miss Verity's farm are, as is perhaps only natural, in a most extraordinary state. A fault of detail which is the more irritating as it might be easily avoided, is the arrangement by which Gilbert Hythe drags about with him through the first two acts a great double-barrelled gun, for no conceivable reason, except that he may have the wherewithal to shoot at Thorndyke at the end of the second act.

One of the merits of the play is the clever drawing of several of the minor characters, and altogether the piece is one of the most interesting and promising the stage has seen for long. It shows that Mr. Pinero is a thoughtful and conscientious writer with artistic aims, if not yet with full command of his artistic means. The latter, doubtless, will come in good time. It may seem a strange piece of advice to give, but I cannot help thinking that Mr. Pinero would do wisely to try his hand at one or two adaptations before giving us his next original play. He would learn much from the analysis and reconstruction of a well knit French drama. His originality has been proclaimed as his great merit, and so, no doubt, it is; but a little study of French methods, without diminishing his originality, would be almost certain to improve his form.

MR. ROBERT REECE.

MR. REECE has of late years been one of the most untiring workers in the dramatic field, but unfortunately much of his energy has been given to what is little better than hack-work—I say unfortunately, for in several ways he has manifested a talent worthy of better things. It was his fate to come to the front in the dramatic world just as the rage for burlesque was at its height, and a little before the fever for opera-bouffe had set in. To these thankless, not to say ruinous, forms of production, he has devoted the greater part of his energies, with the result that, in spite of his undoubted wit and ability, he has not produced a single work which will live even the ephemeral life of a successful English comedy or drama.

It is difficult to imagine anything more destructive to dramatic style than the practice of adapting opera-bouffes. Many of the French librettos are in themselves clever enough, some of them remarkably so; but the English adapter's first indispensable task is to remove all the cleverness and point of the plot so that it may pass the watchful eye of the Lord Chamberlain. He has then to write dialogue full of puns and local allusions, for the British public classes opera-bouffe with burlesque, and demands the same cockney witticisms in each. He knows, too, that it is useless to devote any care to making even this style of dialogue neat and telling, as it is certain to be overlaid with a fungoid growth of inane "gags" and horse-play "business." Then in the lyrics he has to fit our more rigid forms of verse to the light rhythms of the French composer, and is thus forced in most cases to produce rhyming jingles of indescribable puerility, compared with which the legend of the Jabberwock is full of meaning and coherence. Three or four opera-bouffes a year is by no means a large allowance for one adapter, and it is no wonder if he comes out of the struggle with nothing but wild puns and senseless rhymed-endings chiming and jangling in his exhausted brain. Mr. Reece, with or without the aid of Mr. H. B. Farnie, has probably done as much of this sort of work as any man in England. That he has not entirely worked out his wit and reduced himself to the level of a punning-machine, speaks well for his original intellectual stamina,

In original burlesque Mr. Reece is, perhaps, the most satisfactory, or more correctly the least objectionable, writer of the day. His versification is unusually good, comparing very favourably with that of either Mr. Burnand or Mr. Byron. Nor are his puns quite so childish as some with which these remarkable writers have favoured us. They are wild enough as a rule, but there is sometimes a gleam of humour in their very wildness.

When Keemo-kimo says to the quack Gallipotz in "Brown and the Brahmins"—

> D'ye think I can't detect sham magic lore, sir—or
> A *cupper* who pretends to be a *sorcer*-er?

or when King Tomidod remarks,

> No Roman emperor shall be severer
> I mean to merge the *father* in the *Nerer*,

one cannot help smiling at the mere audacity of the word-plays. Even in the construction of his burlesques Mr. Reece shows quite as much comic invention as is to be found in any work of Mr. Byron's or Mr. Burnand's, with the exception perhaps of such parodies as "Over-Proof" and "Diplunacy." "Romulus and Remus," one of Mr. Reece's most successful extravaganzas, contains some really clever ideas, and the same may be said of some of his little one-act absurdities, such as "The Wizard of the Wilderness" and "The Musical Marionettes." In short, I confess that in seeing and reading Mr. Reece's burlesques I have, like Sir Charles Coldstream, "smiled thrice distinctly." He cannot be altogether acquitted of the charge of taking up themes which no man of any literary reverence would subject to the desecration of burlesque. "Prometheus, or the Man on the Rock" and "Agamemnon and Cassandra, or the Prophet and the Loss of Troy," deal with subjects surely too great and beautiful to be distorted in "the small cracked mirror" which serves as the burlesque-writer's joking apparatus. But, whether from accident or design, Mr. Reece has been unusually sparing in his selection of such materials; while the taste with which he treats his themes is certainly not worse, and sometimes better, than that usually exhibited by his fellow-workers in the same exalted sphere of art.

In comedy Mr. Reece has done little original work, but has made several very clever adaptations. His forte is his dialogue. Of constructive skill he has very little; so little, indeed, that he has spoiled some of his adaptations by making the dialogue a misfit, as it were, for the plot. The stuff is excellent, of a bright pepper-and-salt pattern, and the cut is good in style, did it only suit the form it is intended to clothe. Unfortunately it bags here, wrinkles there, puckers in front, and trails behind. The most amusing scenes are quite unconnected with the plot, and are dragged in merely for the sake of some good points they contain. The points are often really excellent as farcical dialogue goes, but in the drama, as in real life, to know what to say is scarcely more important than to know when to say it. These remarks apply specially to "The Guv'nor," which was also marred by a good deal of vulgarity, and to "Out of the Hunt." In the latter there were some admirable touches of satire. One of the characters, for instance, is Miss Orinthia FitzOrmond, a young lady who has abandoned the music-hall stage, where her rendering of the ballad, "It's 'andy to 'ave it in the 'ouse," made her illustrious, and has taken to "the legit.," in which she purposes to delight the critics with new readings of Shakespeare, "showing everything the fellow *didn't* mean." This is a palpable hit very neatly delivered.

The same superiority of dialogue to construction characterizes Mr. Reece's few and slight original efforts. "An Old Man," for instance, is a two-act comedy almost puerile in point of idea and construction, but with a few happy touches of humour. "Dora's Device" is much superior in conception, but even it is very naïve in its methods. It contains some really excellent dialogue, however, and one of its characters is cleverly observed and might have been carried out on a larger scale. It is that of an amiable but somewhat commonplace young man who goes through life uttering truisms under the impression that they are rather profound discoveries. The type is common enough in real life, but I do not remember to have met it elsewhere upon the stage, though the heroes of several modern comedies belong unconsciously to the same genus.

MR. GEORGE R. SIMS.

THE saying that journalism is the grave of genius is true in two senses. It may mean that much actual genius is buried, beyond all possibility of resurrection, in the columns of our newspapers; or it may mean that the habit of writing for newspapers prevents the development of potential genius, bringing it to a premature end before it can fairly claim that lofty title. The former sense is the more obvious, though not the more generally true. To express the latter effect with greater precision, I may perhaps be allowed to invent a new phrase and say, "Journalism is the step-mother of genius." It distorts and stunts the tender nursling, gives it stones for bread, puts it to menial offices, and in time makes of it an overworked drudge. It is a pity we cannot frame and apply a spiritual Factory Act to meet the evil, which is in all probability on the increase.

Were I to hint to Mr. Sims that the fable is narrated about him, he would probably deny the soft impeachment, and claim journalism as his beneficent mother rather than his step-mother. For there is this peculiarity in the case, that her victims are generally unconscious of the spiritual distortion they undergo. Perhaps, too, Mr. Sims would be right, and I wrong. Perhaps his talent is precisely of the sort which the nervous, rapid, hand-to-mouth labour of journalism developes rather than stunts. It may be that repose and culture would merely have left his ability dormant, instead of facilitating its normal growth. There are no doubt natures which require the perpetual stimulus of that more-than-Egyptian task-master the printer's devil to make them productive at all. Mr. Sims' organization may be of this type. In any case, since habit is a second nature, it has probably ere now assumed this form. But I can scarcely doubt that there were originally better possibilities in his constitution which more auspicious circumstances might have developed into actualities. A little culture, a little *Selbst-Kritik*, an occasional respite from the necessity of ministering to the ever-recurring hunger of that insatiate monster the press, might have enabled Mr. Sims to make some permanent additions to English literature. As it is, his production has been often remarkable, generally clever, but always ephemeral.

It is all the more interesting to examine the conditions, limitations, and prospects of Mr. Sims' talent, as he is, for the moment at any rate, one of the potentates of the English stage. His reign has scarcely begun, and is perhaps not yet firmly established, but there is every probability that the future of the drama for the next ten years or so lies in a considerable measure in his hands. His personal popularity is very great, and his energy and power of production are apparently inexhaustible. He has, justly enough, secured a reputation for good fortune, and the British manager is proverbially superstitious. Altogether it is scarcely rash to prophesy that we shall see at least as much work by Mr. Sims as by any other dramatist during the coming decade ; and a glance at his short but busy career in the past may enable us in a certain degree to anticipate the future. I do not presume to hope that any advice or warning which may incidentally be given or implied will influence the course of Mr. Sims' development. To the British playwright all criticism except that conveyed by the manager's offers and the treasurer's accounts, is as the warnings of Cassandra—unpleasant to hear, but not for a moment to be regarded seriously.

One fact which meets us at the outset in examining Mr. Sims' career, is perhaps the determining fact of his whole talent—that in which his merits and defects are implicitly predicted. He is a Londoner of the Londoners. I do not use the commoner and almost synonymous term, because it conveys a shade of disparagement which is apart from my intention. It is no secret indeed that, until quite recently, literature was to Mr. Sims what Sir Walter Scott recommended that it should always be, a staff and not a crutch. It was the work of his leisure moments, and meanwhile he was actually "something in the city," a business-man in the busiest commercial town in the world. Hence that intimate knowledge of the world—of London—which is peculiar to him, in which no writer, perhaps, has equalled him, since the death of Charles Dickens. His Asmodeus has unroofed for him the whole metropolis east of Charing Cross. In the West-end he is not so much at home, seeming in fact to have gathered his knowledge at the respectful or dis-respectful distance prescribed by the area railings. Whenever his characters appear in evening dress they seem to be studied not from nature, but from the *London Journal.* So too with country life. Mr. Sims' England is the England of a Londoner's outing, modified by reminiscences of elaborate landscape "sets" at the leading theatres. What Mr. Ruskin has said of a very different writer might a good deal more fitly be said of Mr. Sims—and here I am not speaking only of his plays, but of his tales and sketches. "In the English cockney school," says the Jeremiah of Coniston, "the personages are picked up from behind the counter, and out of the gutter; and the landscape by excursion train to Gravesend, with return ticket for the City Road." He adds something equally severe about "the characters being the sweepings out of a Pentonville omnibus"—violent phrases which my readers will scarcely believe to have been applied by their author to the works of George Eliot. Even as applied to Mr. Sims they are exaggerations, but withal they have a spice of truth. The minutiæ of middle and lower class life in London—its heroism, its pathos, its humour, its rascality, its barbarism—are known to Mr. Sims from personal observation and from the minute and daily study of what M.

Zola would call the "documents" relating to them. When he gets beyond his charmed circle he is always more or less conventional.

So it is, too, with his views of the abstract relations, duties, and ideals of life. His mother-milk has been watered from Aldgate Pump, and he has learnt his letters from the *Daily Telegraph.* He despises the *Daily Telegraph,* but its ink has entered into his blood. There is something parochial in his very radicalism. It is of the undoubting, unhesitating type which "shrieks and sweats in pigmy wars," profoundly unconscious of being

> Before the stony face of Time,
> And looked at by the silent stars.

I say this in no spirit of disparagement. Such radicalism is by far the most effectual, has done great things in the world, and has an infinity still to do. It is certain that nothing will be effected by standing apart, to use the phrase which Mr. Oscar Wilde has conveyed from Mr. Pater, " neither for God nor for his enemies." The enervating doubt as to whether the game of life is worth the candle has never seriously presented itself to Mr. Sims' mind. He can get up interest, indignation, admiration, conviction, on any given subject. Yet even in this respect the peculiar action of modern journalism upon the mind of its slaves can be traced very clearly in Mr. Sims. He looks at everything from the point of view of its effectiveness in print, addressed to the apprehension of Brown, Jones, and Robinson. Nothing human is alien to him unless it be alien to Brown, Jones, and

Robinson. He is above all prejudices, except those of Brown, Jones, and Robinson. He is a man of that world whose hub is Fleet Street, and whose circumference is the four-mile circle.

But with all its limitations his is a genuine and striking talent. His work has been, whether in tales, poems, or political and social "paragraphing," to give a picturesque and humorous running commentary upon the daily papers. And with what infinitude of skill, readiness of invention, spontaneity of wit, and effectiveness of pathos has he not fulfilled this mission! He has seized upon the externals of modern middle and low-class life, and has transmuted them from the crudity of newspaper prose, into artistic form, humorous, picturesque, or pathetic. His art is of the simplest and most naïve. In very few cases will it bear the least examination or analysis. But it admirably serves its purpose as a picturesque interpretation of every-day English life, which he who runs may read. The fact that he writes almost exclusively for lower-middle-class readers in no way counteracts the bias towards vulgarity which is implied in some of the characteristics I have pointed out above. It is not to be denied that Mr. Sims is often vulgar. Occasionally, too, he is almost puerile, but always one can see his excuse in the evident necessity he has been under of making "bricks without straw," one of the curses of journalism. But one can seldom take up a paper in which he writes without finding some touch of spontaneous wit, perhaps buried among a good deal of very mechanical joking, or a truly picturesque "bit," perhaps hidden in a pile of forced or commonplace pathos. His facility of versification renders his comic verses as a rule admirable, but in his serious "ballads" it detracts from any chance of permanence they might otherwise possess. They entirely lack style. One feels that the artist is working in too soft a medium. He models freely and vigorously in clay, but he cannot transmute his design into the permanence of marble. Still, if we put aside any very high requirements either as to art or refinement, Mr. Sims' work is seldom otherwise than pleasant to read. It is impossible to grudge him his popularity, for, in fine, whatever may be their short-comings, the tone and tendency of his writings are always honest and healthy. He has brought into every-day journalism some of the genius of Bret Harte and Charles Dickens.

It may be asked what all this has to do with the special subject of this paper—Mr. Sims as a dramatist. Everything, I reply; for the characteristics of his journalistic work reappear in his plays, and his training in journalism has, for better or worse, distinctly modified his dramatic manner.

Mr. Sims is a novel phenomenon in our dramatic literature in respect that he had earned a personal popularity by means of his tales, ballads, and political and social feuilletons before he made his first attempt upon the stage. But that attempt could not be long delayed. His irrepressible exuberance of humour and rich vein of melodramatic pathos, if they should prove to be combined with the indispensable instinct for stage effect, were precisely the qualities necessary to secure success on the modern boards. Consequently Mr. Sims' success was from the first unquestionable, for the instinct for stage effect was there in full measure. At the commencement of his career, influenced no doubt by the demands of managers as much as by his own taste, he drew exclusively upon his stores of humour. His first four plays were farces, one entirely original, one an adaptation of a French play, done to order, and the remaining two suggested by French originals, but in a great measure remodelled. It is a characteristic fact that three out of the four dealt with those time-honoured subjects for farce—"My wife's relations." The first, "Crutch and Toothpick," might much more appropriately have been called "Father-in-Law." The second was actually entitled "Mother-in-Law," and the same title would have applied to the third just as well as that which it in fact received, "The Member for Slocum." This circumstance aptly indicates the sort of material with which Mr. Sims dealt. The mother-in-law is the traditional butt of English middle-class humour. She is the consecrated evil-genius, if such a phrase can be used, of domestic life in Paddington and Pentonville. Her malign influence is supposed to reign supreme in suburban semi-detached villas and cottages *ornées*. She is always present to the popular imagination as a lady with a large umbrella and false fronts, who precedes the doctor and the monthly-nurse and usually insists on remaining long after these have vanished. The conventional figure of the mother-in-law, like most other conventional figures, has no doubt its counterpart in nature and fact. But her habitat is essentially the narrow, cramped, sordid, semi-detached life of our lower middle-classes. She and her surroundings are always shabby-genteel—and it is into the shabby-genteel world, with its shabby-genteel tone of thought and feeling, that Mr. Sims introduces us. True his scene-painters treat us to interiors, which, with all the splendours of Tottenham Court Road, are certainly not shabby, and can scarcely even claim to be genteel—but for this Mr. Sims is not responsible. One of his characters is an alderman, and another a Member of Parliament, but they are the most shabby-genteel alderman and M.P. one can possibly conceive. His personages are all small shop-keepers in disguise, and his dialogue is too often of a style to be appreciated by the shop-keepers' shop-boys. It is to be noted, however, that the vulgarity of his dialogue never trenches upon indecency. Compared with certainother dramatists, Mr Sims abstains most laudably from emphasizing the questionable possiblities of a dangerous situation.

It is mere vulgarity, in the ordinary sense of the word, with which I cannot help charging Mr. Sims. His young men are what Mr. Gilbert calls "jolly Bank Holiday young men." The tone of their conversation reminds one of the music-hall, or at highest of the Gaiety bar. Vulgarity, as I have before remarked, is one of those impalpable defects which scarcely admit of proof, and which it consequently requires some courage to allege at the risk of being held superfine, if not snobbish. Nevertheless, I cannot help stating that this, more than anything else, mars my enjoyment of the good spirits, the ingenious word-plays, and occasional true wit of Mr. Sims' stage-work. To take a single instance—the imperious mother-in-law of the member for Slocum refuses to let him take a trip up the river on the ground that he has to study the speech she has written on the Married Women's Property Bill, adding, "Onesimus takes a deep interest in all that concerns our sex," or words to that effect. This being said to a bachelor friend, the opportunity for a point is obvious, but it might be made in fifty different ways. The way Mr. Sims chooses is to make the bachelor friend nudge Onesimus, wink to him, and say, "Yes, he always was fond of the ladies," a phrase which ought to be, if it has not already been, utilized as the refrain of some lion comique's "last great comic song," but is quite out of place on any other stage but that of a music-hall.

As for the quality of his dialogue in other respects, its word-plays seem to me to possess what may be described, though imperfectly, as spontaneity, when compared with the word-plays of older and more hardened perpetrators of "verbicide," to use Dr. Holmes's expression. It must be confessed that, radical though he be in politics, Mr. Sims is a conservative in puns. The hoarier their antiquity the more he respects them. "Let us go to St. Petersburg and be blown up," says one of his characters, to which the reply of course is, "I'll be blown up, if I stay." One of the many mothers-in-law is described as "a tartar—in fact, the cream of tartars." A tenor singer is recommended to "abandon the evil tenor of his ways," and a lady leaving the room to fetch an ink-bottle remarks that she is "going upon an ink-quest." It is useless to protest against these antediluvian monsters, for an English dramatist's worst puns, like a mother's deformed children, are, by a law of nature which seems to run right in the teeth of the Darwinian theory, always the dearest to his heart. Why is it, I have often wondered, that that noxious weed, the pun, flourishes so much more largely in English literature, and especially on the English stage, than anywhere else ? The French *mot*, which is too often translated "pun," is something infinitely higher. Even a very good *mot* may be, and often is, extremely out of place and undramatic. That is one of M. Zola's great objections to the style of M. Dumas *fils* ; but what would M. Zola say if he read a comedy by Mr. Byron, Mr. Burnand, or Mr. Sims ? Is it the influence of Shakespeare, arch-corrupter of the English drama, which has rendered punning a national vice ? If it be, he has much to answer for, and some of the lines in Mr. Sims' farces should lie almost as heavy on his conscience as his own atrocities in that direction. On the other hand, Mr. Sims very frequently treats us to really new and good word-plays, and sometimes to whole passages of genuine wit, in which the *mot* replacesthe pun. I may instance the scene in "Crutch and Toothpick" in which two lovers discuss "business" as carried on in the city, and, proceeding from the definitions supplied by the young lady's father, arrive logically at the conclusion that business consists in "selling something you haven't got to some one else who doesn't want it." But again there are some occasions on which Mr. Sims, striving after originality in wit, descends beneath puerility. When some one says, "I'll be there in two twos," merely that some one else may answer, "Oh, this is too too!" we feel that civilization is a failure, and long for a return to inarticulate barbarism.

If his training in comic journalism has affected his dialogue in one way, his training in the more serious branches of the craft has modified it in another. His manner may be defined as that of a feuilletonist writing for the stage. More than even the rest of our farce-writers, he relies upon allusions to contemporary topics of ephemeral interest. The very title of his first play, "Crutch and Toothpick," was borrowed from a craze of the moment. Already we have almost forgotten the meaning of the phrase, and five years hence it will be quite obsolete. The piece, I understand, is even now sometimes played in the provinces, but must, I should imagine, have been in part rewritten to keep it abreast of the times. So, too, with "The Member for Slocum." The whole action turns upon those "all-night sittings" which have recently been a prominent feature of political life, but which, we may hope, will be things of the past even before the end of the short span of life usually allotted by fate to a successful modern comedy. Every second line of the piece contains an allusion which will be incomprehensible in a year or two, or a piece of slang which will have died out before the play is gathered to its fathers. Even Mr. Byron and Mr. Burnand do not shoot folly as it flies with this Carver-like celerity. It is possible to imagine a revival of "Our Boys" or of "Betsy," five, or even ten, years hence. Audiences would then understand the allusions without much modernization, though they might not be able to understand the taste which had formerly made them so popular. Not so with Mr. Sims' farces. Their whole point lies in their actuality. They will be as obsolete in ten years as Mr. Sims' last column of political paragraphs, and a great deal more obsolete than the "School for Scandal" and "She Stoops to Conquer." If they should ever be revived, Mr. Sims will have to write "second editions," as in the case of a pantomime in which a new verse per week is added to the "topical song." A good deal of the impression of vulgarity which they produce is probably due to this fever of hot-and-hot actuality.

Of his four farces the last, "Flats," separates itself in a measure from the other three, because in it he appears as an adapter pure and simple, whereas he had formerly merely taken hints and ideas from the French. It is an adaptation of Chivot's Palais-Royal farce, "Les Locataires de M. Blondeau," and was only a modified success at the Criterion.

M. Labiche has a great deal to answer for in having invented what may be called the bead-and-string style of farce—the style, that is, in which the situations are quite independent of each other, except that one or two characters run, or rather scramble, through all. The incidents touch each other, but do not even interlink in a chain, far less intertwine in an elaborate filigree work like that presented by a well-constructed piece of Scribe or Sardou. The beads may be of pearl or of common glass—indeed, on the same necklace one may be a brilliant jewel and the next a dull piece of paste. A play so constructed has always length, and, unlike a mathematical line, it has very often "breadth," but it has never form or consistency. It might run on for ever, so far as the dramatic material is concerned, its only practical limit being the physical endurance and intellectual tolerance of the audience. Mr. Sims gave the Gigglethorpe mansion four stories, M. Chivot gave the Maison Blondeau five, but the house might have been made as high as an Edinburgh "land" or the Tower of Babel, and it would have taken but little extra ingenuity to supply Gigglethorpe-Blondeau with fresh adventures on every story, until, like Mrs. Browning's Euripides, through touches of things common he rose to touch the spheres. To illustrate my meaning, I may name an important scene in each of the first three acts which might be bodily cut out—or, to return to the bead metaphor, dropped off—without in the least affecting the coherence of the play. They are as follows: in the first act the passages between Gigglethorpe and the hairdresser: in the second the whole action which follows the entrance of Count Bodega: and in the third the passages which deal with the domestic differences between Mr. and Mrs. Deeds. All these episodes might be simply missed out and no one would be a bit the wiser; and to dispense with any other scene whatsoever only a little change in the subsequent dialogue would be required.

Mr. Sims showed considerable skill in dealing with the moral short-comings of his original; and indeed the frank extravagance of the whole was rather a relief after several recent productions at the Criterion. The farce was no more moral or immoral than a harlequinade. It left no bitter taste in the mouth, simply because there was not a single touch of seriousness in the whole play. It was a saturnalia of practical fun, and in the saturnalia, as we know, the gods themselves were considered legitimate subjects of sport. This is one of those plays to which, *mutatis mutandis*, Lamb's defence of the artificial comedy of last century might be applied, without even the touch of paradox which it actually possesses.

But even taken as what it actually was, the most unmitigated farce ever presented in Piccadilly, it had one great fault, and that was its indescribable noisiness. Mr. Sims pandered to the modern taste for broken china in the most lavish fashion. Had he been composing a burlesque Wagnerian opera, instead of writing a farce, he could not have indulged more freely in bangs, crashes, and discords in general. I lay this to Mr. Sims' account, for the author is the conventional scapegoat in these matters, but the Criterion stage-management was probably mainly responsible. Perhaps it would be still more precisely just to attribute the number of crashes to MM. Chivot and Sims, and their loudness and duration to the stage-management. Be this as it may, if "*p p*" had been substituted for "*f f*" in the stage directions whenever a basket of crockery had to be broken or a tea-tray to be thumped, I believe the play would have taken the rank it deserved among Criterion successes.

Besides these farces Mr. Sims has written a burlesque called "The Corsican Brothers Babes in the Wood" and a "specialty play" for a company of gymnasts, entitled "The Gay City." Neither of these has been seen in London, and they are probably not works of much importance; so we may pass at once to the two serious plays with which Mr. Sims has followed up his lighter efforts.

"Wait till he gets a chance in melodrama," was always the remark of those who had studied Mr. Sims' talent and knew it best, when his extraordinary success in the field of farce was commented upon. We had not long to wait, nor was our waiting in vain. "The Lights o' London" proves that Mr. Sims' undoubted melodramatic talent is as well suited to theatrical as to narrative form. By its means he stepped at one stride into the front rank of contemporary dramatists. His materials are not novel—where can one find novel materials within the narrow limits assigned by the taste of the British public, which practically taboos the two great and fertile regions of religion and morals? Between these two lies the neutral territory of domestic sentiment and commonplace crime and misfortune, aided or not, as the case may be, by more or less novel mechanical auxiliaries. Every corner of this territory has been explored long before Mr. Sims ever set foot in it. His merit lies in using the old materials in novel and original combinations, with almost unerring taste, and with a true and keen observation in details which imparts a freshness of interest to even hackneyed scenes and situations.

"The Lights o' London" is a picture of low-class life painted with a fidelity which is almost without precedent on our stage. The melodramatic framework in which it is placed is more conventional, less truthful, and consequently less valuable. It savours not a little of Charles Dickens, and still more of the *London Journal* and *Family Herald.* Still, it is made to suit the picture with not a little skill; or rather, as in the case of Mr. Whistler's productions, the frame is artistically contrived so as to form an effective part of the picture, and not a mere arbitrary accessory. Such pictures have been common enough on canvas. Mr. Fildes' famous painting of the Casual Ward is recalled by one scene, Mr. F. Barnard's lurid "Saturday Night" by another. Many attempts, too, in the same direction have been made upon the stage, but they have generally dealt with sensational externals, and not with the real essential spirit of popular life. We have had the Aquarium with its frequenters, a racecourse with its betting men and welchers, a house on fire with real fire-engines. We have even seen the eminently realistic spectacle of a single hansom cab almost knocking down Regent Quadrant, the pavement of which was so narrow that a foot-passenger's umbrella stuck between the lamp-post and the houses. But Mr. Sims, though aided, and very ably aided, by his scenic artists and his stage-manager, does not rely upon them alone, but makes use of his own sympathetic observation to give us many of those touches of nature which raise such scenes above the level of mere mechanism. "Sympathetic observation," I repeat, for in the first of these words lies the clue to the extraordinary directness with which Mr. Sims' work goes home to the heart of his audience. We feel—and this "we" is not the impersonal pronoun of literature, but is meant to designate the audiences which Mr. Sims' touch of nature makes so thoroughly kin, that it is no presumption to speak in their collective name—we feel that this writer is not a mere manufacturer of scenes, treating the life of the "lower orders" as so much useful and paying material, but a man whose eye leads straight to his heart and brain, whose intimate knowledge of the people has produced that tolerance, pity, and admiration which are summed up in the word sympathy. This, of course, was not absolutely a new discovery. Most of us were familiar with much admirable work of Mr. Sims', which evinced this sympathy in the fullest measure. But it was a new discovery on the stage. We felt that there was an unwonted touch of true humanity in the work, and felt it none the less strongly because the feeling was in most cases vague and unformulated. Hence the almost unexampled enthusiasm with which the drama has been greeted.

The dramatic action has been compared above to the frame in which the picture of life is set. I must now take the liberty of altering the metaphor, for the sake of convenience, and supposing the actual plot to occupy the foreground of the picture, with the scenes of real life filling in the background. In the design of the foreground, then, there are several details which are worthy of notice. I have already disclaimed all intention of objecting to the lack of absolute originality in the incidents. I might be profoundly erudite in pointing out resemblances to this, that, or the other previous melodrama, a highly entertaining exercise, which might be of practical use if Mr. Sims had failed to weld together his materials into a homogeneous whole. This he has in no sense failed to do. His drama is not a patchwork. If he has consciously borrowed any incident, which I doubt, he has proved his right to it by assimilating it thoroughly, and putting it to its most effective use. The end of the fourth act bears an external resemblance to the cave scene in the "Colleen Bawn," which it might possibly be worth while to obviate by a different stage arrangement. The suggestion lies merely in the fact that the curtain falls upon Harold Armytage and Seth Preene in the very attitude of Miles-na-Coppaleen and Eily. The essentials of the situation are quite different, and it should not require much ingenuity to modify even the external similarity.

To pass to more important matters, it seems to me that the title, good in itself, does not precisely fit the play. Taken in connexion with the verses which Mr. Sims uses as a sort of motto, it suggests a totally different drama. A very interesting play might be written, and Mr. Sims should be the very man to write it, dealing with the struggles of an ambitious young man, a modern Chatterton or Johnson, attracted by the lights of London "that gem the city's crown," who finds her after all a stony-breasted step-mother, and wastes the best energies of his life in wringing from her recognition and sustenance. This, or something like it, is the play which the title and motto would most aptly fit. As it is, the glamour of the Lights of London, and the struggle under their heartless glare, are past and done before the play commences. Harold Armytage and Bess are supposed to have gone through the losing battle of London life in the three years which intervene between Harold's quarrel with his father and his return in the first act, defeated and dispirited. The drama shows us a man unjustly accused and hunted down, and the fact that some of his sufferings take place in London is a mere accident, quite insufficient to justify the title, or at any rate to give it its full significance. We are shown nothing of the weird attraction possessed by the lights of London for so many young and ambitious spirits, nothing of the disappointment and disillusionment which in ninety-nine cases out of a hundred await them under the "cruel lamps." All this is supposed to have gone before the opening of the play, and it is a significant fact that the phrase "Lights of London" only occurs once, and that once in the first act. The title is good and the play is good, but they do not precisely fit each other. It is far from improbable that Mr. Sims will some day write a play much better suited to this title, and then he will regret having used it before its time. Wearing the right boot on the left foot entails the corresponding necessity of forcing the right foot into the left boot.

The action of the first act depends too much on an elaborate and impossibly arranged scene; but after a slightly conventional exposition, it moves freely and naturally up to the concluding situation, which strikes me as unduly hurried. Over-compression is almost as great a fault as flabbiness, and the rapidity of a sequence of small events should not be allowed conspicuously to transcend possibility. The second act is throughout admirable. The opening scene is one of genuine comedy, and the interview between Clifford Armytage and Seth Preene is really well written; while the scene in which the escaped convict takes refuge with the Jarvis family is a piece of vigorously conceived drama, in some respects the best in the play. Would it not add strength and probability to this scene if the showman's wavering inclination to shield the suppliant were clinched by the discovery that it is his wife who has been nursing the rising hope of the Jarvis family? I make the suggestion with all diffidence, and can appreciate Mr. Sims' motive for not allowing the discovery to be made at that point. But the effect of surprise on the recognition between husband and wife in the next act is scarcely enhanced by the fact that the surprise is mutual. It would be almost if not quite as great were the surprise reserved for Bess alone. At such a juncture we are forced to concentrate our attention upon one or other of the characters, and we naturally concentrate it upon Bess. Moreover, it is a stretch of probability that Harold should have travelled all the way to London with his benefactors without the discovery being made. It involves several strained suppositions—that he did not tell the Jarvises his name, that he did not learn theirs, or that he did not recognize it as the name of the people with whom his wife was lodging, and that he never inquired the address of the house he was being taken to. Lastly, the scene in the second act would be made decidedly more probable, if not more effective, by the revelation of his identity. As it is, the faith and generosity of the showman in sheltering an escaped convict of whom he knows nothing, and who has not the slightest claim upon him, strike one on reflection as Quixotic to the verge of impossibility.

The principal scene of the third act is marred, to my mind, by an absurdity whose reason I did not see until the very conclusion of the act, and which then seemed scarcely compensated by the effect produced through its means, though it is one of the great effects of the play. I refer to Harold's appearance in his convict clothes, only partially concealed beneath a green overcoat, which, with the striped convict hose visible beneath it, gave him an extremely bizarre appearance. The first thing he would naturally have done on taking refuge in the caravan would have been to burn his broad-arrow uniform, or sink it in the nearest pond, even although the only garb he had to substitute for it had been that of the ghost alluded to by Mr. Jarvis. To enter London and drive through the streets in the guise in which he presents himself at "No. 7, Boston Street, Borough," would merely have been to tempt providence and the police. The absurdity is perpetrated in order to secure a concluding effect, when Jarvis is hurried off to prison in the convict dress, and Harold, saved once more, rushes to his wife's arms as the curtain falls. The theatrical effect is very striking, and perhaps it is a fault in my mental constitution to be unable to be carried away by it, knowing as I do that it is obtained through an impossibility. It is, in a sense, an instance of Mr. Sims' apparently instinctive mastery of his art, for the vociferous approval that greeted it showed that he had not exceeded the liberty which may safely be taken with a popular audience. This knowledge of the exact amount of departure from absolute consistency which will be tolerated by the public, some dramatists have failed to acquire after years of experience. Mr. Sims in his first farces showed that he possessed it, and has done so again and again in "The Lights o' London."

The intrigue of the jewels, upon which the first scene of the fourth act turns, is well conceived and carried out. In this scene, however, Mr. Sims for once perpetrates a slight anti-climax. It does not close at the right point, Seth Preene's last words serving merely to weaken the effect. This is the act which, on the first night, needed most compression. To my taste, however, the pathetic passages between Harold and Bess stood most in need of cutting, the effects being too much repeated. The episode of the Irish policeman merely needed to be played a little quicker. In the fifth act, with its unceasing motion and excitement, the only thing which called for special remark was the admirable stage-management, which in the opening scene produced as near an approach to absolute illusion as I remember to have seen on the stage. I need not here inquire into the artistic merits or defects of such a scene. It is certainly, at first sight, remarkable that a reproduction on the stage of the squalor and bustle of a Seven Dials slum should give pleasure and excite enthusiasm. It even seems ludicrous and degrading that such should be the case ; but a very little analysis is sufficient to show that the pleasure excited is neither quite irrational nor altogether contemptible. Even to indicate the course of this analysis would involve too long a digression ; as it is, I neither entirely defend nor entirely condemn the scene from the point of view of art, but content myself with "constating,"[1] as the French would say, its merits from the point of view of stage-technique, together with the vivid effect it produced upon the audience.

The great success of "The Lights o' London" is now a matter of dramatic history. Its first night presented a scene of almost unexampled enthusiasm, and the enthusiasm has borne solid fruit in the shape of pounds,

[1] *Constater* is a word which should surely, in one form or another, be introduced into English. Neither "stating" nor "affirming" fully supplies its place.

shillings, and pence. The fact that the play, or at least a considerable part of it, had for years gone begging from manager to manager, before Mr. Wilson Barrett had the penetration to see its merits, has been very largely commented upon as proving the extent of managerial blindness in London. It is not my habit to take up the cudgels for the British manager, but in this case I think he is evil entreated. It is perfectly comprehensible to me that a manager reading the first three acts of "The Lights o' London," unpolished, unelaborated, unnamed, should see in it nothing but a *Family Herald* melodrama. I am quite sure that had a scenario of the piece been handed to the most penetrating dramatic critics in London they would have laughed at the idea of its becoming a success at a west-end theatre. For the plot and situations, though well knit, are commonplace; and the effect of small touches of character and dialogue, admirable stage-management, and admirable acting, especially in some of the minor and episodic parts, could not be foreseen, or at any rate could not be calculated upon. Had the piece fallen into the hands of a less liberal and intelligent manager than Mr. Wilson Barrett, it is not only conceivable but probable that it would have been a failure. Its history proves unusual insight on Mr. Wilson Barrett's part rather than remarkable density on the part of the other managers.

So much for Mr. Sims' first venture in melodrama. He followed it up very quickly with a first venture in original domestic comedy, not, unhappily, with equal success. I understand that "The Half-way House" proved a remunerative production, but the fact only shows that with the British public a bad play is no more certain to fail than is a good play to succeed. I have not seen the piece since the first night, when defects of representation at a theatre proverbially slovenly in that respect no doubt prevented its appearing to full advantage. But, making every allowance on this score, I cannot see in the piece such a work as we seemed almost to have a right to expect from Mr. Sims.

The paradox that "nothing succeeds like success"—is it a paradox or a truism?—resolves itself, stated without epigram, into the fact that personal popularity covers a multitude of sins. The authors who believe in "organized oppositions," and hold that a certain section of the public takes a malicious pleasure in damning a play, need only have assisted at the production of "The Half-way House" at the Vaudeville to be completely cured of any such belief. The contrary is the case. A popular audience is almost always predisposed to make a piece a brilliant triumph, if the author will only afford it the slightest excuse for so doing. There is no feeling more delightful than the thrill of exhilaration which runs through the house when a new play is recognized as a great success. The enthusiastic play-goer feels that in applauding and shouting he is "making history"—the history of the stage. He looks forward to boasting some day to his children and grand-children that he was "in at the birth" of this or that famous and immortal work. True, he has every chance of outliving the immortality of any play he is likely to see in these latter days, but the momentary exhilaration is none the less stimulating. The production of "The Lights o' London" was one of those charming scenes of unbounded enthusiasm, and it pleased the first-night public so much that they determined at all hazards to repeat it at the Vaudeville. There is to be seen on the shore of some Highland firth a board announcing that the ferry-boat will cross "on Mondays and Fridays, God willing, and on Wednesdays whether or no." The Vaudeville audience had evidently determined to make "The Half-way House" a storming success "whether or no." It is better than some pieces which have recently been presented on the same stage; but it can easily be better than "Punch" or "Jacks and Jills," and yet be a bad play.

In one respect Mr. Sims has been the victim of a misunderstanding, whether attributable to his defective exposition, to the actors' defective delivery, or to the obtuseness of the critics, I cannot tell. Every one insisted on believing that Mrs. Hesseltine, wife of the selfish squire who forms the central figure of the piece, had escaped from a lunatic asylum. Now Mr. Sims intended to convey that she had been living under the care of a private family, and not among the patients of a regular asylum. This, in a certain measure, removes one or two apparent impossibilities which were much objected to. But the mere fact of Mr. Sims having chosen such a difficult and ungrateful theme, shows that for once his instinct for stage effect had failed him. The unhappy lady in question never appeared on the scene without exciting either painful or ludicrous associations. This was very generally, but I think very unjustly, laid to the account of the actress who played the part. To my mind it seems unavoidable, from the very nature of the case.

The play is like life in this respect, that it raises innumerable questions which only its author can answer, and which I am not very sure that even he can answer satisfactorily. What have the difficulties of the landlord to do with the story of "The Half-way House"? Is his insolvency merely an excuse for the introduction of the broker's man? Has the latter any function in the piece, except to lock up Mrs. O'Shaughnessy in the porter's lodge—the fundamental function of saying funny lines being always presupposed? Why should Philip Hesseltine have gone under an assumed name in London? Is it merely so that a momentary effect of surprise may be produced on his meeting with Ivy Hope? If his mother was sane, why did he not procure a medical certificate to that effect, instead of smuggling her about all over the country as if she were an escaped convict? What has the situation at the end of the first act got to do with the piece? Is the situation at the end of the second act supposed to be serious, or comic, or thrilling, or pathetic, or "everything by turns and nothing long"? Would not a simple effect, whether of drama, comedy, or farce, have been more telling than this hopeless mixture of the three? Why did not Mrs. O'Shaughnessy destroy the letters she had intercepted? Or, if she had any reason for not doing so, why did she carry them about with her so that they could be lost and found at a moment's notice? Why should not Mrs. Hesseltine have been produced and sent off on her second honeymoon to Wiesbaden in the first act just as well as in the third? Was it necessary to have eleven names in the bill instead of nine, or for what other conceivable reason were Bertie Scott, R.N., and Madge O'Shaughnessy added to the *dramatis personæ?* Might not Bertie Scott have been promoted with advantage to the place in the lunatic asylum, or "private family," left vacant by the retirement of Mrs. Hesseltine? These are a few of the questions I should like to put seriously to Mr. Sims. Some of them may be capable of satisfactory solution, but the fact that they present themselves at all to an attentive auditor is sufficient to prove that there is something either feeble or confused in the construction of the play.

The character-drawing is a little better than the construction. John Hope is merely the conventional type of a wealthy tradesman brought into contact with the upper ten thousand, familiarized by Mr. Byron in a score of "comedies." To Squire Hesseltine, on the other hand, Mr. Albery, and not Mr. Byron, stands sponsor. As a portrait of the English country-gentleman, he is, to say the least of it, eccentric, but as a study of a peculiar development of selfishness he promises well at the outset. He is a marked variety of the species Digby Grant, his kinship to that aristocratic personage, showing itself even in the modified use of the catchword "You annoy me—you annoy me exceedingly." Unfortunately, the character is not well sustained, and loses in individuality as the play proceeds. Mrs. O'Shaughnessy, again, is descended from Thackeray through T. W. Robertson; and Obadiah Dell, the tender-hearted man in possession, walks living from the pages of Dickens, whence he has already been borrowed more than once by Mr. Paul Meritt and others.

It was undoubtedly the dialogue which secured the success of the play, and it was indeed very fair dialogue of a very bad school. I had hoped to find Mr. Sims strike out a new line in this, his first effort in original comedy; but I was grievously disappointed. He adopted the old manner of Mr. Byron and of his own farces, merely bringing to it a certain freshness of treatment and originality of detail. His dialogue is of the style which the Vaudeville company knows so well how to deliver, waiting patiently for the laugh if it does not come at once. And its faith is always rewarded, whether the majority of the audience understands the joke or not. For instance, when Squire Hesseltine says, "You may regard my son's marriage as a *fait accompli*," and John Hope replies, "If you want any flowers for that *fête*, apply to me," it is certain that not many of the gods were sufficiently versed in the arcana of the French tongue to appreciate the wit; yet they saw that a laugh was expected, and they rose to the occasion heroically, as they would no doubt have done had the joke been in Chinese. Again, one of the best points in the piece—where Hope, being asked if he is Beck's solicitor, replies, "No, I'm his friend"—would have been entirely lost had not the actor paused and looked round the theatre with the peculiarly sheepish expression of a man who has ventured on a little joke and is uncertain of its reception. On the whole, however, the humour of the dialogue "took" freely enough, and deserved to do so, for the puns, as puns, were of more than average merit, and less than average antiquity. One of his witticisms, however, Mr. Sims might have spared us—that about the "shady" family tree of the Hesseltines. I heard it last in Mr. Byron's "Courtship," and then it was an old familiar friend.

Whatever may have been the measure of its pecuniary success, "The Half-way House" cannot but be regarded as a check in Mr. Sims' career. Its reception by the press was deservedly cool, for a long time its fate trembled in the balance, and it has in no sense added to his reputation. At worst, however, it is a temporary check. The theatrical world lies before him, and there can be little doubt that he will avail himself to the full of his opportunities. Will he improve upon "The Lights o' London" or will he degenerate from "The Half-way House"? This is a question of immense importance for the immediate future of the English stage. It is possible, but not probable, that he may attain the repose, concentration, and freedom necessary for work of abiding literary value, such as his talent undoubtedly qualifies him to produce. It is more likely that in answering the perpetual claims made upon a popular dramatist he will abuse the facility which is one of his main characteristics, and produce works of varying temporary value, but of no lasting merit. For facility, to use Guarini's beautiful illustration, is a sharp sword which can work miracles if grasped by the hilt, but only destruction to its possessor if grasped by the blade. For the present M. Zola's characterization of Victorien Sardou applies only too aptly to Mr. Sims. (It seems to be my fate to apply to Mr. Sims the severe things which one great writer has said of another great writer—and the greatness of both must be my excuse). Thus saith M. Zola,—"M. Sardou est simplement un amuseur. Il a beaucoup de verve, beaucoup de mouvement, le flair du théâtre et de l'actualité, un esprit de petit journaliste lâché à travers les ridicules contemporains. Mais il ne pense pas, il n'écrit pas, mais il est incapable de rien créer de solide et de vivant." I would eliminate the word "incapable" from this passage, but otherwise it applies a great deal more exactly to Mr. Sims than to M. Sardou.

In his latest work, "The Romany Rye," produced since the above was written, Mr. Sims, misconceiving the causes which led to the success of "The Lights o' London," has committed the error of trusting entirely to effects, which, in the earlier work, were but secondary and contributory to the main result. No doubt the episodic but keenly-observed pictures of low life in "The Lights o' London," and the stirring tumultuous action of the last scene, contributed greatly to its success; but they would have gone for little had not the play, with all its conventionality, been on the whole well-knit and interesting. In "The Romany Rye," on the other hand, Mr. Sims has held himself bound to surpass his former effort in choiceness and piquancy of slang, and in external movement and tumult; but he has not taken equal care to tell an interesting story and to tell it well. The action of the first three acts is rapid, but little else, and Mr. Sims has boldly brought the curtain down three times on what is practically the same situation. In the fourth act occurs the only strongly dramatic scene in the play, that in which the "Romany Rye," bound and helpless, overhears his brother hiring the two miscreants who have waylaid him to "find him drowned" in the Thames. This is a passage of powerful melodrama, the effect of which is greatly heightened by the well-drawn figure of the old hag "Mother Shipton," though it is weakened again by the sentimental conventionality of her repentance on recognizing in the victim a likeness to her "long-lost son." In the fifth act, Mr. Sims, apparently at a loss how to conclude his drama, takes a leaf out of Mr. Meritt's book, and has recourse to the old expedient of a shipwreck. This is merely an arbitrary device for finishing off with an effective picture. The picture was indeed very effective in itself, but it was instructive to notice that the audience, with an instinctive feeling that this was good scene-painting rather than good drama, remained comparatively unmoved by it.

The play has been accused of too much realism, but

that is not the reproach I would bring against it. On the contrary, it is unreal to a degree, except in a few isolated touches, which are simply episodes, one might almost say anecdotes, taken from the life. There is, indeed, an immense preponderance of blackguardism in the characters, but that by no means constitutes realism. The unbroken villainy of the majority of the *dramatis personæ* is as unreal as the impossible virtue of the "Romany Rye" and Gertie, and the equally impossible delicacy and fidelity of Boss Knivett, a gentleman who illuminates the profession of burglary by his chivalrous attachment to his "pal," and by the use of the choicest slang, which has often to do duty for humour. If Mr. Sims had been a little more realistic in essentials of plot and character we might have spared some of the elaborate external realism of details. At any rate, the cry of "Zola-ism" is equally unjust to Mr. Sims and to M. Zola.

MR. S. THEYRE SMITH.

ANY account of the modern English drama would be incomplete without a reference to the author of "My Uncle's Will;" and yet there is very little to be said about him. The list of his writings, so far as they are known to me, comprises five one-act pieces, none of them with more than three characters. Their subjects are invariably of the most frivolous and conventional order—a hard-hearted uncle captivated by the young wife whom his nephew has married against his will; an old bachelor on the point of proposing to a lady, rudely convinced of the folly of his design; a pair of lovers brought almost to hate each other because their uncle has left them a large property, which is to be forfeited if they do not marry. The sole merit of these trifles lies in their dialogue, which is delicately woven around an ingenious framework of small details of stage-business. In this art Mr. Theyre Smith is almost unrivalled. His pieces fairly scintillate with wit, and that of no mean quality. It is always perfectly unnatural, and often extremely ill-mannered, but it is genuine wit, not mere word-plays, vulgarisms, and distortions of language. Mr. Smith seems to have taken as his model the scene of reproach, reconciliation, and quarrel between Sir Peter and Lady Teazle in "The School for Scandal." An immense proportion of his work is made up of similar fencing-bouts of wit between a husband and wife, or between two lovers. And it must be said that in point of neatness of repartee he sometimes rivals Sheridan himself. "Cut off with a Shilling" and "Uncle's Will" seem to me his most thoroughly successful efforts, but "A Happy Pair," "Which is Which?" and "Old Cronies," also contain many brilliant passages and admirable lines. Mr. Smith may be said to have founded a school, for several writers have imitated his manner to a greater or less degree, and the result has been a small repertory of really clever one-act plays, finer than mere farces, but too slight to be called comedies, which are, in their way, among the most satisfactory products of the modern stage. They are trifles light as air, but they are carefully written and good of their kind, with the additional merit of affording opportunity for some excellent acting.

It has often struck me as a matter for regret that short pieces of this, or indeed of any, sort are so little regarded on the English stage. A one-act piece is generally put on merely to fill up a too short bill. It is intended either to "play people in" or to play them out. It is carelessly placed on the stage, and carelessly acted. "There is no money in a one-act piece," is the common phrase. But why is there no money in it? Simply because it is seldom given a chance. I am not sure that even as it is, a good one-act piece would not often be found to put a good deal in the treasury, if a manager could analyze his receipts. But, admitting that it does not, the reason is plain. It is not put on to make money, but to fill up time. If the public is led by the management to understand that a piece is not worth seeing, the public will certainly take the management at its word. By not advertising the piece, or merely giving it a line in the very smallest letters, by putting it on at an unreasonably early or unreasonably late hour, and by giving the parts to inferior members of the company, the management tacitly asserts that the piece is not worth much, and the public never thinks of doubting or testing the assertion.

Of course, if a three, four, or five-act play is in the bill, a one-act piece must be either a *lever de rideau* or an afterpiece; and except on special occasions, audiences cannot possibly be got to give proper attention to the piece which either precedes or follows the main attraction. But would it not be possible occasionally to compose a bill of three or even four one-act pieces, making them co-ordinate in importance? Something of this sort used to be done on the English stage, generally with mere farces however, and it is very common to this day in France and elsewhere on the Continent. At the Théâtre Français, for instance, an evening's performance very frequently consists of one-act plays, with occasionally a two or three-act piece of Molière, played without entr'actes so as practically to constitute one act. Nor is this to be wondered at when we remember that the repertory contains such plays as "La Joie fait Peur," "Gringoire," "Les Ouvriers," "Le Petit Hôtel," "L'Etincelle," "L'Eté de la Saint-Martin," "Le Luthier de Crémone," and many others, in which the foremost members of the Comédie Française find some of their best parts.

Much of the best dramatic work, both here and abroad, is to be found in the list of one-act plays. It is natural that this should be the case. Life abounds in dramatic moments and motives which, though of the greatest value, do not contain material for development beyond one act. Indeed, it is much to the prejudice of the English drama that the fact of one-act pieces being supposed to have "no money in them" often forces authors to spin out into three acts, and so injure or destroy, a motive which would have suited admirably for one act. There are many men, too, who have the ability to do finished dramatic genre-studies, if the expression be permissible, but who break down whenever they attempt a great picture on a wide canvas. Thus it would be in every way to the advantage of the English drama if a method could be devised by which more prominence could be given and more justice done to one-act plays. Let us suppose a bill composed as follows:—Mr. Theyre Smith's "Which is Which?" might form the opening dish. Then, for solider fare, Mr. Sydney Grundy's "In Honour Bound," a comedy as full of matter as any three-act piece on the stage; and to wind up, by way of dessert, Mr. F. W. Broughton's "Ruth's Romance," or, if broader fun be thought desirable, Mr. Paul Meritt's "Tale of a Tub." Let all these pieces be thoroughly well mounted, thoroughly well played, and thoroughly well advertised, and I venture to assert that such a bill, slight as it may appear, would "draw the town." Of course, the attraction would be all the greater if one or two of the pieces were novelties, but as I do not know what one-act masterpieces may be reposing in the desks of our dramatists, I can, of course, only make my "selections," as the sporting prophets say, from pieces already known.

The already existing store from which to select is by no means small. Mr. Theyre Smith, Mr. F. W. Broughton, Mr. H. A. Jones, Mr. Sydney Grundy, Mr. Pinero, and Mr. Herman Merivale, have all written plays which would answer admirably for the treatment I suggest, while Mr. Wills' "Iolanthe" and Mr. Tennyson's "Falcon" must not be forgotten. Of course, older pieces, among them several by Mr. Tom Taylor, and adaptations from the French, would by no means be excluded; and two-act plays, such as Mr. Gilbert's "Sweethearts" would come in extremely well.

But the great advantage of this scheme, if it were ever adopted, would be that it would not only give us an opportunity of becoming familiar, under improved circumstances, with many of the best plays we possess, but would also lead to an immense increase of good work in the lighter branches of the drama. As matters now stand, a dramatic idea, to have any money value, must be cast into three acts, and is very likely to be spoiled in the process. Even if it is not, the experiment of putting it on the stage is so expensive and precarious that it is ten chances to one it never sees the light at all. I am convinced that any manager adopting even for a little time such a scheme as is here sketched would be doing a service to the British drama, and I am much mistaken if playgoers would not testify in solid pounds, shillings, and pence their sense of the service done.

MR. ALFRED TENNYSON.

In this paper I have to maintain what may seem, nay is, a paradox; not, I hope, from any love of paradox for its own sake, but from sincere, though perhaps mistaken, conviction. I believe that of the four plays which as yet constitute the Poet Laureate's dramatic works, the best has never seen the stage, the worst has been the most successful, and the remaining two have met with quite unmerited neglect. Perhaps this may be an overstatement of the case. I am not prepared to assert positively that "Harold" is a better play than "Queen Mary;" but I am sure that they, and with them the much-ridiculed "Falcon," are infinitely better plays than "The Cup," which alone has secured anything like success.

He is a bold man who, except in the morning papers, dares to talk seriously of Mr. Tennyson as a dramatist. The critical world, having made up its mind and said its last word upon the poet some twenty years ago, felt itself unwarrantably trifled with when its last word was found to have been spoken too early, and it was called upon to stretch its formula. This it resolutely refused to do. It would have been little less than desecration to spoil the symmetry of a formula, simple, graceful, and portable in the waistcoat-pocket. So, as it could not absolutely ignore the two importunate volumes that claimed to be taken into account, it contented itself with adding a trifling pendant to the original formula, tacked on with a disjunctive "but" and consisting of a contemptuous dismissal of the poet's claims to the title of dramatist. Truly it was an unheard-of phenomenon that the aftermath of Mr. Tennyson's genius should take the ever-troublesome dramatic form. There had been traces of dramatic force, that most intangible of essences, in "Maud" and some of his minor poems. But *à priori* it was in the highest degree improbable that Mr. Tennyson should be able to write a good drama; and the *à priori* method necessarily plays an important part in periodical criticism.

Let us try, however, to free our minds from all preconceptions as to what Mr. Tennyson probably might, could, would, or should have written, and turn our attention to what he has actually written and published. "Queen Mary" has undoubtedly many faults and weaknesses which it is not difficult to reckon up. In the first place it is rather a chronicle-play than a drama properly so called. There is nothing in it of the conflict essential to a true drama. The scenes follow each other without vital connexion. It is a dramatic panorama of a period of history, its sole claim to organic unity lying in the elaborate and interesting character-study which gives the play its name. The poet has perhaps been too industrious in reproducing, without strict attention to their relevance, the small touches of actuality and local colour provided for him in history, chiefly in the elaborate study of Mr. Froude. But all these accusations could be brought with equal truth against many plays of Shakespeare, "Julius Cæsar" being a noteworthy example. As Mr. Tennyson has dramatized Mr. Froude, so Shakespeare dramatized Plutarch. Each has given us a vivid picture of a great historical crisis. The one, no doubt, is much more instinct with life and colour than the other, but the difference is of degree and not of kind. In each the historical importance of the action compensates for the lack of unity, which in more regularly constructed dramas is supplied by the development of a single character or of a dramatic conflict. Perhaps I should rather say that in each we are conscious of a genuine conflict through our knowledge of what has preceded the action and of what is to follow it. The conflict is that between the two scales of the balance in which Fate is weighing out the history of the world. In "Julius Cæsar" liberty and empire are trembling from the beam, and its last word is spoken by the astute youth who was afterwards to be worshipped as Divus Augustus. In "Queen Mary" the die is being cast which is to decide whether Alva and the Inquisition or "the spacious times of Great Elizabeth" are to fall to the lot of England.

There are many minor defects in "Queen Mary," which, for the stage, would necessitate a considerable amount of re-arrangement. Crudities of construction, I may even say puerilities, occur now and then. There are certain passages which would defy the art of the most ingenious and skilful stage-manager. Mr. Tennyson has imitated Shakespeare, perhaps too closely, in diction and manner, and imitates him likewise in writing for a stage almost totally unconditioned by modern exigencies of scenery and stage-management. But a slight exercise of tact and skill might reduce the play to such limits as would fit it even for the modern stage. This done, the most striking effects for leading and minor actors, for scenic artists, and for the stage-manager, might be got out of the play. I shall not quote from a work which is in the hands of everyone, but shall merely indicate the leading passages. For Mary herself the last scenes of the first two acts, the second scene of the third act, with its great lyrical monologue, the sixth scene of the same act, and the whole of the concluding scenes—all these passages should afford admirable opportunities. True, it would demand a really great actress to take advantage of them—an actress whose taste should be at least equal to her power. For such an actress the very originality of the character should constitute its attraction, and she should aspire to a novel triumph in attacking a novel problem. A very different actress, much easier to find, but still not to be met with every day, might make of Elizabeth a fresh and charming study. As for Philip, the opportunities for character-creation which lie in his part have been sufficiently proved. Cranmer and Gardiner, Cardinal Pole and Simon Renard, Sir Thomas Wyatt and Sir Ralph Bagenhall would all afford to really able artists opportunities for historical silhouettes of the first value. For the stage-manager I would indicate Act I., Sc. 1 and Sc. 3; Act III., Sc. 1 and Sc. 3; Act IV., Sc. 3, as passages in which the achievements of our recent guests from Saxe-Meiningen might be rivalled if not surpassed. As for the scenic artist, there is not one scene in which he would not be able to give proof of study, invention, and skill. In short, I believe that under proper conditions "Queen Mary" might become a most valuable addition to the acting drama of England.

Here I shall be reminded of the fact from which I started in the first paragraph of this paper, that "Queen Mary" has been tried on the stage and found wanting—indeed, proved a notorious failure at a theatre where failures are rare, and where it appeared to have every chance of success. I have not for a moment forgotten the fact, which in no way invalidates my argument. The conditions of success which I have indicated above were entirely wanting to the experiment. I do not believe that even now, if Mr. Henry Irving were to revive "Queen Mary," it would prove a financial success. The great difficulty would remain of finding an actress with sufficient power, taste, and authority to give the title-part its full value. Such an actress may exist in England,[1] but I cannot name her with any confidence.

[1] I have never seen the American actress, Miss Clara Morris, but should judge, from all accounts, that her gifts must be somewhat of the order required for Queen Mary.

There would also remain the minor but still invincible difficulty of finding actors of sufficient ability willing to undertake the very important but comparatively short parts in which the play abounds, and whose adequate treatment is essential to its due effect. The scene-painters and stage-managers of the Lyceum, under Mr. Irving's rule, could probably cope pretty successfully with the problems presented in their departments, but even this was not the case during the former management under which the drama was produced. Mr. Irving, who, whatever may be his merits as an actor, is certainly an admirable *metteur en scène*, was not then monarch of all he surveyed, and his liberal policy of management was not yet inaugurated, perhaps not even dreamt of. The part of Queen Mary was in the hands of an actress of some reputation but of very narrow endowment, quite inadequate to deal successfully with the difficulties it presented. Moreover, the minor parts were filled in a manner anything but ideal. In fine, a problem of extraordinary difficulty was attacked with very ordinary means, and the result was naturally failure.

I am sanguine in the hope that the conditions I have dwelt upon may one day be realized. An actress and a manager—talent and taste—these are the two great essentials. But there is one doubt still lurking in the background of which I must make confession. Supposing the actress and the manager found, would the public also be forthcoming? I hope so, but not with any assurance of faith.

That "Queen Mary" failed is not wonderful; but that "Harold" has never been tried on the stage does seem to me wonderful. In it Mr. Tennyson, to show his impartiality, has dramatized Mr. Freeman as he had formerly dramatized Mr. Froude; yet "Harold" is less of a chronicle-play, and more of an organic drama. Indeed, it might almost claim the rank and title of tragedy. In Harold himself, though not such an original and striking character as Mary, we have the truly tragic spectacle of a noble nature at war with fate, which acts in this case through the medium of superstition. Up to the end of the second act, and especially in the scene of the oath at Bayeux, the play has all the elements of effective drama. With the third act the tragedy commences. We see Harold's own faith in himself, and the faith of those around him, sapped by the remembrance of the fatal oath. He cannot, he must not keep it, and yet he cannot shake off its bonds.

Harold. As far as touches Wulfnoth,
I that so prized plain word and naked truth
Have sinned against it—all in vain.
Leofwin. Good brother,
By all the truths that ever priest hath preached,
Of all the lies that ever men have lied
Thine is the pardonablest.
Harold. May be so!
I think it so, I think I am a fool
To think it can be otherwise than so.

Surely a fine nodus this, and worthy of dramatic solution. What is the material of tragedy if it be not a soul so tangled in the meshes of doubt that its struggles can only end in destruction? With doubt within him and around him, Harold is no longer himself. The dying words of the Confessor confirm the vague feeling, which all try in vain to stifle, that the unseen powers are against him. The influence of such a feeling, however groundless, is one of the best-ascertained facts in history and human nature. With the exception of the visions in the fifth act, there is nothing supernatural in the play, and even they, though I hold their introduction to be a mistake, are merely intended as a visible presentation of Harold's dreams. Apart from its historical and picturesque interest, "Harold" is an almost scientific study in ethical casuistry, complicated and rendered dramatic by the influence of superstition.

It, too, would require re-arrangement for the stage, though not so much as "Queen Mary." With trifling alterations and suppressions, it would present a series of quite practicable and extremely effective stage-pictures. The death of Edward the Confessor (Act III., Sc. I), the whole of the fifth act, and especially the scene between Stigand and Edith while the battle of Hastings is in progress, might be made finely picturesque by skilful stage arrangement, and nobly poetic by worthy acting. For the scene-painter and stage-manager, "Harold" presents as great opportunities as "Queen Mary," and the casting of the play should not prove nearly so difficult, if only from the fact that the *dramatis personæ* are fewer. Surely we may hope one day or other to see it worthily placed upon the stage.

If there ever was a play worthily placed upon the stage, that play was "The Falcon." Its scene was a masterpiece of quiet and tasteful art, every detail was studied and complete, the dresses were exquisite, and the mere stage-picture was, to my mind, sufficient to have provided an "entire evening's entertainment." Moreover, Mr. Kendal looked extremely handsome, and played very respectably as Ser Federigo; and I should exhaust my superlatives and my reader's credence were I to attempt to describe Mrs. Kendal as Monna Giovanna. She was a living poem in her gracious stateliness and queenly yet tender womanhood. Never, in England or elsewhere, have I seen a piece of acting more instinct with the truest poetry. The writing which inspired such a creation could not but possess some merit. And, indeed, it seemed to me to possess many merits. The play was far from being a great or remarkable drama, but it was a very graceful re-telling of Boccaccio's beautiful story, which has been so often re-told in prose and verse, and yet retains a perennial freshness. How came it then that the production was a failure? I answer that it was killed by the Press. One or two errors of taste, especially one childish witticism certainly very much out of place, offended the critics mightily. That Mr. Tennyson should make a bad joke was quite unpardonable. Moreover, the play was not strong enough meat for them, while the falcon, on the other hand, was too strong for their stomachs. They chose to consider Ser Federigo's sacrifice ludicrous if not disgusting, and they said so with the fine outspokenness which now and then characterizes critical utterances. The consequence was that a production which in every way did credit to the English stage was received with indifference by the public. It is a favourite heresy among actors to deny the influence for good or evil of newspaper criticism. Every second production refutes the heresy, but none more signally than "The Falcon."

"The Cup" is the only play of Mr. Tennyson's which has attained financial success, and, as above hinted, I consider it by far the feeblest of his dramatic productions. Let me now give my reasons for this apparent paradox.

The story on which "The Cup" is founded comes originally from Plutarch—not from the "Lives," but from the treatise "De Claris Mulieribus." It simply relates how a priestess of Artemis, wife of a Galatian lord, was loved by another noble of the country, who killed her husband for love of her. Thereupon she devoted herself to vengeance, and feigned to yield to her husband's murderer, but poisoned the sacred cup which it was part of the marriage ceremony that the new-made spouses should drink. I have not been able to find Plutarch's tale in English, but here is the conclusion of it in the quaint French of Amyot, beginning with Camma's speech immediately on drinking the poison :—

Je t'appelle à témoin, dit-elle, très honorée déesse, que je n'ai survécu à Sinatus pour autre intention de voir cette journée, n'ayant eu ne bien, ne plaisir de la vie en tout le temps que j'ai vescu depuis, que l'espérance de pouvoir un jour faire la vengeance de sa mort; laquelle mainctenant faicte, je m'en vais gayement devers mon mari. Mais toi, le plus méchant homme du monde, donne ordre maintenant que tes amis et parents, au lieu de lict nuptial, te prépare une sépulture.

Le Galatien, ayant ouî ces propos, et commençant desjà à sentir que le poison faisoit son opération et lui troubloit tout le dedans du corps, se fit mettre dans une litière, et ne sceut si bien faire que le soir même il ne rendit l'âme, et Camma ayant passé toute la nuict et entendu comme il estoit desjà trespassé, s'en alla volontairement et gayement hors de ce monde.

The dramatic material in this is obvious, and has already attracted the attention of several dramatists. Thomas Corneille wrote a tragedy called "Camma," said to be in his very worst style, and there is also a German play on the subject. But the best known treatment of the theme is the "Camma" of Giuseppe Montanelli, in which Ristori made one of her greatest triumphs. This is not only the best known, but also the best treatment of the theme, Mr. Tennyson's tragedy, I am sorry to say, not excepted. A comparision between the two is extremely instructive, as showing how to write and how *not* to write a drama.

First, let me relate, as concisely as possible, the story of Montanelli's play. It is in three acts and in verse, and its great fault is a poetic inflation of the dialogue which impedes the dramatic action. It opens in the court of the temple of Artemis, or rather of Corivena, the Celtic counterpart of Artemis; for Montanelli has made the religion of the Galatians, what it probably was, in the main Celtic and Druidic, only modified to a certain extent by the influence of Hellenic surroundings. At the very commencement of the play news is brought to Camma, the chief Druidess, that her husband Sinato, tetrarch of Pessinunto, has been murdered by an unknown assassin. She is on the point of devoting herself to death so as to join him in the stars—for a belief in immortality was a cardinal point of the Celtic religion—when the old bard Talese reminds her of the sacred duty of vengeance. Meanwhile, the people have proclaimed Sinoro, a noble suspected of unpatriotic leanings towards Rome, the new tetrarch. He comes to the temple, and Camma at the sight of him feels, by a supernatural thrill, the presence of her husband's murderer.

Camma (*aside*).—
What sudden tremor thrills me to the heart?
Sinoro.—
The yearly session of the avenging judges
Will soon be called to meet in Pessinunto.
(CAMMA, *with terrible restlessness, gazes from face to face of the people on the stage.*)
Talese (*to Camma*).—
Camma! you tremble.
Camma. Tremble! nay, I thrill!
Sinoro (*to the Druids*).—
The murderer, hereby condemned to death,
Slay, in the sacred lunar hour, oh Druids,
A victim surely grateful to your god.
Camma (*to herself*).—
I feel *my* victim near.
Sinoro. Your zeal, oh elders,

Must aid my power by stern avenging justice
To wipe away the stain of this foul deed,
And seize the murderer.

Camma (*to herself*). 'Tis he! 'tis he!

(*Envelopes herself in her veil and goes alone into the temple.*)

The second act shows Camma convinced in her heart of Sinoro's guilt, but determined absolutely to prove it before taking vengeance. To this end she feigns to be in some measure inclined to favour his suit, much to the horror of her sister Druidesses and Talese, by whom Sinoro is hated for his Romanizing proclivities. She summons Sinoro to an interview in the temple precincts, and receives him alone. His passion for her has moved her, she tells him, but she cannot return it, for she loves another. Sinoro, enraged, demands to know his rival, but she replies that she herself does not know him. Little by little he extorts from her the avowal of her criminal passion. She has learned, she says, by supernatural means, that love of her was the motive of her husband's murderer, and she has been seized with an irresistible love for the unknown man whose passion was so strong as to drive him to crime. Sinoro walks blindly into the trap. He not only confesses that he was the murderer, but he gives incontrovertible proof of the fact:—

Camma (*aside*).—

. . . Oh, horror! I can bear no more.

Sinoro.—

Still do you doubt?

Camma (*with a forced smile*).—

No, no!

Sinoro. Then crown at last

My boundless love. As pledge of nuptial faith,
Give me your hand.

Camma (*aside, giving him her hand with an expression of terrible joy*).—

At last I hold my prey!

The last lines of the act can only be given in the original :—

Sinoro.—

M' accompagni un tuo detto, un tuo sorriso.

Camma (*in modo da far capire che parla del suo amore per* SINATO).—

Amo!

Sinoro (*partendo*).—

Oh delirio! Il talamo pressento!

Camma (*tra se*).—

Mostro! il talamo tuo sarà la tomba.

The third act resembles, on the whole, that of Mr. Tennyson's play, except that its effect is heightened by a scene in which the old bard Talese denounces the marriage between Sinoro and Camma so violently that Sinoro is on the point of ordering his death, while Camma cannot interfere to save him for fear of arousing Sinoro's suspicions and so losing her vengeance.

This play, with all its faults of diction, and despite the classic slowness of its movement, seems to me, in point of construction, an almost perfect handling of the theme. A dramatic idea is not enough to make a drama. It must be moulded and fashioned so that the interest is sustained from incident to incident. This is what Montanelli has done with rare skill. He has worked up Plutarch's material with a true power of invention and selection, and the great scene of the second act is of the most genuine dramatic force.

Did Mr. Tennyson know Montanelli's play? I can scarcely think that he did, or he would surely have avoided some of the errors into which he has fallen. On the other hand, he may have read "Camma," and felt himself hampered by the necessity of treating in a novel fashion a theme which had already been treated almost to perfection. If so, he would have done better to have thrown originality to the winds, and simply adapted and beautified Montanelli's play, as he might easily have done.

As it is, what has he done? He has constructed a first act which is quite outside the dramatic motive, he has left the development of the motive to the imagination, and in the second act has merely given us its culminating point. The play really begins as the curtain falls upon Act I. Camma's vengeance is its true subject, not the plots of Synorix, with which, in a vague fashion, the first act is occupied. It is only when Sinnatus is dead that the dramatic problem, the psychological nodus, really presents itself. That Sinnatus should appear at all on the scene weakens the play inexpressibly. Montanelli leaves him to the imagination of the audience. We know him only from Camma's devotion to him, and we accept his character without difficulty as heroic and worthy that devotion. Mr. Tennyson, on the other hand, shows us a Sinnatus whose character is by no means calculated to excite any devotion whatever. He is a rash, empty-headed youth, whose one prominent attribute is vanity of his prowess in the chase. Perhaps the actor to whom the part was assigned may have made him more contemptible than necessary; but Mr. Tennyson's own lines present him in a by no means admirable light. He is painfully the inferior of Synorix in everything except virtue, and even his virtue we have to take upon hearsay. But Mr. Tennyson is not content with dragging this superfluous Sinnatus upon the stage merely to show that Camma's devotion was about as rational as that of Amelia to George Osborne. He even destroys the motive for her revenge by making Sinnatus die, not by deliberate assassination, but in the heat of open fight. True, he is protecting his wife, but the fact remains that Synorix kills him in self-defence and without forethought, so that half the justification of Camma's treacherous vengeance is destroyed. Thus, at the end of the first act, we find the dramatic motive entirely undeveloped and fatally weakened.

In the second act, six months later, Camma, to the mildly-expressed surprise of her sister priestesses, consents to marry Synorix, who has just been proclaimed King of Galatia under the protection of Rome. No hint is given of her purpose in thus consenting. So far as Mr. Tennyson is concerned, the audience is as much in the dark as the priestesses. It was pretty generally known, of course, by means of advance notices, that Camma was to poison Synorix, but it is not good art for a dramatist to rely upon newspaper paragraphs for the mere telling of his story. She does poison him, however, most effectually, and after consigning his soul to Hades —she uses a less classical expression—herself departs to join Sinnatus in the Blessed Isles, though that Galatian Nimrod would probably feel more at home in the Happy Hunting-Grounds.

Thus it will be seen that Mr. Tennyson's first act ends exactly where Montanelli's begins, and his second act begins about the middle of Montanelli's third. Of the beginning of Camma's thirst for revenge, of the religious enthusiasm which justifies it, and of the conception of the scheme by which she carries it out, he affords no glimpse. In short, he gives us an unnecessary prologue and an unmotived catastrophe—the drama he misses out.

Of minor crudities of construction it is needless to speak—unnecessary changes of scene, a long soliloquy intervening between a situation and the fall of a curtain, with others of a like nature. Even the catastrophe is clumsily managed. Camma, who has drunk the poison considerably earlier than Synorix, watches his convulsions almost unmoved, and then, when he is fairly dead, "goes off" herself, the effect of the double climax being almost ludicrous. Meanwhile, by a very extraordinary piece of stage management, for which Mr. Irving and not Mr. Tennyson was probably responsible, the Roman soldiers, after watching the scene in silence for some time, apparently came to the conclusion that they had had enough of it, and sneaked off to the left one by one in an irresistibly comic fashion.

This was, so far as I know, the only defect of the production which can be attributed to Mr. Irving. He mounted the piece with a taste and lavishness positively unexampled. Each scene was a masterpiece in itself, but the supreme effort was the Temple of Artemis, in which the last act takes place. In the gloom of the background we saw the great Diana of the Ephesians—"Artemis polymastos," the many-breasted mother—looking down upon the fore-court, with its double row of solid, richly-sculptured marble pillars, and its roof of sandal-wood inlaid with gold. The air was heavy with incense, and the priestesses moved noiselessly among the sacred lamps. I doubt if a more elaborate and perfect stage-picture of its kind has ever been seen, and if so, certainly not in England. It almost seems as if stage-decoration could go no further.

All this is very praiseworthy. While we are waiting for the coming dramatist any improvement in the medium, scenic or histrionic, in which he will have to work, is to be welcomed with gratitude. At the same time one cannot but regret that this extreme care and skill were not devoted to one of the earlier and worthier works. Rumours have been abroad for some time of Mr. Tennyson's having completed a fifth drama, on the subject of Thomas à Beckett. If this be true we may look with some confidence for a play of greater value than "The Cup." Mr. Tennyson's forte evidently lies not in the construction of dramas but in the dramatic interpretation of history. He can write a series of dramatic scenes for which the material lies ready to his hand, but he cannot logically develope a drama from a given germ. The chronicle-play is not the highest form of dramatic art, but neither is it despicable. Mr. Lowell's saying, "Not failure but low aim is crime," does not apply to the drama. On the stage it is better to hit a low mark than miss at a high one.

MR. W. G. WILLS.

THE writer of a new "Rosciad" could have no more promising subject than Mr. W. G. Wills. I should like, had I the ability, to draw his literary character in a score or so of balanced pentameters after the manner of "Absalom and Achitophel," each line an epigram, and each couplet an antithesis. His is one of those self-contradictory talents which seem made for definition in rhymed paradoxes. He is so strong and so weak, so manly and so puerile, so poetic and so commonplace, so careful and so slovenly, that one hesitates whether to regard him as the greatest or the worst of modern dramatists. In truth, he is neither. He is a man of poetic and artistic temperament, with occasional moments of dramatic inspiration. Unfortunately he does not always wait for these moments to take up his pen, and, when he writes without inspiration, his deficient taste and lack of genuine dramatic instinct betray him into deplorable solecisms. He is an exception in the dramatic life of the day, or rather, as it were, a freak of nature. He does not, to any extent, share the faults and tendencies of the reigning school, but still less can he be regarded as in advance of it, or in any sense the precursor of better things.

The secret of his limitations, perhaps, lies in the fact that he requires to be inspired by his material. He now and then chances on a fine situation and works it out dramatically, but he must find his situation ready made. He has not the skill to extract the dramatic possibilities which lurk in a given theme. They must lie on the surface, or he will miss them. Idyllic work is his forte. Here the vein of poetry, which he certainly possesses and is sometimes inclined to overwork, stands him in good stead. In grappling with a really serious situation his strength too often fails him.

Several of Mr. Wills' plays are unfortunately unknown to me, among them being one which I have heard described as his masterpiece—namely, "The Man o' Airlie." "Buckingham," too, and "Bolivar," written in collaboration with Mr. W. Wilde, I have been unable to procure; but apart from these there remains a long list of works by which to gauge Mr. Wills' capabilities.

It is difficult to discover any principle of classification under which to arrange all these various works. Some are historical, some romantic, but, as Mr. Wills has a profound contempt for history, this does not constitute any real distinction. Some are in verse, some in prose, and a considerable number are in neither prose nor verse. Some were successes, others failures, and several hovered between the two extremes. They do not fall naturally into groups, and I shall thus be forced to take them up almost at random.

In one of his earlier works, now almost forgotten, Mr. Wills has narrowly escaped producing a great play, and a lasting addition to English dramatic literature. "Medea in Corinth" deals with a genuinely tragic theme, and, so far as construction goes, deals with it in a really able fashion. Mr. Wills has freely and skilfully remoulded the matter afforded him by Euripides, and has ably fitted the action to the material requirements and conditions of the modern stage.

What, then, spoils the play, and renders the oblivion into which it has fallen scarcely unmerited? Two causes, I think, explain the phenomenon. The first is the totally unworthy fashion in which the character of Jason is treated. There was room for a piece of genuine analysis in this figure. The author might have depicted the struggle in the hero's mind caused by genuine horror of Medea's crimes, remorse for his own share in them, and longing for the better life which Glaucea's love opens to him. The unconscious sophistry of desire might persuade him that all means are justified by which he can cut away his evil past and cling to his better future, nay, that it would even be a crime to let the ties he abhors restrain him from the good he longs for. Here we should have a phase of the old and yet ever new tragedy which lies in our inability to sever to-day from yesterday, and what we are from what we have been. Even as it is, the play of course gains its tragic import from this source, but Mr. Wills has done his best to spoil it by concentrating the whole interest on Medea, and making of Jason an empty blusterer, with no motive higher than the merest selfishness, heartless, and vulgar-minded. Such a treatment of his character is perhaps more in accordance with the spirit of the legend than the one suggested above; but if there is one thing more impossible than another it is the revival of the antique tragedy, in its habit as it lived, for modern audiences. Of this Goethe's "Iphigenie auf Tauris" is a sufficient proof. With all its classic purity of form, its spirit is the opposite of classic, as a comparison with the drama of Euripides will show; and it pleases precisely in proportion to this divergence from the antique. Nor has Mr. Wills attempted the empty feat of reproducing the classic spirit. The shortcomings of his Jason do not savour of the moral crudity of the ancients, but of the dramatic feebleness of the moderns.

A still graver fault lies in the form of the play. I have no doubt that, if questioned on the subject, Mr. Wills would say that "Medea" is written in blank-verse. But why write a play in blank-verse at all if every second line is to be incorrect? I do Mr. Wills the justice to believe that this irregularity is intentional, and that he could, if he liked, write blank-verse as correct as any poetaster that ever counted his ten syllables upon his ten fingers. It is no doubt with the view of avoiding monotony that Mr. Wills writes such passages as the following, at the conclusion of Act I :—

Medea (advances upon Glaucea, who retires).—
Why does your eye quail before mine?
Why does my name strike you dumb?
I see around me here the nuptial preparations,
They are thine! And the bridegroom, where is he?
Speak! I would see him; let him come!
You tremble! Ah! blind that I was!
I see it! Thou art that accursed one
Whom I have sought. And he, the coward—
Glaucea (lifting her head with energy).—
Silence! In my presence honour him!
Medea. Dost thou love him?
Glaucea. Yes, I love him!
And to-morrow the priest shall name him as my lord.
Medea. He thy lord! It may be.

Here Mr. Wills has deserted verse altogether, with the result that his spasmodic periods remind one of the elegant translations which render Italian-opera libretti in their way curiosities of literature. Still more irritating is a passage like the following :—

Orpheus. Oh, Jason, I am troubled;
An aching pity for thy wretched wife
Which will not let me smile.
Hast thou seen Medea?
Jason. What is her mood? Angry or clamorous?
Orpheus. No, Jason; silent, gentle, and resigned;
Thrice beautiful in grief, grand in despair!
Jason. 'Tis well Eurydice is out of hearing,
Or she would question thy fidelity.
Does she talk of her children?

Orpheus. Not a word ; she sits and seems to wait,
With a large melancholy patience,
Like some afflicted goddess.
Sometimes she muttered to me of her home
Among the cedar forests, and the hill-tops blank with snow.
But of her children, not a question or a word.

Of these sixteen lines exactly half are blank-verse. Three are incomplete fragments of blank-verse, and one, by means of several false emphases, can be tortured into a correct fragment. The remaining lines are no verse whatever, but prose cut into perfectly arbitrary lengths ; and it is to these lines that I particularly object. An occasional unfinished line pleasantly prevents monotony. Shakespeare uses the device very frequently, as a glance at any, say, of Hamlet's soliloquies will show. But lines of pure prose in the middle of blank-verse speeches are unspeakably jarring. Little as I love blank-verse, I am willing to admit that it is perhaps the fittest medium for such a theme as that of "Medea;" but if we are to have blank-verse, let it be moderately correct. The poet who cannot give his verse variety without making it incorrect merely proclaims his lack of mastery over the metre.

The passage last quoted I have selected because it illustrates another weakness in the play. If Mr. Wills has refrained from putting modern morality in his work, he has not failed to endow it with occasional touches of modern commonplace and even vulgarity. The speech of Jason quoted above is perhaps the worst instance. To place in the mouth of the leader of the Argonauts a piece of vulgar "chaff"—that is the only word for it—with reference to the love of Orpheus and Eurydice, is surely a defect of taste worthy of a burlesque writer rather than of a serious dramatist. A nudge and a wink would be the "business" appropriate to such a speech. And such anachronisms, to use no stronger term, are not rare, though they are not generally so glaring. When Glaucea remarks,

> That which
> We give to the needy we consecrate to the gods,

it is nothing short of ludicrous to hear this paraphrase of one of the most selfish of Christian proverbs in the mouth of the daughter of Creon. Now and then, it is true, we come across a line of weighty meaning and worthy expression, as, for instance, Jason's saying,—

> Creon, who wavers, him the gods control;
> But he who promptly acts, controls the gods.

This might be a translation from the "Iphigenie," in which Goethe has given such an incomparable model of the style in which classic subjects should be treated for the modern world. But as a rule Mr. Wills has despised or ignored this model. It was not, of course, to be expected that he should give us matter worthy of Goethe; but, at least, the master's example might have taught him to avoid his most glaring faults of manner.

In "Charles I." Mr. Wills has shown that he can,

when he pleases, write excellent blank-verse, which to my ear seems to possess all the variety necessary even in dramatic works. This play, despite the one great blot upon it, remains the finest of its author's work. Since it was not hissed off the stage on its first performance, it will probably live as long as any poetic play of this century. That an English audience listened without exasperation to the second act speaks ill for its sense of historic justice, but well for the dramatic power of the composition.

The subject was one which admirably suited Mr. Wills. He had not to construct a drama, but to write four dramatic scenes, each exhibiting a different phase of one pathetic character. He has shown genuine sympathy and insight in his portrait of Charles I. He paints in living colours the gentle, feeble, well-meaning, and ill-doing monarch, born out of his due time, and mistaking the wall of prejudice around him for the divinity which doth hedge a king. He shows us the cultured, loving, and brave gentleman, and the short-sighted, illogical, unprincipled politician. I am not sure how far the revelation of the latter side of Charles's character may be unintentional on Mr. Wills' part. One has a suspicion that it is in spite of himself that he has dealt such even justice to his hero. Be this as it may, it needs no preconception to read in the sophistries and fallacies placed in the mouth of Charles the jesuitical tendencies of his obstinate absolutism. "We must be crafty for an honest end," he says,—

The path seems crooked while we toil along it,

> But left in distance, all the petty curves
> Melt from the vision, it looks straight and fair.
> Then let old Justice Time assoilzie us;
> Time is the tardy advocate of kings.

Unfortunately for this hope, Justice Time is not content with the foreshortened view which hides deviations from the straight path. He demands that a geometrical survey of the road be laid before the court, measures all its tortuosities, and will not suffer them to be glossed over as "petty curves."

Thus Mr. Wills has been fain to accept the verdict of history upon Charles. Upon Cromwell, again, he wilfully closes his eyes to the verdict, and studies only the violent philippics of a prosecution which has long since been silenced by a masterly defence from the accused's own lips. He makes him

> A mouthing patriot with an itching palm,
> In one hand menace, in the other greed,

who openly offers, for the earldom of Essex, to sell the cause of liberty. This puerile calumny did not pass without protest in the Press, and Mr. Wills thereupon defended himself by writing, "I really supposed the matter to be familiar to all readers of history." It is perfectly familiar to all readers of history that thousands of malicious lies were told about Cromwell by his political opponents; but that does not excuse an English dramatist's going out of his way to repeat them as truths after their utter baselessness has been made as clear as day. "Furthermore," says Mr. Wills, "considering the unblushing rapacity which he displayed at this very period by accepting from the Government the confiscated estates of a loyal nobleman, the Marquis of Worcester, it seems to me that, in exclaiming against the paltry charge above, we swallow a camel and strain at a gnat." Was ever such extraordinary logic or morality? Cromwell accepted from his fellow-countrymen a recompense for his services which seems to Mr. Wills inordinately large; therefore, we are to believe "the paltry charge" that he was a hypocrite and traitor prepared to sell his country for an empty title! In short, treachery appears to Mr. Wills "a gnat," and rapacity, to leave the term undisputed, "a camel." Mr. Wills probably considers it "a paltry charge" against Judas that he betrayed his Master, but looks with abhorrence on his enormity of carrying the bag.

I have no wish to make an elaborate defence of Cromwell. Mr. Wills, in his letter of explanation, proves to his own satisfaction that he was cruel, high-handed and rapacious. All these epithets might easily be disputed, but they are utterly beside the question. My code of ethics may be antiquated, but it seems to me that there is a vast abyss between cruelty and venality, rapacity and treachery—precisely the abyss which lies between honesty and dishonesty. A man may be actuated to cruelty by good motives, however mistaken. He may grasp too largely at the spoils of war, and yet believe himself to be acting within his right. But he cannot sell a cause to which he professes himself devoted without both being and knowing himself to be a hypocrite and scoundrel. This is what Mr. Wills makes Cromwell, and this is what, as has been proved with scientific certainty, Cromwell never was. Again I say, it is little to the credit of the English public that it should ever have tolerated this belittling caricature of a man who, with all his errors and limitations, remains one of the greatest figures in our history.

Now that the play has taken its place in our modern repertory, however, we may, after due protest lodged, accept the second act as a sort of literary curiosity, for the sake of the other three and of its own unquestionable dramatic force. The worst of it is that only a temporary and minor effect is gained by this degradation of the character of Cromwell. The act, without the few lines which contain the disgraceful accusation, would give a fair enough, if sketchy, view of Cromwell, while it developes admirably an important phase of the character of Charles. The third act is throughout good, and its exquisitely pathetic close is perhaps the finest point in the piece. In the fourth Mr. Wills has treated with excellent taste one of those scenes of perennial pathos which history now and then presents. If Charles did not know how to reign he knew how to die, and that is a knowledge which covers many sins and restores our sympathy with the most erring character. For actors of picturesque and poetic style "Charles I." will probably long continue to possess attractions, and the objectionable passages will either be eliminated or will be regarded as we now regard the treatment of Joan of Arc in "Henry VI."

Along with "Medea" and "Charles I." I may group "Juana" as a play in verse written with some effort after literary form. The materials are strong and original, but there are many ways in which they may be treated, and Mr. Wills has chosen one of the least effective. Perhaps his choice was influenced by the circumstance that the play was written for Madame Modjeska, and consequently the heroine's part had to be made the more prominent. But for this Mr. Wills must surely have seen that the real drama lay in the character of Friar John—in the struggle, which is barely indicated, between his monastic vow and his earthly passion—and not in the love and madness of Juana. Madness in itself is quite undramatic. It may often be introduced with great effect as an expedient, and it may be rendered very pathetic by the skill of the artist. But Mr. Wills makes it an end rather than a means, and does not even give it the interest of a psychological study. Juana's ravings throw no light upon the phenomena of mental disease, and her recovery is quite arbitrary and unmotived, though doubtless very opportune. The same may be said of her death. When she has made her confession she remarks, "That pain again!" and sinks to the ground. I am not aware that she had mentioned the pain previously, but it carries her off after "some gentle words and a few more spasms," as an enthusiastic critic wrote in describing the death-scene of Adrienne Lecouvreur. This happy despatch is eminently well-timed, but if characters could always be got rid of in such a simple and inexpensive fashion, the dramatist's lot would be a comparatively happy one.

The true drama, I repeat, lies in the character of Friar John. A young tutor in the Esteban family has fallen desperately in love with the young mistress of the castle. His passion is hopeless, and he dares not even utter it, but leaves the castle and adopts a religious life. He conquers his love and takes the vows of a Dominican monk. Some years later he returns to the castle as confessor to the family. At the news that Juana is about to be married, his old passion, which he had believed to be quenched for ever, blazes forth again. It would be difficult to imagine finer material for a drama of passion and struggle, which might be developed either in the direction of crime or of heroism, but which would necessarily place the young priest foremost among the characters, and leave the lady a subordinate though still important part. The unhappiness of Juana's married life would naturally place the priest, as her spiritual director, in extreme temptation. He might either obey the dictates of his passion and foment the domestic troubles to his own advantage, or he might sacrifice himself for her good. This he does in Mr. Wills' play, but in an extremely ineffective manner. There is no hint of doubt or struggle. He happens to drop in at the moment when Juana, in an access of frenzy, stabs her unworthy husband, and to shield her accuses himself of the crime. This self-accusation he maintains even at the expense of juggling with the Ordeal by Touch, which a churchman so devout as he must hold the most sacred of oracles. It is plain, too, that his self-sacrifice can only be effectual in the extremely improbable event of Juana's never recovering her reason. He knows that if she does she will at once confess her crime, so that his sacrifice will lose even its "saving grace." Thus his heroism becomes incredible, and consequently ineffective. Mr. Wills does not even work up the melodramatic possibilities of the situation. I am not learned in the history of Ordeal by Touch, but am very much mistaken if it was not a rite which could only be validly performed, with much pomp and ceremony, in a church or consecrated place. Mr. Wills makes it come off in the most haphazard and unimpressive form in a woodland glade, beside a pond which arouses dangerous reminiscences of the second act of "Patience." If this is not an archæological, it is a scenic error. The audience might have been impressed had the scene been the dim and long-drawn aisles of a cathedral, and had the gravity of the situation been denoted by solemn music and ecclesiastical pomp. As it is, the whole affair has an unpremeditated and informal appearance. There is an air of a funereal picnic about it.

In the verse of "Juana" Mr. Wills has relapsed into the manner of "Medea," and in his diction he adopts a very irritating affectation, which he happily avoided both in "Medea" and in "Charles I." Why in the name of wonder should a modern playwright use a language made up of reminiscences of Shakespeare and the Bible? Shakespeare wrote the language he spoke, giving it, of course, poetical form, but using the vocabulary and idioms of his time. His language differs no more, and probably less, from the ordinary speech of his age than the language of "Enoch Arden" differs from our modern English. Why should Mr. Wills and other dramatists adopt Shakespeare's language as the unalterable dialect of poetry? Why should they desert Victorian for Elizabethan English whenever they mount the poetic tripod? Their Elizabethan is very incorrect, and would have been as unnatural in 1581 as it is in 1881, but that does not affect the principle of the thing. There would be some excuse for Mr. Wills if the scene of his play were laid in mediæval England. In that case an exact reproduction of contemporary forms of speech would be a curious and interesting piece of pasticcio. But the characters in "Juana" are Spaniards of the close of the fifteenth century, whose Spanish Mr. Wills is supposed to translate into English. Why, then, should he adopt a dialect which was never spoken by mortal man, but which most nearly resembles the English of the beginning of the seventeenth century? His characters never "wait," "stay," or "go"—they "bide," "tarry," or "hie."[1] "In sooth," "i' faith," and "go to" are their favourite

[1] Charles Lamb says, writing to a beginner in poetry: "Ween" and "wist" and "wot" and "eke" are antiquated frippery, and unmodernize a poem rather than give it an antique air, as some strong old words may do. "I guess," "I know," "I knew," are quite as significant.

expletives. When Juana finds Carlos embracing Clara he remarks,—

> Blame me, not her. I scarce can ask thy pardon.
> I sought thee here, and—by mischance—gramercy!—

From such a use as this of the word "gramercy"—a use which is repeated in another passage—one is forced to conclude that Mr. Wills does not know the meaning of the word, but puts it in at random as being picturesque and mediæval, just as transpontine dramatists use "By my halidame" and "Ifakins." Such roundabout phrases as:

> And gratulation plays the hypocrite,
> Rejoicing in an unknown jubilee,

are mere imitations of Shakespeare: but, though Shakespeare's grammar is not immaculate, he would scarcely have perpetrated the following solecism:—

> Of late 'tis a sick mother near Toledo,
> *Whom* I know well is of a lusty health.

Occasionally it is the Bible which Mr. Wills honours with the sincerest form of flattery, as in Pedro's speech, "My heart goeth out after that maid. Oh she is exceeding fair, and her palm is like unto silk." What can be the object of all this strained archaism? Its one result is to make a good deal of the dialogue and a great many of the allusions incomprehensible to the majority of the audience.

This Shakespearizing tendency is especially obtrusive in the humorous portions of the play. They are, indeed, of an even older period than Shakespeare, for he generally gave his comic scenes more or less connexion with his plot, and we have to go back to Marlowe, or even further, to find such absolutely irrelevant comic "interludes" as those between Pedro and Katrina. The idea is an old one, but I do not remember to have seen it so unpleasantly carried out before. It is surely nothing less than repulsive to see a girl, without common modesty, making fierce love to a youth of preternatural stupidity, while a lusty old friar looks on and makes delicate allusions to "coneys" and "bluebottles" and "Potiphar's wife"—the last comparison being as inapt as it is tasteless. This is one of those not uncommon instances in which Mr. Wills' tact and good sense seem entirely to desert him.

In popular drama Mr. Wills has made some successes and several failures. The now almost forgotten adaptation from Madame Birch-Pfeiffer, "Hinko, a play in five acts, with a prologue, entitled 'The Younger Son,'" is simply a heavy German melodrama of the most old-fashioned type, though containing some strong scenes. "Herman the Fatalist," though it possessed a charming vein of poetry, was too fantastic and intangible in idea to hold the stage, and was marred by Mr. Wills' metrical eccentricities. "Jane Shore" was rendered a great success by means of a snow-scene, but was a tedious and inartistic play. "England in the days of Charles II.," was, and deserved to be, an enormous fiasco, only equalled in this respect by the lugubriously puerile "Ellen, or Love's Cunning," resuscitated a few weeks after its timely death, in the almost imbecile form of "Brag." That such plays should have been written by a rational man, much more by the author of "Charles I." and "Medea," is almost inconceivable. "Forced from Home," again, was a melodrama of the East-end type, not quite despicable in its kind, but scarcely the sort of drama one would have expected from an exhibitor in the Grosvenor Gallery, and a writer of general high-art aspirations. But the genius of Mr. Wills is not of that grovelling order which confines itself to one path. He would have been eminently qualified for the post of dramatist-in-ordinary to that celebrated combination troupe which visited Elsinore in the reign of the late King Claudius, and which, on the authority of an enlightened dramatic amateur of the day, was thoroughly competent for tragedy, comedy, history, pastoral, pastoral-comical, historical-pastoral, tragical-historical, tragical-comical-historical-pastoral, scene individable or poem unlimited. He is equally at home in the empyrean and in the gutter—in the council-chamber of Whitehall, the vicarage of Wakefield, and the toll-house of Waterloo Bridge. In some of the above-mentioned cases, and especially in "Forced from Home," one is tempted to suspect that Mr. Wills, like the elder Dumas, has an apprentice or apprentices at play-manufacturing, to whose work he now and then puts a few finishing touches, and his name.

The most interesting of these popular dramas are "Ninon," and "Sedgmoor." The motive of "Ninon" can be told in a few words. A young woman during the French Revolution undertakes to avenge upon the seducer the seduction and death of her sister. She is to do so by worming herself into his confidence and then betraying him to his political enemies. While she is playing her treacherous part, she herself is seized with a passion for the man she is about to betray. Her vow of vengeance, however, and the recollection of her sister's fate, prevent her yielding to it. She determines, after a struggle, to carry out her plot, and betrays him to his foes, only to learn when it is too late that he is not the seducer of her sister, but has, on the contrary, avenged the unhappy girl's fate by killing the actual criminal. The chief faults of construction probably arise from the necessity under which the dramatist found himself placed of developing his matter into a picturesque melodrama of the guillotine and gunpowder type. Its motives are anything but closely knit, its scenes hang loosely together, and many of its situations are worked in purely for their own sake, without developing the action in the smallest degree. Perhaps the worst fault of all is that Mr. Wills seems totally innocent of the art of suggesting psychological development in action and dialogue. He is perpetually having recourse to long soliloquies, which, Shakespeare notwithstanding, are the weakest of dramatic devices. One is often reminded of the Chinese drama in which the characters confide in the audience somewhat after this fashion :—"I am Wong-Li the son of Ho, and I am an abandoned character, though supposed by my friends and relations to be virtuous. I hate my mother-in-law, the wise Loo-Foo, and I have made up my mind to poison her," &c., &c. Mr. Wills' revelations are not quite so direct and unsophisticated as this, but they sometimes attain an almost Celestial pitch of naïveté. Moreover, the fourth act of the play, which should be its climax, was, on its first production, extremely feeble. Mr. Wills had deemed it necessary to bring his plot to a happy ending, and thus ruined both the logic and the scenic effect of his conclusion. I understand that the piece has since been produced in the provinces, with a tragic ending, and it is possible that in this revised form the really strong motive is developed to proper advantage.

"Sedgmoor," written by Mr. Wills in collaboration with his brother, the Rev. F. C. Wills, is that saddest of spectacles, a bad play on a good subject. A bad play on a bad subject does not matter. It makes its failure or success—very often the latter—and is forgotten. But a bad play on a good subject is a sort of dog-in-the-manger phenomenon. It appropriates a certain quantity of the essentially limited dramatic material presented by life, it does not put it to good use, and it prevents its being put to good use in other forms. A good subject badly treated is like an exceptionally fine block of marble in the hands of a bad sculptor. The marble is spoiled, and no one is a whit the better. An ordinary seamy slab of mantelpiece stone would have served the sculptor just as well, and he would not have deprived some more skilful or fortunate brother-artist of the opportunity offered by the rare block of Parian.

The Messrs. Wills have absorbed in "Sedgmoor" a subject which might have made an extremely neat and effective little quasi-historical play. They have made of it a very long and ineffective, broken-backed, blank-verse drama. There is a god named Terminus in the Latin mythology, whose divinity Mr. Wills must surely have offended, and who has retaliated by afflicting Mr. Wills with blindness as to the ends and limits of things. He does not know where one play ends and another begins, where a situation ends and an anti-climax begins, where poetry ends and bathos begins, where the patience of his audience ends, and utter tedium begins. "Sedgmoor" is not one, but three plays, and the day for trilogies has passed. The first play ends about five minutes before the close of the second act, and, barring a good deal of superfluous matter introduced so as to hook it on to the second play, it is a strong and ably constructed drama. Its motive lies in the treachery displayed by the fugitive Duke of Monmouth towards Sir Gilbert and Lady Evelyn, who had concealed him after his defeat. His baseness is foiled, and recoils upon himself, by means of a very ingenious touch of diplomacy on the part of Lady Evelyn, which affords in the second act a scene of powerful and admirable drama.

The second play consists of the third act and the first scene of the fourth. It is a very trivial domestic drama of misunderstandings, founded upon a wife's foolish and almost criminal obstinancy in keeping an oath of secrecy, which she has made for no reason whatever, and from which, if her conscience is so very tender, she could easily procure a formal release. The third play begins and ends in act four, scene three. The domestic misunderstandings are satisfactorily cleared up, but the husband has meanwhile got condemned to death (for the third time) and the wife is tempted to save his life by renouncing her legal claim upon him and giving him up to the arms of a rival. This third play is fortunately suggested rather than worked out, for it is summarily cut short by the Revolution and the arrival of the Prince of Orange. Such is the incoherence of the construction that when a tableau was formed at the end of the first scene of the fourth act, I, for my part, considered the play as satisfactorily wound up as it was ever likely to be, and never doubted that the curtain was going to fall. My astonishment was extreme when a carpenter-scene descended instead, and it became evident that we had a third play to look forward to. This carpenter-scene, however, afforded opportunity for the one gleam of humour which relieved the sombreness of the entertainment, and which, as a theatrical curiosity, I cannot refrain from describing. The troop of soldiers which is told off to shoot the hero marches into a corridor outside his cell. After some desultory conversation it becomes painfully apparent from noises behind that the necessary change of scene has not yet been effected, whereupon a bright idea strikes the captain. "Do you remember," he says, "that song which he (the prisoner) used to be so fond of?" The soldiers signify that, though they have not brought their music, they believe they could manage to join in the chorus. "I'll sing it, then," says the captain. "It may cheer him up"—and he forthwith proceeds to do so, the soldiers, all standing at "attention," joining duly in the chorus.

There remain to be noticed Mr. Wills' various adaptations and dramatizations of novels. Of the latter "Eugene Aram" and "Olivia" are the most noteworthy. "Eugene Aram" consists of a good first act, an excellent second act, and a very feeble third act. It is altogether an interesting play, and affords an opportunity for one of Mr. Irving's very finest creations. "Olivia," again, has been praised much above its deserts. It is by no means the best dramatic version we possess of "The Vicar of Wakefield." It contains some beautiful touches, but also several errors of taste, and the last two acts, especially the last of all, are extremely faulty.

One of his adaptations, "William and Susan," brought down much obloquy upon Mr. Wills' head, to my mind very unjustly. Mrs. Kendal wished to play at her own theatre one of her most delightful parts, a perfect embodiment of healthy English womanhood, but was conscious at the same time that Jerrold's play was too antiquated in manner to suit the taste of her audiences. Mr. Wills consequently undertook the delicate task of transforming a transpontine nautical drama into what may be called a nautical idyl. His characters are about as real as the shepherds of Guarini or Watteau, but they are none the less pleasantly and gracefully drawn. He refined both the humour and the pathos of the older play, and gave it a touch of delicate and fanciful poetry. The honest sentiment and homeliness remained with an added grace and charm. This is the style of work in which Mr. Wills excels, and here he excelled himself. It says much for the taste with which the play was written, that though the public mind was still infected with the burlesque associations of "Pinafore," not to mention the burlesque of the original play itself, these associations were almost forgotten. I am by no means sure that Mr. Gilbert "deserved well of the republic" by bringing even the conventional Jack-tar into contempt; and in any case it is pleasant to find that audiences have still a smile of sympathy as well as a smile of ridicule for that delightfully ideal personage.

Another of Mr. Wills' adaptations, "Iolanthe," is so interesting that I must give it what may perhaps seem disproportionate space. The story of Henrik Herz's "Kong Renés Datter" has been rendered familiar in England through Sir Theodore Martin's translation, and by the talent of his distinguished wife. King René's daughter, Iolanthe, having become blind through an accident in infancy, has been allowed to grow up in a secluded valley of Provence, under the care of two faithful servants of the king, and *in total ignorance of the fact that she is blind*—that she lacks a sense possessed by those around her. A Moorish physician, Ebn Jahia, is about to attempt her cure, but he states that a necessary condition of the experiment is that she shall be informed of her blindness and made to feel the want from which she suffers. Her father refuses thus to imperil her peace of mind for the sake of an experiment, which is at best doubtful. By chance, however, Tristan of Lorraine wanders into her garden, and reveals to her, by allusions to colour, to the number of distant objects, &c., that there are things in heaven and earth undreamt of in her philosophy. Her eyes being thus opened metaphorically, their literal cure soon follows, and the curtain falls within five minutes of her restoration to sight.

This is the theme of the play, and a very pretty and original idea it is. But it has one fault—it is a purely fantastic subject, placed by an error of judgment in a historic frame. Herz admits that his piece has no foundation in historic fact—only the names are historical. On the other hand, the whole machinery is supernatural. In the first place the cure is performed by amulets and the stock-in-trade of mediæval empiricism. This of itself does not necessarily imply anything supernatural, for the physicians of those days were apt to give the appearance of magic to very simple operations—a practice from which their modern brethren have not entirely departed. The main element of the supernatural lies in the major premiss of the play—the assumption that Iolanthe could grow up to the age of eighteen, educated, and in a sense accomplished, in daily intercourse with several people, and occasionally coming in contact with strangers, yet without a suspicion that she differed in any essential respect from those around her. This is an impossibility, only to be accounted for by supernatural means, and yet in this assumption lies the whole beauty and force of the play. It is true that Herz has managed with wonderful skill to throw the impossibility into the background and prevent it from jarring upon us. Only in one case, so far as I remember, is it brought into prominence by the dialogue—to wit, in the following passage :—

René. I bring with me your teacher, Ebn Jahia.
Iolanthe. He too? Where is he?
(EBN JAHIA *gives her his hand.*)
Welcome, master, welcome.

Here Iolanthe must understand that Ebn Jahia has some power which she has not, since he knows where she is and can give her his hand at once, while she does not know where he is. Such incidents must have occurred a score of times a day, even in her quiet life, and the inference from them must have forced itself years ago upon her quick apprehension. This is almost the only place where the dialogue and action obtrude upon us the impossibility; but it must be clear enough to any one who reflects how largely the most ordinary language is made up of references to sight and colour. Even if it were possible for René, Bertrand, and Martha to have schooled themselves to omit from their talk all such references, it is absurd to suppose that the strangers who, as we are expressly told, now and then visited Iolanthe, could do so. Would it not have been much more artistic to have appealed frankly to our credulity, to have given the play a fantastic locale, in some "castle east of the sun and west of the moon," and to have made it, in short, a fairy-comedy, like Mr. Gilbert's "Pygmalion" or "The Palace of Truth?" We can *imagine* a blind girl growing up to maturity and perfect womanhood, yet ignorant of the existence of such a faculty as sight. Such a character forms an interesting and graceful psychological study, as does the vivified Galatea. But we can no more believe in Iolanthe as a real personage than we can in Galatea. The cases are somewhat analogous. Herz has worked out his problem far more tastefully than Mr. Gilbert, yet Mr. Gilbert's play is the more artistic of the two in so far as it is frankly mythological, while the very name of "King René's Daughter" gives the Danish poet's work a false appearance of intended reality.

There is room, indeed, for a reconstruction of the idea on lines quite different from those of Herz. On the one hand the play should be made more openly fantastic; on the other hand the psychological problem should be worked out more in detail. Herz has looked only at the romantic and romantico-religious aspects of the case, and has left its philosophy almost untouched. Such a reconstruction might even, by the introduction of new elements into the plot, be made effective on the stage. Mr. Wills, however, has not attempted anything of the sort. His dialogue is better than Herz's, and much better than Sir Theodore Martin's. It suits to perfection the idyllic character of the piece. But so far from working out more carefully the philosophy of the problem he has not even been so careful as Herz to eliminate all allusions which tend to bring into relief the impossibility of the theme. Tristan's allusions to the stars, for instance, are a little out of place, as Iolanthe's astronomy must necessarily have been limited.

There are many negative defects in Mr. Wills' talent—his lack of firm taste, his lack of moral force and purpose. His great positive defect is that he is a writer of dramatic scenes, not an inventor or constructor of dramas. It is characteristic of his method that he should so often remould and touch up his plays after they have left his hand. I have already referred to his "second editions" of "Ellen" and of "Ninon." He has promised to "remove the gloom of the closing acts" of "Juana" and reproduce it; and I believe a reconstruction of "Sedgmoor" has been contemplated, if not executed. Such attempts to smuggle a well-damned play from the dramatic Hades into the sunlight once more are almost always a mistake.

A good play should be an organic entity, which can no more be fitted with a new catastrophe than a man can be fitted with a new pair of legs. The situation should lead to one logical *dénouement*, and one only. There should be no possible toss up between a happy ending and an unhappy one. The illustration used above is very apt. No doubt some of my readers have already observed "a man *can* be fitted with a new pair of legs." So he can—or with a dozen new pairs of legs in succession. But no man ever had more than one pair of legs which formed an organic part of him—through which his blood circulated and his nerves ramified. He may have wooden legs, or cork legs, or elaborate mechanical legs which look very like the real article—but he is none the less lame for life. So it is with a play. Every drama which deals with a moral problem, as all serious dramas should, has one logical solution. It may be shirked in a hundred ways by the arrangement of ficelles, or the introduction of *coups de théâtre*, but if so, the play will come to a lame and impotent conclusion. This is a test of the strength and completeness of a serious motive. If it presents a choice of radically different catastrophes, all equally effective, there is something weak and deficient in its antecedent structure. The conclusion of a play should never depend, as Mr. Wills seems to imagine it does, upon the taste of the audience, but upon the moral and psychological necessities of the theme.

THE END.

INDEX.

[*Lists of Plays by Mr. Burnand, Mr. Byron, Mr. Paul Meritt, &c., which are merely mentioned without comment, and are therefore not included in this index, will be found on pp.* 113, 121, 122, 123, 226, 227.]